A
Sociology
Writer's Guide

Linda L. Yellin
California State University

PEARSON

Boston   New York   San Francisco
Mexico City   Montreal   Toronto   London   Madrid   Munich   Paris
Hong Kong   Singapore   Tokyo   Cape Town   Sydney

Executive Editor: Jeff Lasser
Series Editorial Assistant: Lauren Macey
Senior Marketing Manager: Kelly May
Production Editor: Karen Mason
Editorial Production Service: GGS Book Services PMG
Manufacturing Buyer: Debbie Rossi
Electronic Composition: GGS Book Services PMG
Cover Administrator: Joel Gendron

For related titles and support materials, visit our online catalog at www.pearsonhighered.com.

Between the time website information is gathered and then published, it is not unusual for some sites to have closed. Also, the transcription of URLs can result in typographical errors. The publisher would appreciate notification where these errors occur so that they may be corrected in subsequent editions.

Library of Congress Cataloguing-in-Publication Data
Yellin, Linda L.
   A sociology writer's guide / Linda L. Yellin.
      p. cm.
   Includes bibliographical references and index.
   ISBN-13: 978-0-205-58238-9
   ISBN-10: 0-205-58238-9
   1. Sociology—Authorship—Style manuals. 2. Sociology—Research—Handbooks, manuals, etc. 3. Report writing—Handbooks, manuals, etc. I. Title.
   HM85.Y45 2009
   808'.066301—dc22

                                                                    2008014318
Printed in the United States of America

10   9   8   7   6   5   4   3   2   1   12   11   10   09   08

To my parents
with love and appreciation

This is the book I needed when I was in college.

Back then, there seemed to be a secret "code" or set of unwritten rules that some students knew and the rest of us didn't. Nowhere was this more evident than in writing papers for our various courses. I remember thinking to myself *why don't they just tell us how to do it?*

Amazingly, little seems to have changed since that time. Now I see the students in my classes confronting the same code. Needless to say, some know it, and they breeze through their college courses. The rest don't realize what they don't know until the first poor grades arrive. Then, those that don't give up try to discover and learn the unwritten rules they never were taught. If asked, they talk about their struggles to decipher the code and master it. Of course, they don't use those exact words. Instead, they say, "how are we supposed to find out all the things we need to know?" and "why didn't anyone tell us this before?"

Yes. Why not? Isn't it time?

Well, that's why I wanted to write this book—to pass on the code to those who never learned it. This book also can help those who know the code brush up on recent changes in style and usage, as well as add sophistication and polish to their writing.

You may notice that there are no big, wordy chapters or long motivational passages in this book. Sorry. I personally don't find either one very useful, and I imagine that neither do you. General suggestions or remonstrations, such as "write clearer" or "develop better thesis statements," are also pretty worthless, in my view. From what I can tell, most students want to write clearer and better—they just don't know how. So, with this book, don't worry about improving your "overall writing." The small, simple rules and tips suggested here cumulatively will produce improved writing, and clearer and better papers.

I probably should disclose that this book has an agenda. It can be summed up in four words: Work Smart, Not Hard. I didn't always believe that, but over the years, I have grown to respect the wisdom of that simple adage, and it is reflected here in the text, which—for instance—

1. lists very easy, specific pointers to help you fix your papers.
2. walks you through each step in writing a college term paper, start to finish.
3. shows you how to revise your papers in 10 simple, systematic steps.
4. provides a complete list of examples for citations and references in current sociological format.
5. includes a complete list of examples for handling quotes and paraphrases.
6. offers chapters on writing quantitative and qualitative sociology papers, as well as other types of writing assignments.
7. uses Tips and other features to highlight key points.

This book has been inspired by the thousands of students who have taken my courses over the years. Their questions sparked this project and brought it to life, even as their enthusiasm and love of learning made every class an adventure. Now it's your turn. Take a moment to get involved. If you have any ideas for improving this effort, e-mail me at socwriter@gmail.com. If you think something is missing, or if you found an idea that helps, I'd like to know about it.

Acknowledgments

I am deeply grateful to the people who contributed to this book in different ways. I want to thank Jeff Lasser for his editorial vision and support in nurturing this project. Thanks to Karen Mason, the critical nexus of the endeavor, for her helpful ideas and warm, welcoming book design. My sincere appreciation to Connie Strassburg for her ultimate professionalism, endless patience, and infectious good spirits. Also, thanks to Connie's production team for always being willing to jump into the breach to creatively solve problems at a moment's notice. I am indebted to Allison (Ayelet) Fischer who granted permission for her work to be adapted and used for illustrative purposes. My gratitude to Adam and Kineret for reading drafts of chapters and offering helpful insights from the student perspective, and to Yael for her thoughtful questions. Above all, my profound thanks to Bill for reading every draft and checking minute details with loving care. His unfailing enthusiasm and warm, constant support helped make this work possible.

Linda L. Yellin

1 Starting Your Paper

Without doubt, getting started writing is a challenge for most of us. It requires marshaling our creative energies, harnessing our competitive drive, rolling up our sleeves, and throwing ourselves headlong into the task, while disciplining ourselves to see the project through to completion. Yet, we all need to write many papers during our years in school, and even after education is completed, the highest paid professions usually require excellent writing skills to get a job, keep a job, and advance in the field. Writing is something that we may not always love, but we need to handle successfully—and even try to master.

1a What Type of Paper Are You Writing?

In getting started, the first question to ask yourself is what kind of paper is it:

- a term paper or research paper?
- an essay?
- an analysis of a text?
- a book review?
- a paper reporting your original quantitative or qualitative research?
- a thesis or dissertation?

Each of these papers has a distinctive structure and format that you need to incorporate as you write. Also, if you have a choice of topic, be aware that certain topics will yield better results than others with some types of papers—and some topics won't work at all.

1b Using This Book

This book is designed as a hands-on guide to writing a college paper. Its goal is to help you improve your skills by walking you through the steps of preparing a paper, from nascent idea to final version.

As such, an effort has been made to present information in a straightforward and accessible manner. However, thinking, researching, and writing are rarely tidy or linear, so jump around a bit and chart a course through the book that fits your own personal style. It is hoped you will find the information you need clearly marked and logically placed—and if all else fails, check the index.

This chapter will help you start any new paper. Subsequent chapters will assist you in revising your draft, doing library and Internet research, preparing citations and references, and writing specific types of papers, such as research papers or term papers, quantitative or qualitative research papers, critiques or text analysis papers, book reviews, or essay exams.

If you are writing a term paper based on library and Internet research, start here. After reviewing this chapter, go to Chapter 5, "Writing a Library Research Paper or Term Paper." Also, consult Chapter 3, "Library and Internet Research," as well as Chapter 4, "Citations and References." You may wish to return to this chapter for help with your thesis statement, outline, and first draft. For assistance in revising your paper, Chapter 2, "Structure and Style in Writing," provides an easy way to find and fix all sorts of problems and prepare the final polished version.

For other types of papers, start here. After reviewing this chapter, consult the chapter that covers the specific paper you are preparing. If you need to do library or Internet research, you will find Chapter 3 useful. Also, check Chapter 4 for assistance with citations and references. When you are ready to begin writing, you may wish to return to Chapter 1 for help developing your thesis statement, outline, and draft. To aid in revising your paper, Chapter 2 shows an easy way to find and fix all sorts of problems and prepare the final version of your work.

And now, let's get started . . .

1c   Selecting and Narrowing a Topic

Your choice of a topic is crucial to writing a successful paper. The subject must not be too general (such as "Gender Roles"), but should have a specific angle or aspect that you can explore (such as "Gender Roles in Dual-Career Families"). Usually, students have little trouble thinking up a general idea, but considerable difficulty narrowing one to a manageable size appropriate for a paper topic.

These steps will help you choose an idea and shape it into a focused topic.

1. Brainstorm for Ideas

Look at the assignment for suggestions. Review your course syllabus and your textbook's table of contents for ideas. Consider two sources of ideas that professional researchers often draw on in their search for topics: *personal concerns* and *social problems.*

In thinking about **personal concerns,** consider experiences or problems that you, your family, or your friends may have encountered. What interests you, bothers you, worries you? What do you wish you could change or understand? This does not mean you will be writing about your family or your personal experiences. Rather, you will research the thing that worries you, or the thing you wish you could understand.

In thinking about **social problems,** consider some of the major issues facing society today. Reading the daily newspaper, watching the nightly news on television, or reviewing the table of contents in a social problems textbook should give you a number of ideas.

2. Shape and Refine Your Best Idea

Once you have a general idea, you need to translate it into a precise, researchable question by limiting its scope to manageable proportions. Narrow your focus so the idea can be addressed within the page limits set by the instructor. Also, consider the following questions:

- Is there time to do the research for this topic properly?
- Will it cost more money than I want to spend to research this topic?
- Am I in a location where I can practically carry out the research?

If your idea is too broad and unfocused, or the answer to any of the preceding questions is no, you will need to further narrow your idea. The following steps can help you do so. Proceed through as many of the steps as necessary, ordered as you wish, until your topic is manageable and focused. Note that at each step, you need to do preliminary research on your subject (see "Reviewing the Literature" in the following text for more information). Keep track of the sources you consult either on your computer or in a notebook in case you want to return to them later.

3. Reduce the Time Frame

Instead of discussing events over a century or more, limit yourself to a shorter time period. Focus on a 20-year period, a decade, or less. Before committing to the topic, check that sufficient published research related to the subject is available for the time period you select. If not, you will need to change your topic's time frame to a period of time for which published research is readily accessible.

4. Reduce the Spatial/Geographic Coverage

Instead of discussing events internationally or nationally, limit yourself to a state, city, or neighborhood. The availability of published research will be key in making this decision, so check before committing to a topic. Check that sufficient published research related to the subject is available for the geographic area selected during the time period chosen. If not, change either your geographic location or time period.

5. Choose a Unit of Analysis

What are you going to investigate? The **unit of analysis** is the subject of your study and the "thing that you count." Most researchers tend to focus on the **individual** as the unit of analysis, comparing and contrasting individuals' behavior. There are other units of analysis, however, that you may select for study. You could examine **groups,** such as families, peer groups, and social groups. You might focus on **organizations,** such as corporations, schools, universities, and churches. You could analyze **programs,** such as Head Start or DARE. You might research **social artifacts,** such as magazine articles, newspaper editorials, movies, song lyrics, or court documents. Check to be certain that sufficient published research is available for the subject chosen.

6. Add a Variable

To limit your idea further, add another variable, or factor, to investigate in conjunction with the main idea. Let's see how this might work.

General idea	Delinquency
More focused	Delinquency in the United States
Reduce time frame	Delinquency in the United States 2000–2005
Reduce spatial coverage	Delinquency in Los Angeles 2000–2005
Unit of analysis (individual)	Delinquents in Los Angeles 2000–2005
Variable added (gender)	Female delinquents in Los Angeles 2000–2005

7. Add Another Variable (or Two)

As your idea crystallizes into a topic, keep adding variables to further limit it until it reaches a manageable size.

Broader topic	Female delinquents in Los Angeles 2000–2005
One variable added (type of offense)	Female runaways in Los Angeles 2000–2005
Second Variable added (type of abuse)	Types of abuse and the decision to leave home among female runaways in Los Angeles 2000–2005

Remember to check that published scholarly research is available for your final topic. If not, you will need to adapt your topic accordingly.

1d Reviewing the Literature

Once you have selected a topic, you will need to review the literature, or search for scholarly work published on your topic, in order to formulate a tentative thesis statement and gather information for use later in the writing process. In the natural and social sciences, the term **literature** refers to all published research studies on a particular subject in a particular discipline. When you review the literature in sociology, you will be looking for (1) articles in sociology journals, (2) books, and (3) authored chapters in edited volumes. General books (e.g., *Men Are from Mars, and Women Are from Venus* [Gray 1993]) and articles in popular magazines (e.g., *Mademoiselle, Newsweek, GQ*) or newspapers (e.g., *New York Times, Wall Street Journal*) are not considered part of the sociological literature even if they discuss subjects of sociological interest and quote from research studies. The actual research studies mentioned, however, are part of the literature.

A review of the literature will give you a sense of how your topic has been treated by scholars. Is this subject viewed as an important one, or has it been neglected? Is there a great deal of work on the subject, or very little? How has the subject been approached by sociologists? Has the subject been dealt with so extensively that your topic seems simplistic in its present form?

Keep track of your literature review using a research log, either in electronic or print form. This will make the task of locating and documenting your sources easy and quick. Take careful notes on key points, and record URLs for online sources. You may need to consult the same sources later when doing research to assemble evidence in support of your thesis statement.

1e Constructing a Thesis Statement

As you review the literature, start looking for the idea that will serve as your thesis statement. A **thesis statement** is an assertion that answers these questions: What point does the paper make? What opinion does it offer? What stand does the writer take? What does the writer want us to focus on as we read this paper? The thesis introduces the key point(s) of the paper—the side of the argument you will argue or the statement you will try to prove. As you write your paper and develop your ideas, it is expected that you may refine or revise your initial thesis statement. Once you have crafted a clear and comprehensive thesis statement, the writing of the rest of your paper should flow easily.

The following example illustrates the relationship between a paper's topic and thesis statement.

Topic	"In this study, I follow Atkinson's lead to investigate suicide from the perspective of death investigators to understand how these key professionals decide the official suicide record" (Timmermans 2005:313).
Thesis statement	"After reviewing the basics of the U.S. death investigation system and the methodology of this study, I will show how medical examiners address the equivocality of suicide, deal with the stigma of suicide, and manage pressure of relatives and public health officials on their decision-making" (Timmermans 2005:314).

Often, a good way to start off your thesis statement is to employ one of the following phrases.

This paper examines . . .

This paper investigates . . .

This study explores . . .

Then, complete the thesis statement by clearly stating the point(s) you are planning to make in your paper. Depending on your topic and the type of paper you are writing, it may be appropriate to construct a thesis statement with a main point and three subpoints (three is an arbitrary choice—it could be two or four depending on the length of the paper and the complexity of your thesis). Keep in mind that if you don't end up actually discussing or finding supporting evidence for all of these subpoints, or if you revise them later in the writing process, you will need to go back and update your thesis statement.

If your thesis statement's main point is long or complex, it is acceptable not to list your subpoints as part of the thesis statement. Still, you will need to identify your subpoints at this time, for they are key elements in structuring your paper. If you are testing a hypothesis, you may substitute it for the thesis statement.

Remember the topic we developed in the previous section? Here is an example of a thesis statement for that topic.

Topic	Types of abuse and the decision to leave home among female runaways in Los Angeles 2000–2005
Thesis statement	This paper examines the two main types of abuse associated with female runaways' decisions to leave home and discusses implications for intervention.

1f   Outlining

After you have done some preliminary research on your topic, draft a broad topic outline that includes the major points and subpoints you plan to cover in your paper. An **outline** is an orderly plan, in writing, showing the division of ideas and their arrangement in relation to one another. Outlining requires you to determine which ideas are most important, which are less important, and the best way of grouping them.

An outline serves as a guide for planning the architecture or "bones" of your paper. The outline of a paper sets down your arguments in defense of the main point and subpoints of the thesis statement. Evidence introduced in a logical, orderly way clarifies your argument for readers. Each main idea, in turn, is bolstered by secondary details (e.g., facts, data, citations). The different levels within an outline force you to make choices about which points are most important and which are less so, while considering the order of their presentation. Working from an outline allows you to be flexible and try different ways of raising issues before committing to one way.

Informal Outlines

Use an **informal outline** as a guide when starting to write a paper. An outline constructed for personal use does not need to be perfectly typed or even utilize a formal outline structure as long as you can understand and follow it. As your paper progresses, rework your outline if necessary to accommodate your changing ideas. On the other hand, don't let outlining become a substitute for writing your paper. You can easily spend hours constructing and revising your outline, but you will not necessarily write a better paper as a result.

Formal Outlines

Sometimes, an outline is used in presentations to other people. Often, a **formal outline,** carefully organized and neatly typed, is incorporated into handouts and other visual displays accompanying oral presentations in the classroom or workplace. A formal outline also may serve as a table of contents for a report or a collection of articles.

A formal outline can be a **topic outline,** composed of words or phrases, or a **sentence outline,** composed of grammatically complete sentences. The outline's visual layout shows the order and relationship of ideas. An alternating number-letter system (roman numeral, capital letter, Arabic numeral, lowercase letter) is commonly used in sociology. Ideas of equal importance are identified by the same level symbol (for example, roman numerals for main ideas). All subdivisions must have two parts, so if there is an *A*, there must be a *B*, and if there is a *1*, there must be a *2*. Symbols are followed by a period, and the first letter of the first word after each symbol is capitalized. All symbols of the same kind should be arranged in a vertical line. Begin succeeding lines of writing under the start of the first word following a symbol. Outlines are typed double-spaced.

Only principle points appear in an outline. The introduction and conclusion are not included, and usually illustrations, amplifications, or development of the main points are excluded, as well. The thesis statement is placed as a preface to the formal outline. Table 1.1 shows formal outline format.

TABLE 1.1 A Formal Outline

Thesis statement
I.
  A.
  B.
    1.
    2.
      a.
      b.
        (1)
        (2)
          (a)
          (b)
II.

1g   Writing a Draft

After outlining your paper, the next step is to sit down and write a draft of your *entire* paper on your computer. Get all your sections in place, any headings, and all main ideas. No matter how bad it is, get it written. Save it. Then go for a run, or go to sleep. Leave it for a day. When you come back to it, you won't have to write your paper—you simply will need to *edit* it. Now, how hard is that?

1h   Revising the Draft

Once you have a draft of your paper, you simply need to revise it. Revising is always easier than writing, and Chapter 2 will walk you through the steps.

2 Structure and Style in Writing

Once you have written a draft of your paper, you will need to edit it. This chapter breaks down the process of revising your document into simple, manageable steps.

2a The 10 Revision Cycles

The easiest way to revise your paper is to fix one aspect at a time. **Revision Cycles** help simplify the process. For each cycle, start at the beginning of the document and make a complete pass through your draft focusing on one—and only one—element at a time. Once you finish revising for that aspect, go back to the beginning of the paper and start the next Revision Cycle.

1. Content
2. Clarity
3. Conciseness
4. Elimination of slang, colloquialisms, trite expressions, and jargon
5. Tone
6. Bias-free language
7. Spelling
8. Grammar
9. Uniformity
10. Format

2b Revision Cycle 1: Content

Read though your entire paper, editing the content of your draft. Make sure that you have positioned the sections of the paper correctly and have placed the correct information in each section. Check your ideas for quality, order, balance, emphasis, and transitions.

Sections of a Paper

Confirm that the sections of your paper are located in the correct order and include the needed information.

• Sections of an Essay, Research Paper, or Term Paper

A paper structured as an essay—for example, a research paper or term paper—has three sections: the introduction, the body paragraphs, and the conclusion. For a short paper, do not use headings to begin these sections. If your paper is complex or long (over 20 pages or so), headings may be created for subsections of the paper's body to make reading easier. However, never place headings before the introduction and conclusion paragraphs. In a very long paper, such as a thesis or dissertation, each section of the paper will comprise a full chapter or more. For more information on writing a research paper or term paper, see Chapter 5.

• Sections of a Paper Reporting Original Quantitative or Qualitative Research

A paper that reports your original quantitative or qualitative research is structured as a research article and has five sections. Headings announce the beginning of each section, except for the introduction which has no heading. In a short paper, the discussion and conclusion sections often are combined into a single section titled discussion/conclusion. As a rule of thumb, a paper is "short" if the discussion section is two paragraphs or less in length. For more information about writing a quantitative research paper, see Chapter 6.

Ideas

Focus on your ideas. Did you develop them sufficiently? Are they understandable? Do you need to add more information? Review your arguments carefully. Insert new ideas, and revise or eliminate old ones.

Make sure every sentence says something necessary and important. If not, combine it with another sentence, or delete it altogether. The following sentences are poorly written.

Juvenile delinquency is a social problem.

In the last one hundred years, there has been much social change.

Order

Make sure your paper progresses in an orderly way. Check to see if the organization of your paper follows your outline. If you neglected to construct an outline earlier, do so now. An outline will help you see where you arguments are weak or insufficiently supported with evidence.

Balance

Maintain a balance between description and analysis in your paper, with somewhat more space devoted to analysis. Supply sufficient evidence, but not too much. For example, to support a point, use two good quotes, as opposed to five redundant quotes.

Emphasis

Repeat major points for emphasis using different words. Don't make the reader do the work of figuring out how your paper progresses or what is important. Help the reader by distinguishing your main points from your subpoints through repetition and summary.

Transitions

Add appropriate transitional words and phrases to indicate the logical relationships between sentences. Use them to indicate to the reader that you are shifting to a new idea, or to highlight how certain material should be understood. Transitions help the reader follow the progression of your argument.

Table 2.1 lists some commonly used transitional words and phrases.

TABLE 2.1 Transitional Words and Phrases

To Indicate Addition

additionally	equally important	moreover
again	finally	next
also	further	similarly
and	furthermore	then
and then	in addition	too
besides	last	

To Indicate Comparison

again	in the same way	more importantly
also	likewise	similarly
by comparison		

To Indicate Contrast

although	in spite of	on the one hand . . . on the other hand . . .
but	in the meantime	otherwise
contrastingly	instead	regardless
conversely	meanwhile	still
despite	nevertheless	though
even though	nonetheless	whereas
however	notwithstanding	yet
in contrast to	on the contrary	

TABLE 2.1 Transitional Words and Phrases *Continued*

To Indicate Concession

although it is true that	it may appear that	while everyone agrees that
certainly	naturally	while no one disputes that
given that	of course	
granted that	undoubtedly	

To Indicate Examples

as a matter of fact	indeed	the following example
as an illustration	in fact	thus
after all	in other words	to demonstrate
even	namely	to illustrate
for example	specifically	
for instance	such as	

To Indicate Location

above	far	there
adjacent to	farther on	to the left
around	here	to the right
below	near	to the north
beyond	nearer	to the south
closer to	nearby	
elsewhere	opposite to	

To Indicate Sequence

again	first, second, third	moreover
also	formerly	next
and	furthermore	still
finally	last	too

To Indicate Result

accordingly	consequently	therefore
as a result	hence	thus
because	so	to this end
clearly	then	

TABLE 2.1 *Continued*

To Indicate Time

after	earlier	presently
afterward	eventually	previously
as	finally	simultaneously
as long as	gradually	since
as soon as	immediately	so far
at last	in the meantime	soon
at length	in the past	subsequently
at once	lately	then
at that time	later	thereafter
at the same time	meanwhile	until
before	now	when
by	once	while

To Indicate Repetition

as has been argued (demonstrated, indicated, mentioned, noted, said, shown, stated)	as this paper has demonstrated (argued, indicated, noted, shown, stated)
as I have argued (demonstrated, indicated, mentioned, noted, said, shown, stated)	in brief
	in other words
as mentioned earlier (argued, demonstrated, indicated, noted, shown, stated)	in short

To Indicate Summary or Conclusion

accordingly	in any event	so
as a result	in brief	therefore
at last	in conclusion	thus
consequently	in sum	to conclude
hence	in summary	to summarize
in any case	on the whole	

2c   Revision Cycle 2: Clarity

Now, go back to the beginning of your paper and read through the document again, this time revising for clarity. Make sure your ideas are expressed clearly enough to be understood by a reader not familiar with your topic. Check the logic of your arguments and clarify them where necessary. Define your key concepts and terms if they are complex or technical.

Use a definition from the sociological literature, not a dictionary. Make sure you use terms consistently throughout your document. Don't switch your usage just because you reference a source that employs the term differently.

Paragraph Structure

How can you know whether your writing itself is clear? The easiest way is to check your paper systematically, one page at a time, focusing on the structure of each paragraph. This approach isn't as time-consuming as it may sound, and it can help you quickly diagnose more serious problems—for example, that you don't know what to write so you simply repeat one point over and over in different words.

A paragraph should begin with a clear and meaningful topic sentence that summarizes the main point of the entire paragraph. The remaining sentences of the paragraph explain and support the topic sentence using (1) facts, (2) explanation, (3) examples and illustrations, and (4) testimony. By fitting these elements together in an orderly way, you create logical, clear, powerful paragraphs. There are six principal patterns of ordering information in paragraphs.

Six Patterns for Organizing Paragraphs

1. Time

Start with a topic sentence, and then organize the remaining sentences of the paragraph chronologically. This approach is useful when describing a method or steps in a process.

> A recurrent event was the arrival of a red two-door sedan in midafternoon. After parking directly in front of the bar, the driver would open the hood and then unlock the trunk. He would be joined by several people. After about ten minutes of activity, the driver would get back in the car and leave. This routine would take place two more times in late afternoon. (Whyte 2002:176)

2. Space

Start with a topic sentence, and then organize the remaining sentences of the paragraph around spatial order, using words such as *across, over, under,* and *near.* This approach is used when describing a location.

The shrines may be found anywhere in the yard area—front, back, or along the sides — although the front yard, especially near the sidewalk, appears to be a favored location. Regardless of placement, however, the front of the shrine always faces the street. Since these are personal shrines, built to suit the religious needs and preferences of individuals, no two are exactly alike; diversity is the standard. In size, the shrines range from about two to ten feet in height, and two to six feet in width. Most are rectangular in shape, although octagonal and circular structures are not uncommon. The most frequently used building materials include brick, cement, stone, and glass; wood is rarely, if ever, used except for trimming. Exterior walls, though, are often stuccoed or tiled. A single cross may adorn the top of a shrine, and use of latticework and other forms of ornamentation are occasionally found, but in general the degree of exterior embellishment is more austere than ornate. (Curtis 1996:488)

3. General to Particular

Start with a topic sentence, followed by sentences with details, examples, and explanations that provide supporting evidence.

I interviewed all fifty-seven ex-nuns for approximately two hours each, using the focused interview as a prototype. There were a number of specific issues I wanted to explore with each interviewee; however, the sequence in which I introduced them was unstructured and determined by the flow of the interview. In addition to asking predetermined questions, I followed up and explored any areas that seemed pertinent and meaningful to the person being interviewed. If one individual brought up an issue that seemed especially important with regard either to the role-exit process in general or to the specific order from which she had exited, I introduced that issue in subsequent interviews in order to obtain additional information. In this sense, I used a grounded theory approach (Glaser and Strauss 1967). (Ebaugh 1988:26)

4. Particular to General

Start with several sentences that present specific details or examples. The final sentence of the paragraph is the topic sentence. This technique is not commonly used in sociological writing, and is more typically found in popular writing. The fact that a sociologist of considerable stature wrote the following paragraph makes it all the more fascinating.

People who like to avoid shocking discoveries, who prefer to believe that society is just what they were taught in Sunday School, who like the safety of the rules and the maxims of what Alfred Schutz has called the "world-taken-for-granted," should stay away from sociology. People who feel no temptation before closed doors, who have no curiosity about human beings, who are content to admire scenery without wondering about the people who live in those houses on the other side of that river, should probably stay away from sociology. They will find it unpleasant or, at any rate, unrewarding. People who are interested in human beings only if they can change, convert or reform them should also be warned, for they will find sociology much less useful than they hoped. And people whose interest is mainly in their own conceptual constructions will do just as well to turn to the study of little white mice. Sociology will be satisfying, in the long run, only to those who can think of nothing more entrancing than to watch men and to understand things human. (Berger 1963:7)

5. Climax

Start with a topic sentence, and then arrange the details or examples in order of increasing importance. This strategy is commonly used in arguments and debates.

Consider, for example, a northern California police who rode with the Hell's Angels for a year and half. He was responsible for a large number of arrests, including previously almost untouchable higher-level drug dealers. He was praised for doing a "magnificent job." But this came at a cost of heavy drug use, alcoholism, brawling, the breakup of his family, and his inability to fit back into routine police after the investigation was over. The result was resignation from the force, several bank robberies, and a prison term. (Marx 1991:285)

6. Compare and Contrast

When you compare two elements (such as two authors, works, or ideas), you focus on the ways they are similar. When you contrast two elements, you look at the ways they are different.

There are two approaches you can use to compare and contrast within one paragraph.

a. The block method: You present information first about one element, and then the other within the same paragraph.

b. The alternating method: You discuss each of the elements with regard to Point 1, then Point 2, then Point 3, and so forth within the same paragraph.

Because the level of ideas presented in sociological writing tends to be complex, it is fairly rare to find compare and contrast within one paragraph used in sociology. Many general writing handbooks talk about this approach, and therefore it is noted here as well—but mainly to warn you. This approach is difficult to handle. Instead, the preferred and much easier method of comparing and contrasting is shown in Chapter 9. There, points of comparison and contrast are discussed in separate paragraphs, allowing room for the full and unhampered development of ideas. Outlines for two versions of the compare/contrast paper (similar to the block method and the alternating method) can be found there.

TABLE 2.2 Wordy Phrases and Concise Alternatives

Wordy	Concise
beginning to learn	learns
is able to start	starts
really low self-esteem	low self-esteem
actually motivated	motivated
pretty interested	somewhat interested
persons of the masculine sex	males

`2d` Revision Cycle 3: Conciseness

In Revision Cycles 1 and 2, you added additional material to your paper. Now, in Revision Cycle 3, read through your document and eliminate wordiness. Make sure each word in your paper counts. Get rid of the fluff, the filler, the useless words, the meaningless sentences. (Don't worry that you won't have anything left! The upcoming cycles will help you bulk up your paper in substantive ways that you will make your paper sound more sophisticated and erudite.)

Table 2.2 shows a few examples.

`2e` Revision Cycle 4: Elimination of Slang, Colloquialisms, Trite Expressions, and Jargon

College papers should be written using a formal academic tone. To achieve this tone, one key step is the elimination of all informal language, including slang, colloquialisms, trite expressions, and jargon. In this Revision Cycle, review your document, replacing all nonstandard English terms with standard usage.

To check if a word or expression is classified as informal, consult a dictionary—either online or in print (be sure to use a recent edition). Find the definition for the term you wish to use, keeping in mind that many words have multiple meanings, some of which may be slang or informal whereas others are not (the word *break*, for example). If a term is categorized as informal, slang, colloquialism, idiom, interjection, or jargon, this information will be noted in the dictionary's definition, and the term should not be used.

Remember, in a college paper your goal is not to sound "cool" or "hip." Instead, try to sound like your instructor. After all, who is going to grade your paper?

Slang

Slang is a short-lived style of language usually characteristic of subcultures within a society, such as age groups, localities, and social or cultural groups. Because slang changes fairly rapidly much like a fad, and since it usually identifies

TABLE 2.3 Slang Terms and Formal Standard English Alternatives

Slang	Formal
(totally) awesome	splendid, remarkable
bash	party, celebration
cool	very good, socially adept, skillful
chill	calm down, relax
decked	knocked down
dope	illicit drugs, narcotics
dude	fellow, chap, person
figure out	calculate, consider, conclude, decide
stinks	low quality, the appearance of dishonesty
uptight	nervous, very conventional
wired	tense

the user as a member of a subculture—or as one who "tries too hard to relate" to the in-group—it is more appropriate for casual speech than for the written word. Imagine a set of college course readings where theories are described as *fab*, *boss*, *groovy*, or *the cat's meow*. (In case you are curious, the previous four words are synonymous with *totally amazing*.) Slang is dramatic, flamboyant, emotionally charged, and highly changeable, and for all those reasons should not be used in formal writing. Table 2.3 lists some slang terms and more formal alternatives.

Colloquialisms and Other Informal Terms

Colloquialisms and informal language are words or expressions typically used in ordinary informal conversation. As a varied and richly nuanced language, however, English offers more shadings of meanings than can be expressed in the simple dichotomous distinction between "formal" and "informal." A thesaurus entry for the word *go*, for example, yields a rich lode of alternate words and expressions conveying varying degrees of formality, from very formal to slang (see Table 2.4). Additionally,

TABLE 2.4 Formal and Informal Synonyms for the Word *Go*

More formal—depart, withdraw

Formal—go, leave

Informal—run along, get going

More informal—skedaddle, scoot, scram

Slang—split, vamoose, take a powder, make a getaway

TABLE 2.5 Colloquialisms, Informal Terms*, and Formal Standard
English Alternatives

Colloquialism	Formal
booze	an alcoholic beverage
cops	police officers
kids	children
flunk	fail
teenager*	adolescent
babies*	infants, toddlers
mama*	mother
pretty good*	good, fine, average
figured out*	discovered, realized
a great idea*	a first-rate, or fine, idea
in all honesty*	actually
a lot*	very much, a great deal
she is something*	she is a remarkable person
she has something to say*	she expresses an important viewpoint
upwards of*	more than

as you can see by looking at the synonyms for the word *go*, colloquialisms and other informal terms themselves vary in their degree of formality, spanning a range from more to less formal (*get going* versus *skedaddle*).

Colloquialisms and other informal terms differ in the length of time they have been in use, and whether they have undergone transformation in degree of formality over time. Many of the words listed in Table 2.5 actually have been in use a century or more (for example, *skedaddle* and *scoot*), unlike slang which often becomes outdated within a decade or less. Still, colloquialisms and informal language are not appropriate for academic or business writing and must be avoided.

Trite Expressions

Trite expressions include (1) overused phrases, and (2) expressions that have no empirical referent. Overused phrases, also known as clichés, are expressions that were once colorful and descriptive, but now are boring and uninteresting because they are used so frequently. They are usually viewed as a sign of lazy thinking by the writer. If you find them in your paper, replace them with less dramatic, but simpler and more straightforward wording (see Table 2.6).

Expressions with no empirical referent are descriptive phrases that are not logical, or do not have a reference point, in the real (empirical) world. They are colorful and

TABLE 2.6 Clichés and Formal Standard English Alternatives

Trite	Formal
law and order	law abiding, a lawful society
from coast to coast	nationally
the good times and the bad times	throughout life
trials and tribulations	difficulties, hardships
powers that be	the authorities, the government
sadder but wiser	matured, seasoned, realistic
last but not least	last, finally

TABLE 2.7 Expressions with No Empirical Referent and Formal Standard English Alternatives

No Empirical Referent	Formal
an *off the wall* idea	an unusual, novel, innovative idea
the room was *crying out for* a cleaning	the room needed cleaning
jump at the opportunity	eager
waiting in the wings	available
the program was *in full swing*	the program was operating at full capacity
a *black-and-white example of*	an example of
a *clear-cut* example	an example
she was *torn apart by*	she was distressed, grieved, hurt by
it was *raining cats and dogs*	there was a rainstorm, it was raining
the book *goes into*	the book describes, discusses, details

flamboyant, which makes them enjoyable to use, but they are not appropriate for formal academic or business writing (see Table 2.7).

Jargon

Each discipline and occupation (as well as hobbies, sports, and other areas of endeavor) has its own specialized terminology, or **jargon**—a technical language for insiders in the field. When writing a paper, however, you should not use the jargon of your specialty area. You should imagine the audience for your writing to be broader than just people from your field who are familiar with the jargon (see Table 2.8). Jargon, like other types of casual language, should be reserved for conversations where you are trying to give the impression of informality and affiliation with the in-group.

TABLE 2.8 Jargon and Formal Standard English Alternatives

Jargon	Formal
the program has *impacted*	the program has affected, influenced
she *fed back* to me quickly	she responded to me quickly
he *worked through* it	he handled it
he *acted out* his frustration	he expressed his frustration
the *perpetrator*, the *perp*	the suspect
the *collar*	the arrested suspect

2f Revision Cycle 5: Tone

In the university and the workplace, as mentioned earlier, you need to use a formal academic tone in your writing. Your goal is to sound serious and thoughtful, not chatty or hip.

In this Revision Cycle, review your entire document, improving the tone of your writing. There are five specific steps you can take in this Revision Cycle to achieve a formal academic tone in your paper.

Eliminate Contractions

Contractions (such as *don't* or *isn't*) lend a sense of informality to your paper, and should not be used in formal writing.

Eliminate First-Person and Second-Person Pronouns

Rid your writing of the following pronouns:

I, me, my, mine
We, our, ours
You, your, yours

Changing these pronouns will force you to restructure your sentences, thereby making your writing more complex and sophisticated.

Eliminate Extreme Language

Use a *moderate* range of variation in your choice of words. Intelligent people do not get carried away by their emotions often, and certainly not when they are discussing a serious subject. When you use colorful, emotionally laden terms, such as *great, fabulous, terrific,* or *excellent,* you sound passionate and not very scientific. Your goal in formal writing should be to sound balanced, calm, thoughtful, and scientific.

TABLE 2.9 A Continuum of Extreme Language

Extremely bad			Extremely good
awful	average	fine	fabulous
horrible	competent	insightful	marvelous
terrible	suitable	thoughtful	wonderful
ugly	passable	attractive	magnificent
catastrophic	troubling	important	amazing

It might help to think of your word choices as arranged on a continuum with extremely positive at one end, and extremely negative at the other. Use terms drawn from the middle of the continuum to make your writing sound intelligent, as shown in Table 2.9.

Avoid Big Words for Their Own Sake

Students often think their writing will impress if they pull a big word out of a thesaurus and plant it in their paper. However, unless the word is used correctly, this strategy will backfire badly, so don't do it! Do not use any word you are not *absolutely* sure you are using properly. There are many embarrassing stories of students who made "slight" errors that proved unforgettable to their readers. Don't be one of these cases.

Also, keep in mind that the larger and more distinctive the word, the more memorable it is. Words that attract attention in that way should be used only *once* in a paper. In fact, a student who used the same big word in every paper he or she wrote would probably become something of a joke. Think of words such as *indomitable, exclusivity, extrapolate, trope,* or *weltanschauung.* These are words that should be used only rarely.

Never Say *Never* (or *All* or *Every*)

Do not use broad generalizations such as *never, all,* or *every.* After all, human behavior is not easy to classify, and as sociologists, we know that there are almost always exceptions to every rule, and deviance in a population is to be expected. Intelligent readers will question everything you say, so avoid words that convey absolutes.

Don't Use	Do Use
never	tends not to
all	most
everybody	seems to, appears to, tends to
absolutely	it may be
always	it is apparent that, it is likely that

2g Revision Cycle 6: Bias-Free Language

Do a complete review of your document, eliminating all biased language. Today, more than ever, there is no excuse for using terminology that reflects stereotypes or bias based on gender, race, ethnicity, age, social class, disabilities, religion, family status, sexual orientation, or other personal characteristics. It is important to master bias-free language, since it is the standard in sociological writing, as well as in business and government communication today. Your wording should not be offensive or distracting to a reasonable reader, and you should use demographically identifying terms only when they are essential to the meaning you are attempting to convey. (For more information, see *The Chicago Manual of Style* 2003:233.)

Gender-Neutral Language

Unless you are writing about specific individuals of a particular gender, use gender-neutral terms. The guidelines presented here are the widely accepted standards for nonsexist terms in both academic and business writing today. For additional details, see McGraw-Hill's (1979) *Guidelines for Equal Treatment of the Sexes*, and the University of Wollongong's (2003) Web site for policy and guidelines on nondiscriminatory language.

1. Don't use *man, men,* or *mankind* as generic terms. Instead, replace with *person, individual, people,* or *humankind.*
2. Replace terms that incorporate the word *man* or *father.*

Don't Use	Do Use
man-made	synthetic, artificial, handcrafted, manufactured
manpower	workforce, staff, labor
mankind	humankind, humanity, the human race
manned ("he manned the phones")	staffed, handled
manhandled	assaulted, pushed, shoved
prehistoric man	prehistoric humans, ancient civilization
average man in the street	average person, ordinary person
forefathers	ancestors
founding fathers	founders, pioneers

3. Replace terms that incorporate the word *man* in the name of occupations.

Don't Use	Do Use
chairman	chairperson, chair, convener, moderator
statesman	leader
assemblyman	member of the assembly
congressman	member of Congress
newspaperman	reporter, journalist
businessman	business executive
salesman	sales clerk, salesperson
fireman	firefighter
policeman	police officer
mailman	mail carrier, postal worker
foreman	supervisor

4. Do not distinguish people based on gender when it is not relevant to the matter under discussion.

Don't Use	Do Use
The men and women attended the concert.	The people attended the concert.
	The residents attended the concert.
Girls and boys still play in the old gym.	Children still play in the old gym.
	Students still play in the old gym.

5. Avoid gendered pronouns (*his, hers*). Instead, use *the*, or try restructuring to use the plural *they*. This approach is preferred to using the slashed gendered pronouns (*his/hers*), repeating the conjunction *or* (*he or she*), or switching gendered pronouns middocument (using the pronoun *she* in the first half of the document, then switching to the pronoun *he*).

6. Refer to males and females in equivalent terms. Males should not be presumed to possess stereotypically masculine characteristics nor females stereotypically feminine traits. Don't discuss men in terms of their accomplishments and women in terms of their appearance. Refer to a woman by her own name, and not by her husband's name.

Don't Use	Do Use
Of course, he did not cry.	He did not cry.
Steve Smith lets his wife work.	Judy Smith works at the bank.

Naturally, Sally is a good cook.	Sally is a good cook.
John is a skilled mechanic and his girlfriend Alice is an attractive redhead.	John is a skilled mechanic and Alice is a talented artist.
	or
	John is a handsome blond and Alice is an attractive redhead.
This is Mrs. John Smith.	This is Susan Smith.

Writing about Race/Ethnicity

Do not use racial or ethnic stereotypes. Describe an individual's race or ethnicity only when necessary, and then use precise terms if known.

She is Vietnamese American.	is better than	She is Asian.
He is Puerto Rican.	is better than	He is Hispanic.

When discussing subjects in a research study, however, individuals may be designated by their race or ethnicity, and grouped together with others in pan-racial or pan-ethnic categories of analysis (*20% of black males . . . , like other Hispanic females . . .*). For additional information, see the American Psychological Association's (2007) Web site.

The following names should be used for racial and ethnic groups, according to the *American Sociological Association Style Guide* (2007).

African Americans (no hyphen)
blacks, whites (lowercase)
Hispanic, Chicano, Latino/Latina
Asian, Asian American (no hyphen)
American Indian, Native American (no hyphen)

When writing about racial and ethnic groups, a key factor determining your choice of terminology is the purpose of your description. Sociologists write to share ideas with others in the field, so commonly understood terms must be used. Also, a major goal of sociology is to study and generalize about social trends. Describing a single case in great detail has limited use; after all, a single case may be unique or at least different than the majority of cases. For both these reasons, terms must be used that allow comparisons between your work and that of other researchers.

Thus, for example, asking subjects how they wish to be identified and then using their chosen label is not necessarily the best way to handle the issue of a group name. You need to check how sociologists have labeled the group (by reviewing the recent literature). If the subjects' and literature's approach differ, it is best to use the approach of the literature and then discuss the divergent views of the subjects in your paper (which itself may become an important contribution of your work).

Today, most sociological studies that discuss racial and ethnic group membership in the United States tend to identify four main groups: whites, blacks (or African Americans), Hispanics, and Asians.

Note that three of these groups are racial groups (whites, blacks, and Asians), and one group is an ethnic group (Hispanics). Sociologists since the 1990s have dealt with the issue of handling these two variables (race and ethnicity) by combining them into a single variable called race/ethnicity, which is usually conceptualized as having the four categories previously listed (white, black, Hispanic, and Asian).

Writing about Age

Refer to age only when necessary, and then state it in a straightforward manner. Avoid terms such as *mature, seasoned, well-preserved,* and *senior citizen,* or a surprised tone about the accomplishments of older people.

Don't Use	Do Use
Although in his 70s, John has finally been recognized as an accomplished painter.	John, at 75, has finally been recognized as an accomplished painter.

Writing about Social Class

When writing about social class, avoid bias. Don't assume most people are from the same social class as you, or share the same values. Concepts of "meaningful work," entertainment, and sports differ among the classes, so don't impose your views. If you want to make the point that a person considers one job superior to another, indicate that you are reporting that person's viewpoint, *not* your own.

Don't Use	Do Use
After two years of working in a factory, Joan quit to take a more meaningful job.	After two years of working in a factory, Joan quit to take a job she found more meaningful.

Also, avoid stereotypical terms based on class, such as *redneck, bumpkin, hillbilly, rube, blue blood,* and *the super rich.*

Writing about Disabilities

Mention a person's disability only when relevant. Use the term *disability* in describing people, and the word *handicap* for the specific limitation. Avoid biased language or terms that imply victimhood (*a cripple*). Don't use euphemisms, such as *mentally* or *physically challenged,* which may seem to trivialize the disability.

The term *people with disabilities* is preferable to *the disabled* or *disabled people*, as these latter terms imply that the person is defined mainly by the disability. Similarly, when mentioning specific disabilities, it is preferable to refer to *people who are blind or vision impaired, people who are deaf or hearing impaired,* and *people who have asthma,* rather than the *blind, the deaf,* and *asthmatics.* Note that the opposite of *disabled* is *nondisabled* (not *normal*). For additional information, see the American Psychological Association's Web site: http://apastyle.org/disabilities.html.

Don't Use	Do Use
She was confined to a wheelchair.	She used a wheelchair.
He suffered from a heart condition.	He had a heart condition.
He was an AIDS victim.	He contracted AIDS.
She was mentally (physically) challenged.	She had (the name of the disease).

Writing about Religion

Mention a person's religion only when relevant. Avoid religious stereotypes and imprecise generalizations, such as *Christians believe in the Bible* or *Catholics oppose abortion.* Keep in mind there is much diversity *within* particular religious groups, not only among different religions and religious denominations. Also, note that there may be a difference between people's religious **beliefs** and their actual **behaviors.**

Writing about Family Status

Refer to a person's marital, family, or parenting status only when relevant. Avoid stereotypes and labels with negative connotations associated with family status.

Don't Use	Do Use
maiden	girl, young woman
unmarried woman	single woman
spinster, old maid	single woman
playboy	single man
divorcée, divorcé	divorced woman, divorced man
housewife, househusband	stay-at-home mom, stay-at-home dad, wife, husband
matronly	mature, dignified, stately
vixen, shrew	temperamental or argumentative person
barren, infertile, childless	does not have children

Also, keep in mind that forms of address should not reflect marital status (unless you are instructed otherwise). For men, the courtesy form of address, *Mr.*, does not denote marital status. For women, however, the traditional forms of address, *Miss* or *Mrs.*, are determined by marital status. For this reason, the alternate term *Ms.* was introduced in the late 1960s to refer to both single and married women, and this form of address has become widely accepted. Today, it is appropriate to use *Ms.* as the courtesy form of address for women, unless you are told that a particular woman wants to be addressed differently. (Note: When you use *Ms.*, do not use a woman's husband's first name.)

Don't Use	Do Use
Ms. John Smith	Ms. Susan Smith

Writing about Sexual Orientation

Refer to sexual orientation only when relevant. Avoid negative stereotypes or terms with negative connotations. Do not assume everyone is attracted to the opposite sex.

2h Revision Cycle 7: Spelling

Check your paper carefully for spelling errors. Using the spell-check program on your computer is an efficient first step, but you still must do a careful read-through yourself to find the errors the computer cannot catch. There is no substitute for an "eyeball check."

Get a good college dictionary and have it available next to your computer as you type. Also, a style guide like Kate Turabian's (1996) *A Manual for Writers of Term Papers, Theses, and Dissertations* is an excellent resource for looking up unusual cases or special formats.

It is useful to have a second person read your paper and help you find misspellings and other errors. Alternatively, try checking your paper from the end, going backward, word by word. That way, your eyes won't gloss over errors as you read quickly and you are more likely to catch your typos.

Below are some common spelling-related problems that are often encountered in academic and business writing. The examples presented here follow the ASA *Style Guide* (2007), but you can feel confident utilizing them in papers and other written communication in a variety of settings.

Abbreviations

- Spell out the words *versus* and *chi-square* in running text. Do not use abbreviations.
- Do not use the abbreviations *etc.*, *i.e.*, or *e.g.* in running text. Do not spell out the word *etcetera*. In the text, replace the abbreviations with the phrases shown here. Abbreviations, however, may be used within parentheses in your text.

Abbreviation	Substitute Phrase for Running Text
etc.	and so on, and so forth
i.e.	in other words, that is to say
e.g.	for example, such as

- Write out in full the names of colleges, universities, and other institutions. If the institution has a lengthy name and it is used several times within your document, spell out the name fully the first time it is used, followed by the abbreviated name in parentheses. Then, the abbreviated name may be used in the remainder of the document. When indicating a specific campus within a university system, use a hyphen to append the location of the specific campus. If the name of campus's location itself is hyphenated, then follow the example for the *University of Illinois* as shown.

The Brookings Institution

California State University-Los Angeles (CSULA)

University of Illinois at Urbana-Champaign

Acronyms

Acronyms are accepted shortcuts of certain names and phrases, formed by combining their initial letters. They are pronounced as words, not as separate letters.

Acronym	Full Name
NASA	National Aeronautics and Space Administration
NORC	National Opinion Research Center
OPEC	Organization of Petroleum Exporting Countries
WASP	White Anglo-Saxon Protestant

If you wish to use an acronym, you need to establish its meaning first. When using an acronym, write out the full term the first time it is used, and follow it with the acronym placed in parentheses. In subsequent uses, the acronym may be used alone.

The National Opinion Research Center (NORC) provided assistance for the research study. NORC data files were used for comparative analysis . . .

Handling Numbers

1. Spell out numbers one through nine in words.

   two, three, four

2. Write numbers 10 or greater in numerals.

   15

   1,687

3. Treat ordinal numbers similarly. Spell out ordinals (*first, second, third*) for numbers one through nine, and use numerals for 10 and greater (*15th, 150th*).

   The second and third stages of the study were completed this year.

   Every 15th document was reviewed.

4. Use numerals with the word *percent*

   Of men, 5 percent are first year students.

5. When numbers are part of a comparison, be consistent in either spelling them out or writing them as numerals. Generally, numerals are preferred.

   Of the 150 students in the class, 8 percent are first-year students and 35 percent are second-year students.

6. Avoid having a number as the first word in a sentence. If you must do so, spell out the number in words.

   One hundred and fifty subjects participated in the first phase of the study.

   Fifteen hundred subjects were followed in a 10-year longitudinal study.

7. Use numerals within tables, figures, equations, and hypotheses.

   Over 75% of self-identifying Catholics . . .

8. Use numerals to refer to tables, figures, equations, and hypotheses.

   The results are summarized in Table 4.

   See Figure 2.

9. Spell out the word *percent* in running text and in parentheses. Use numerals with the word *percent*. In equations, tables, and figures, the percent symbol (%) is used.

   The study found that 8 percent of male students completed the training in less than one hour.

   The 77th percentile

10. Numbers over one million should be written as a numeral followed by the word *million, billion,* and so forth. Numbers less than one million should be written in numerals.

    The population increased by 1.5 million in 2007.

    An estimated 130,000 people died of the disease.

11. Time, money, and sample size should be written in numerals.

    The research team observed from 8:00 a.m. to 5:00 p.m.

    A $20 bill

    N = 1,500

Dates

The date should be presented in the following format: March 20, 1982. No abbreviations are used for dates.

Here are other acceptable forms of dates you may encounter.

twentieth century
nineteenth-century scientists (a compound adjective is hyphenated)

1960s (no apostrophe)
mid-1960s
On December 13, 1983, a special event occurred. (comma after month and year)
December 1983 (no comma)
1945 to 1965 (in the text, use the word *to* instead of an en dash)

Phone Numbers

The ASA has established guidelines for phone numbers. When an address and phone number are listed together, separate them by a semicolon. Phone numbers should be written by placing the area code within parentheses, leaving a space, and then typing the first three digits of the phone number separated from the last four digits by a hyphen.

Wrong	Right
310-555-1212	(310) 555-1212
310/555-1212	
310.555.1212	

2i Revision Cycle 8: Grammar

Editing your paper for grammar is vital. No matter how original or insightful your ideas, if the reader can't understand your paper easily, you won't be taken seriously—and your grade will suffer, as well. There are a number of good references you can consult for help with writing mechanics, such as *The St. Martin's Handbook* (Lunsford 2008).

There are some shortcuts to improving grammar in your paper, which are listed in the following text. They are not a substitute for learning the rules of grammar, but can be used as a quick checklist for raising the quality of your grammar, and thus your writing.

Eliminate All Forms of the Verb *To Be*

In sociology papers at the college level, it may be difficult to rid your paper of all forms of the verb *to be*, but try reducing the number of times you use any form of the verb (*is, was, will be*). Substitute an action verb, or merge sentences to restructure. Just implementing this simple step will improve your writing dramatically.

Eliminate the Word *How*

Eliminate the word *how* from your text.

Don't Use	Do Use
how a child is born	the process of childbirth
how she came to the United States	her migration to the United States

Elements in a List Must Be Equivalent

In formal academic and business writing, when you list elements, they must be expressed in equivalent form. Note that in the first case, nonequivalence can produce an interesting rhythm that could be useful in creative writing, but is not appropriate for formal writing.

Don't Use	Do Use
My breakfast consisted of *cereal, a slice of toast*, and a *really tall mug of steaming coffee*.	My breakfast consisted of *cereal, toast*, and *coffee*.
	OR
	My breakfast consisted of *a bowl of cereal, a slice of toast*, and *a cup of coffee*.

Word Choice and Word Usage

Writing should be clear and concise. Eliminate euphemisms and pompous sentences, and make sure specialized terminology in sociology is used correctly. Euphemisms are mild or vague expressions that replace blunter terms. Some examples are shown.

Don't Use	Do Use
passed away	died
rest room	bathroom
experienced downsizing	was fired

Pompous sentences should be avoided. Simplify overly complex wording (e.g., *It is recommended that the program's relative functionality be subjected to periodic reevaluation*). Additionally, there are certain words that are used in special ways in sociology, and students in the field should be familiar with these terms to use them (or avoid them) appropriately (see Table 2.10).

Punctuation

Always use full and correct sentences. Here is a quick checklist of common punctuation problems. You can use this list to cross-check your paper. For additional help, consult a general writing handbook.

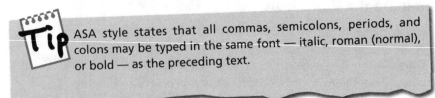

Tip ASA style states that all commas, semicolons, periods, and colons may be typed in the same font — italic, roman (normal), or bold — as the preceding text.

TABLE 2.10 Frequently Misused Terms in Sociology

Term	Acceptable Use
affect	A verb, meaning "to influence."
alienation	Use only following either Durkheim's or Marx's use of the term.
cause	Avoid this word; use instead *affected, influenced,* or *shaped.*
data	*Data* are plural; the singular is *datum.*
effect	A noun, meaning *a result;* a verb, meaning to *make happen.*
prove	Avoid this word; use instead *demonstrates, illustrates,* or *shows.*
significant	Use only in the statistical sense that the null hypothesis has been rejected. Otherwise, use *important, valuable, meaningful,* or *salient.*
socialization	Use only in the sociological sense of "learning the way of life in society"; do not use to refer to partying or having an enjoyable time.
status	Use only in the sociological meaning of "position in society," and not to mean "prestige."
U.S.	Use as an adjective. Use *United States* as a noun.

• Spacing Punctuation

Leave one space after a punctuation mark, including a period and a colon, except in the following cases:

- There is no space before or after a hyphen or en dash (–).

    California State University–Los Angeles

- There is no space before, between, or after an en (–) or em (—) dash.

    Each of the variables—gender, race/ethnicity, age, and social class—is discussed separately.

- There is no space between punctuation marks at the end of a sentence. Note that the period goes inside the quotation marks.

    The text discusses "writer's block."

• Commas

Check that you have used commas correctly. Commas are needed in the following cases:

1. Commas separate words, phrases, and clauses in a series.

When listing three or more items in a series, separate them with commas. If a conjunction (*and, or*) joins the last two items, place a comma before the conjunction.

The paper was coauthored by Able, Baker, and Charles.

2. Commas are placed after an adverbial or participial phrase at the start of a sentence.

Nevertheless, middle-income men supported the program.

According to Jones (1988), the response rate increased with a follow-up mailing.

Working all night on her paper, she finished at dawn.

3. Commas are used before a coordinating conjunction (*and, but, for, nor, or, so, yet*) that joins two independent clauses in a sentence.

The researchers collected data from February through April 2008, and they began data analysis in May.

4. But commas are not used before a conjunction that joins two parts of a complex predicate.

The researchers collected data from February through April 2008 and began data analysis in May.

5. Commas are placed after certain abbreviations.

The abbreviation *i.e.,* meaning "in other words," requires a comma. Likewise, *e.g.,* meaning "for example," needs a comma. These abbreviations should not be used in running text, but may be used within parentheses in the text. The abbreviations are not italicized.

What role did you assume as a researcher (i.e., did you simply observe or did you participate in the group's activities)?

Missing data (e.g., when respondents leave an answer blank) are not usually included in the presentation of frequency distributions.

6. Commas set off individual elements in dates, addresses, and names of places.

A comma is used in a date arranged in order of month, day, and year. If the date appears in the middle of a sentence, place a comma after the year. A comma is not used between a month and a year or a season and a year. In an address, commas follow the street address, and the name of city, but not the state. In a place-name, a comma separates the names of the city and state.

Comma in date	The project began on May 24, 1992, and concluded on June 3, 1993.
No comma in partial date	The research team conducted interviews during August 2001.
Comma in address	616 116th Street, New York, NY 10027
Comma in place-name	Researchers surveyed teenagers in Tampa, Florida.

7. Commas separate two adjectives modifying the same noun.

> In this example, a comma is needed because *young* and *middle-class* modify *city dwellers:*
>
> **Over 50 percent of the respondents were young, middle-class city dwellers.**
>
> In this example, no comma is needed because *young* modifies *city dwellers:*
>
> **Over 50 percent of the respondents were young city dwellers.**

8. Commas set off a parenthetical comment or an aside that is short and related to the rest of the sentence.

> **Delinquency, for example, has been studied extensively by social scientists.**

9. Commas set off a nonrestrictive modifier. A **nonrestrictive modifier** is not an essential part of the sentence and could be eliminated without changing the sentence's meaning, unlike a **restrictive modifier.**

Words in Apposition

Nonrestrictive modifier	The work of Max Weber, the so-called father of sociology, continues to influence sociologists today.
Restrictive modifier	The work of so-called father of sociology Max Weber continues to influence sociologists today.

Clauses That Begin With *Who, Whom, Whose, That,* or *Which*

Nonrestrictive	Sociologists, whose work is constantly put to the test by changing social conditions, are on the cutting edge of new developments.
Restrictive	Sociologists whose work has been put to the test by changing social conditions have had to be on the cutting edge of new developments or they would be left behind.

Use the word *which* in nonrestrictive clauses and the word *that* for restrictive clauses. If either word can be used correctly in the sentence, *that* is preferred.

Nonrestrictive	The study by Smith, which surveyed college students at the three midwestern universities, studied fraternity membership and racial prejudice.
Restrictive	Smith's study of fraternity membership and racial prejudice raised a number of questions about his personal biases.

• Semicolons

Semicolons should be used rarely throughout a paper. Even as you strive for a formal academic tone, too many semicolons will make your paper seem unduly artificial and stilted. So while the list that follows shows you when semicolons may be used, you should try to limit creating situations where they are needed.

Semicolons are used to join two parts of a sentence that are of equal importance. They may be used in the following situations.

1. Semicolons connect two related independent clauses not joined by a conjunction.

    "In 1940, social scientists were asking respondents whether 'blacks' should be allowed to ride on the same bus as 'whites'; in 1975, their surveys contained questions about busing 'black' and 'white' schoolchildren" (Cuba 2002:74).

2. Semicolons separate elements in a series when the elements already contain commas.

    The three coauthors of the paper included John Miller, from Antioch College; Kate Johnson, from Barnard College; and William Hatcher, from Columbia University.

• Colons

Use a colon between two parts of a sentence to indicate that the second part of the sentence is an explanation or elaboration of the first part. Leave only one space after a colon. Colons are used in the following situations:

1. Colons introduce a clause, phrase, or series of elements that elaborates or expands on the part of the sentence preceding the colon.

    The United States is founded on three principles: life, liberty, and the pursuit of happiness.

2. When a colon follows a complete clause and introduces a full sentence, capitalize the first word after the colon. Note that the full sentence following the colon can be a quote.

    The major findings of this study include the following: Most interactions occur between members of the same racial/ethnic group, and where nongroup members interact, the encounter tends to be initiated by a male toward a female.

3. Colons often are used to introduce lists. A clause or sentence will describe the list, followed by a colon. Then a series of elements (numbered or not numbered) are listed. If the elements are short and simple, use commas to separate them. If the elements are long or complex, separate them with semicolons. Do not use a colon when the list is a grammatically essential part of the sentence.

Not numbered	Gordon described two types of assimilation: cultural and structural (1978:157).
Numbered, with commas	"Putting together the equality dimension with the structural dimension, we may thus distinguish four types of societies with regard to ethnic orientation: (1) racist, (2) assimilationist, (3) liberal pluralist, and (4) corporate pluralist" (Gordon 1978:89).
Numbered, with semicolons	". . . classify cognitive capacities into five categories: (1) conceptualization; (2) means-ends apprehension; (3) self-conception; (4) evaluation; and (5) rationalization" (Gordon 1978: 50).
Colon	The study included three variables: gender, age, and marital status.
No colon	The three variables studied included gender, age, and marital status.

• Hyphens and Dashes

Hyphens are typed as (-), with no spaces before or after, as in the word *self-concept.* Dashes are indicated using two hyphens (--) with no spaces before, between, or after them. You also may use an em dash. Em dashes are used to show a break in thought or add an explanation, as in the sentence: *She wrote up her findings—although they were not published for another five years—and subsequently became famous for her discovery.* Dashes should be used rarely in a paper.

Hyphens are used in the following situations:

1. Hyphenate compound adjectives.

   never-married women

   home-based schooling

   working-class families

2. Hyphenate compound nouns and numbers.

   decision-making

   twenty-three

   great-grandson

3. Use a hyphen to separate the name of a university system from the name of a specific campus. However, if the name of the campus itself is hyphenated, use the form shown.

        California State University-Northridge

But   University of Illinois at Urbana-Champaign

4. Don't hyphenate words beginning with *pre, non,* or other prefixes (*anti-, co-, multi-, over-, post-, re-, semi-, sub-, un-, under-*) unless the prefix comes before a proper noun

Not Hyphenated	Hyphenated
coworker	anti-white
nonjudgmental	pro-black
semiretired	non-Hispanic
unambiguous	post-1945
underused	un-American

5. There is no hyphen in the names of racial or ethnic groups.

African Americans, Asian Americans, Native Americans

6. E-Resources are hyphenated.

e-mail, e-journal, e-book, e-commerce

Em Dashes

An em dash, named because it extends the width of the letter *M*, is created by typing two hyphens (--) or by inserting the long dash symbol from the character set in your word processing software (in Microsoft Word, click on Insert and then Symbol).

En Dashes

An en dash (–) extends the width of the letter *N*, and is half the width of an em dash. It is a special symbol that you can insert from the character set in your word processing software. The en dash is used to indicate a range of pages (*Jones 1962:59–60*) or as a minus or negative sign (*it is −10 degrees Fahrenheit or −23 degrees Centigrade today*). In a table, use an en dash to signify a range of dates or variables (*fertility rates 1980–90*). In running text, however, substitute the word *to* or *through* for the en dash.

This study examined fertility rates from 1980 through 1990.

• Apostrophzes

Apostrophes are used to indicate possession and form contractions.

1. Add an apostrophe and the letter *s* to form the possessive for proper nouns and singular nouns.

student's

a sociologist's

Congress's

Cox's

Parsons's

Exceptions: *Jesus'* and *Moses'*

2. Add an apostrophe without an *s* to form the possessive for plural nouns.

sociologists' works

students' backpacks

3. For irregular plural nouns not ending in *s*, add an apostrophe and an *s*.

women's studies

children's programs

4. Apostrophes can be used to form contractions (*don't, wouldn't, hadn't*), which are usually not acceptable in academic papers.

• Quotation Marks

Punctuation marks are placed inside quotation marks as a general rule, whether the quoted words are located in the middle of the sentence or at the end. A semicolon and question mark, however, usually follow a quotation mark.

"Every human society is, in the last resort, men banded together in the face of death," Berger (1967:51) states.

The homeless man said, "my life ain't worth a pile of beans."

But   Who shall determine what is "normal"?

A colon should be used to introduce a long, block quotation. For assistance in organizing quoted material in your paper, see Chapter 4.

• Parentheses and Brackets

Parentheses and brackets are used to place information into the running text that doesn't quite fit but needs to be included nonetheless.

1. Parentheses include explanatory or interjected material.

"As a result, the symbolic accoutrements of one's position are of great importance. That is, by the use of various symbols (such as material objects, styles of demeanor, taste and speech, types of association and even appropriate opinions) one keeps on showing to the world just where one has arrived" (Berger 1963:79).

2. Brackets are used for parentheses within parentheses.

(For additional information, see Thompson [1988] and Billings [2002]).

3. Brackets set off the words of the paper's writer as opposed to the original author of the quoted material.

Few studies have examined the practices of the Society of Friends [Quakers].

4. Brackets enclose missing or unverified information, such as the date of an earlier published source or a change in punctuation.

(Weber [1946] 1971)

"[A]cculturation to Anglo-Saxon norms and patterns had . . . taken place historically, while structural separation of racial and religious groups, and to some degree national origins groups, still remained" (Gordon 1978:66).

• Ellipses

To denote missing words, phrases, or even paragraphs in quoted material, place ellipsis points, or three period dots (. . .). There should be a space before and after each ellipsis point. If the ellipses follow an abbreviation or a full sentence, first place the "true" period. Then, leave a space and begin the three ellipsis points. In ASA style, any change to the original quote must be indicated in brackets. Follow these guidelines when using ellipses:

1. Leave one space between each period. Do not use the ellipsis function on your computer word processor.
2. All periods must be located on the same line. Adapt your text accordingly.
3. Put brackets around any change in punctuation.
4. Indicate omitted information with a space followed by a period.

Here is a section from Peter Berger's well-known book *Invitation to Sociology*:

"Gossip, as hardly needs elaboration, is especially effective in small communities, where most people live their lives in a high degree of social visibility and inspectability by their neighbors. In such communities gossip is one of the principal channels of communication, essential for the maintenance of the social fabric" (Berger 1963:72).

Here is a shortened version of the same section:

"Gossip . . . is especially effective in small communities. . . . In such communities gossip is one of the principal channels of communication, essential for the maintenance of the social fabric" (Berger 1963:72).

5. If words are omitted at the beginning of a quote, usually no ellipsis points are needed. However, if your quote begins with a capitalized word that was not at the start of the sentence in the original, three ellipsis points precede the capitalized word.

Original	"Society provides us with warm, reasonably comfortable caves, in which we can huddle with our fellows, beating on the drums that drown out the howling hyenas of the surrounding darkness. 'Ecstasy' is the act of stepping outside the caves, alone, to face the night" (Berger 1963:150).
First words omitted **No ellipsis needed**	Berger (1963:150) noted that "we can huddle with our fellows, beating on the drums that drown out the howling hyenas of the surrounding darkness."
	". . . [W]e can huddle with our follows, beating on the drums that drown out the howling hyenas of the surrounding darkness" (Berger 1963:150).
First words omitted **Ellipses needed No** **brackets needed here**	" . . . Dr. Jones addressed the committee, reporting on his recent research."

6. If the final words are omitted from a quote, place a period and three equally spaced ellipses points after the last word of material you are quoting.

> "Ridicule and gossip are potent instruments of social control. . . . " (Berger 1963:72).

Capitalization

1. Capitalize the names of racial and ethnic groups. Note that none of the names are hyphenated.

> African American
> American Indian, Native American
> Asian, Asian American
> Hispanic, Chicano, Latino/Latina

2. Do not capitalize the words *whites* and *blacks* when referring to racial groups.

3. Capitalize the regions of the country.

> The Midwest
> The South
> The North

4. When referring to regional groups, use lowercase.

> midwesterners
> southerners
> northerners

5. When discussing the Civil War, however, capitalize *Northerners* and *Southerners*.

6. For the directions of the compass, use lowercase.

   north, south, east, west

7. For regional descriptions, use lowercase.

   southern pride

   northern industrialism

8. When referring to institutions, universities, or newspapers, do not capitalize the word *the* in running text.

   The program was implemented throughout the State University of New York.

   The article appeared in the *New York Times*.

9. Do not capitalize the word *sociology* unless it is part of a proper name or used in a special context, such as in a title.

10. Do not capitalize the titles *chair* or *editor* unless the titles are used as part of a person's name.

11. In a title, capitalize only the first part of a hyphenated word, unless the second part is a proper noun or adjective.

    The Road to Self-discovery

    Pre-Victorian Family Norms

2j Revision Cycle 9: Uniformity

In this Revision Cycle, you need to review your paper to make sure all the elements are handled uniformly. The longer the document and the more time you have worked on it, the more likely it is that inconsistencies will have crept in unnoticed. At this stage, you need to impose uniformity on four aspects of your paper: terminology, citation format, verbs, and treatment of like information. You probably will find it helpful to do four separate passes through your paper in order to focus on each aspect separately.

Terminology

Make sure you have used terminology in a consistent manner throughout your paper. It is easy to make the error of beginning the paper introducing certain terms, and then switching terms mid-document without warning to the reader. The most important thing is to spell out what you are doing for the reader. If you decide to shift to a different definition of a term, say so and explain why.

Citation Format

Review your document to make sure you have correctly cited your sources. Whether you quoted or paraphrased a source, you need to give credit to the author in text citations and a reference list entry. If you have substantive footnotes, check them for accuracy and format. ASA format, the official sociological documentation style, is discussed in Chapter 4.

Verbs

• Active versus Passive Voice

ASA style encourages the use of active voice in sociological writing whenever possible. In active voice, the subject tells *who* did something and the verb indicates *what* happened. By contrast, in passive voice, the verb states *what* happened, but the action is not attributed to anyone. Do not use the first-person pronouns *I* or *we* in formal writing.

Yes	Active voice: The researchers surveyed a sample of 150 high school seniors.
No	Passive voice: A sample of 150 high school seniors was surveyed.
Yes	Active voice: The authors found that . . .
Yes	Active voice: The study found that . . .
No	Passive voice: It was found that . . .
No	First person: I found that . . .
Yes	Active voice: The analysis included 150 documents.
No	Passive voice: All 150 documents were analyzed.

• Verb Tenses

Verb tenses may differ in the various sections of the paper, but must be consistent within each section.

In literature reviews, use the past tense to report a finding from an already completed research study.

> Likewise, Kibria (1993) argued that Vietnamese migrant women in Philadelphia did not use their increased resources relative to men to restructure family life along more egalitarian lines. Rather, women were deeply ambivalent about any change that would undermine the traditional Vietnamese family system, which conferred economic benefits through the extended kin structure and obligations of husbands and children to the family unit. (Parrado and Flippen 2005:608)

However, combining past and present tense within a sentence sometimes makes the meaning clearer. Here, the mixed tenses indicate that the earlier research study's finding is still true today.

> These studies generally argued that migration leads to greater personal autonomy and independence for women, primarily because of their

heightened employment prospects enhancing their control over budgetary and other realms of decision making and providing greater leverage for involving men in household chores (Pessar 2003). (Parrado and Flippen 2005:607)

In the methods section, use the past tense to indicate that your research is completed.

The researchers surveyed a sample of 150 high school seniors.

In the results section, either past or present tense may be used. In the discussion and conclusion sections, the findings of the study usually are stated in the past tense and the implications of the findings discussed in the present tense.

Past	Of the Hispanic seniors surveyed, 30 percent reported making college plans . . .
Present	Of Hispanic seniors, 30 percent report . . .
Past	The hypothesis was supported.
Present	The hypothesis is supported.

• Subject–Verb Agreement

The sentence's subject must agree with the predicate verb in number. Note the following cases often cause problems.

1. The word *data* is plural and requires a plural verb (*the data indicate an upward trend*).

2. Nouns that describe collectivities (*faculty, committee*) require a singular verb when referring to the entire group (*the committee votes tomorrow*). Collective nouns require a plural verb when referring to individuals (*the faculty have diverse viewpoints*). Use the sentence's context to choose the verb.

3. The words *some, any, none, most, part*, and *number* may require either a singular or plural verb depending on the sentence's context. *The Chicago Manual of Style*'s suggestion in this case is helpful and easy to remember (2003:222). When one of the words is followed by a singular noun, use a singular verb. When one of the words is followed by a plural noun, use a plural verb.

> Some of us are leaving now.
>
> Some of my paper needs work.
>
> Any book in this pile is worth reading.
>
> Any books in this pile are worth reading.

Treatment of Like Information

Similar types of information must be presented in a consistent manner. When including lists of information, check that the presentation, appearance, and ordering of information is uniform.

Academic Degrees

On listing academic degrees, use the abbreviations listed in Table 2.11. It is preferred to leave out the periods. Note the unusual capitalization for *EdD* and *PhD*. The plural form is made by adding an *s* (for example, BA*s*). When referring to degrees in general, use *bachelor's degree*, *master's degree*, and *doctoral degree*.

TABLE 2.11 Academic Degrees — Abbreviations

BA (or AB)	Bachelor of Arts
BS	(or SB) Bachelor of Science
EdD	Doctor of Education
JD	Doctor of Law
LLB	Bachelor of Laws
LLD	Doctor of Laws
MA	Master of Arts
MBA	Master of Business Administration
MD	Doctor of Medicine
MS	Master of Science
MSW	Master of Social Welfare; Master of Social Work
PhD	Doctor of Philosophy
Dphil	Doctor of Philosophy (European form)

Academic Rank

In a paper, do not refer to a person's rank unless it is relevant to the matter being discussed. Use only a person's first and last names, or last name only. After the first reference, use the last name only.

Write out all ranks and titles in full, with the exception of *Dr.* (see Table 2.12).

TABLE 2.12 Academic Rank

Assistant Professor
Associate Professor
Professor
Vice President
President-Elect
President

2k Revision Cycle 10: Format

In this final Revision Cycle, check your document carefully for format. It is wise to ask your instructors about their preferences and then apply them exactly. In the absence of such specifications, here are commonly accepted format guidelines for college and graduate school papers that you can use with confidence unless instructed otherwise.

General Appearance

Print or type the final version of your document on 8½ by 11 inch paper. Use good-quality, 20-pound white paper, and avoid colored, lined, hole-punched, spiral-bound, bordered, or scented papers. Type on one side of the paper only, and make sure the ink is dark enough to be read easily. Use black ink only.

Font

Use a 12-point font that is easy to read, such as Times New Roman, Garamond, Arial, or Courier. The same font (type and size) should be used for the text of your paper and the title page.

Italics

Italics are used for

- emphasis—use sparingly.
- the names of books, journals, newspapers and magazines, pamphlets, films and videos, paintings and sculpture, movies, plays, television and radio shows, long musical works, software, Web sites, and other published works.
- the names of specific ships, trains, aircraft, and spacecraft. Do not place types and classes of vehicles in italics (for example: yacht, Learjet, space shuttle).
- foreign words and phrases, but commonly used foreign terms are not italicized. Words from other languages that are in an English dictionary do not need italics.

• Some Commonly Used Foreign Terms — Do Not Italicize

ad hoc	per se
a priori	sine qua non
et al.	

• Mathematical Symbols, Variables, and Equations

If you place equations in your text, type variables in italics and vectors and matrices in bold italics.

Margins

Set your margins as follows: 1½ inches for the left margin, and 1 inch for the right, bottom, and top margins. Do not "pad" your paper with oversized margins or fonts.

Spacing

Double-space all text within and between paragraphs. Direct quotes exceeding five lines may be typed single-spaced. (For more information, see "Indenting.")

Leave only one space between a period at the end of a sentence and the first letter of the next sentence.

Indenting

Indent a uniform number of spaces—either five or eight—at the beginning of each paragraph. Whichever you choose, use consistently throughout the paper.

A long quote of more than five lines (about 50 words) should be aligned in block form. The block is indented from both sides to set it off from the remainder of the text, and it is typed left-justified and may be single-spaced. The first line of the block paragraph begins two single lines below the preceding line of text and is not additionally indented. No quotation marks are placed around the block as the block indenting indicates it is a quote.

Page Numbering

Number pages consecutively. Do not number the title page, or the first page of text. Start numbering with the second page of text, which is page 2. Page numbers may be placed in the upper right-hand corner of the page following your name, or centered at the bottom of the page. Do not put a period after the number or hyphens around it. Page numbers should appear in the same font as the rest of your paper. Do not decorate them with italics, bold, or other features. Pages with references and endnotes are numbered as text. Pages with tables or appendices are not numbered.

Numbering Items in the Text

When listing items in your text by number, write the number as (2). Do not use 2. or 2).

Headers

Your last name is placed as a header in the upper right-hand corner of each page of text (but not on the title page) so that if pages become separated, they can be reassembled correctly. Simply set your computer software to place headers on each page automatically. If you must type headers manually on each page, skip two single lines before beginning the text. Whichever method you use, check that headers are positioned correctly in your paper's final version. Keep in mind that even a slight change to your document may move the headers dramatically.

In most cases, your last name is sufficient as a header for your document. However, if someone in your class or group has the same last name, use your last name and first initial, separated by a comma. If another person has the same last name and first initial, use your last name and first name, separated by a comma as your header.

Preparing the Title Page

It is wise to prepare a title page for every paper you submit unless you are instructed otherwise. Even though it is not required for a short paper, a title page shows you put additional time and effort into your paper and can only help your grade. Guidelines for preparing a title page are as follows:

- Use the same font on the title page and in the text of the paper — a 12-point readable font.
- Don't use bold, underlining, or quotation marks for the full title.
- Don't use italics, unless the name of a book appears in your title.
- Don't add designs or graphics to your title page.
- Don't number the title page.
- Don't place a header with your name on the title page.

• Title Page Layout

Many instructors have a preferred format for a title page. It is wise to inquire, and if a model is available, copy it exactly. Otherwise, the following format is widely used across the disciplines at both the college and graduate school levels.

To prepare the title page, first type the title. To locate the correct line on the page to place the title, place your computer's cursor on the first line of the page you can type on, then move down to the 13th line. Type your title there. If it does not fit on one line, double-space the title.

Next, place your authorship information. Move your computer's cursor to the last line on the page, and then move it four single lines upward. Begin typing on that line, center-justified, the following information:

Your Name

The Course Number

The Course Name

The Date

Single-space the authorship information. See Figure 2.1 for an example of a title page.

Titles

Choose a title that describes your work. Whimsical or cute titles are not appropriate.

Type the title in the same font as the rest of your paper—usually a 12 point font. If the title is longer than one line, double-space it. Do not use bold, italics, underlining, or quotation marks for your full title. If you have a title and subtitle, separate them with a colon. If, however, your title includes the name of a book, the book title should be italicized.

FIGURE 2.1 Title Page

The Decision to Leave Home:

Female Runaways in Los Angeles 2000–2005

Jane Doe
Sociology 150
Introduction to Sociology
September 23, 2008

Nine to Nine?: The American Middle Classes

An Analysis of the Loss of Community in Erikson's *Everything in Its Path*

• Headline Style for Titles

Use "headline style" for titles. Capitalize the first and last words in the title, as well as all other words except articles (*a, an, the*), coordinating conjunctions (*and, but, for, not, or*), prepositions (*among, between, for, into, of, on, over, under, around, through*), or *to* used as part of an infinitive. Follow these same rules for subtitles that follow a colon.

> Types of Abuse and the Decision to Leave Home
> among Female Runaways in Los Angeles, 2000–2005

In a title, capitalize only the first part of a hyphenated word, unless the second part is a proper noun or adjective.

> *Aftermath: An Anthology of Post-Vietnam Fiction*
>
> *Class Formation in Nineteenth-century America: The Case of the Middle Class*

Abstracts

Abstracts are typed on a separate page. Type the heading ABSTRACT in all-capital letters, not underlined, near the top of the page. Move your cursor down three single lines and then begin typing the abstract paragraph. Place a header with your name in the upper right-hand corner of the page. An abstract is not a numbered page. For more information, see Chapter 8.

Chapter Headings and Subheadings

Headings and subheadings are unnecessary in short papers, but are used in lengthy ones to aid the reader in following your argument. The titles given to headings and subheadings should be substantive, indicating the content that follows—and not be humorous or whimsical. In a 30-page paper, three heading levels are sufficient. In a shorter paper, fewer levels are needed.

Headings should be concise and descriptive of the content in the section they introduce. A topic heading or subheading may be stated in a single word (*Education*); in a noun phrase (*Levels of Education*) or gerund phrase (*Measuring Education*); or in a question to be answered (*How Can Education Be Measured?*). The approach you choose should be used consistently for all headings of the same level.

First- and second-level headings stand alone, with text entered on the next typing line (in a double-spaced document, the next typing line is one double-space below the heading). Never place a heading on the last line, or on the next-to-last line, of a page.

Different levels of headings are distinguished by type size and placement. The headings shown reflect *ASA Style Guide* (2007) guidelines.

FIRST-LEVEL HEADING

Second-Level Heading

Third-level heading.

FIRST-LEVEL HEADINGS

First-level headings are typed in all caps, left-justified. (Note: Do not use the heading Introduction in a sociology paper.)

Second-Level Heading

Second-level headings are typed in italics, headline style, left-justified. For more information on headline style titles, see Chapter 2.)

    Third-level heading. Third-level headings are typed in italics and indented at the start of the paragraph. Place a period after the heading, leave a space, and then begin your text. In the heading title, capitalize only the first letter of the first word and proper nouns.

Footnotes and Endnotes

Footnotes or endnotes are used for substantive information that does not exactly fit in the text but is relevant enough that you want to include it in your paper. Footnotes are placed at the bottom of the page, and endnotes are collected and printed on separate pages placed at the end of your text. Keep in mind that since citations are placed within the text, footnotes and endnotes are not used for this purpose. If you use information in a footnote or endnote that requires a citation, cite the source for this information in your footnote or endnote just as you would in the text itself.

Your computer will prepare footnotes or endnotes for you, but it is your responsibility to edit them and make sure the location, format, and spacing are correct. A footnote is indicated with a superscript number (for example, [1, 2, 3]), which is placed in the text at the point the note should be read, and at the bottom of the page to indicate the corresponding note.

If you create endnotes, remember to check their placement. You may need to add or subtract space in order to have the endnotes properly placed on their own page(s). Type the heading NOTES, all-capital letters, not underlined, near the top of page on which the computer placed the endnotes. Move your cursor down three single lines and then arrange for the first endnote to begin. Place a header with your name in the upper right-hand corner of the page. Number and double-space the endnotes. An example of endnotes is shown in Figure 2.2.

Remember to check that text appearing in your footnotes or endnotes is typed double-spaced, spell-checked, and put through all the Revision Cycles.

Appendices

An **appendix** (plural, *appendices*) is a section of the paper where you can place supporting documents. Typically, you will need appendices when you write quantitative or qualitative research papers, or a thesis. If you used a survey questionnaire, supply a clean copy of the questionnaire in an appendix. If you mailed your questionnaire to respondents, place a copy of the cover letter that accompanied the questionnaire in a different appendix. If you sent out follow-up mailings to boost your response rate with a new cover letter, place a copy of the second letter in another appendix. Other documents often placed in appendices include coding sheets, field notes, press clippings about a program, circulars and mailers from an organization being studied, or letters of support for a grant. Documents that share some feature (for example, several press clippings) can be placed together in one appendix.

FIGURE 2.2 Endnotes

Doe

NOTES

1. Roles associated with achieved statuses are more amenable to study than those associated with ascribed statuses, as they usually are acquired at a later age, thereby facilitating more detailed memory of events.

2. In linking elements of role theory and symbolic interactionism, this paper follows George (1993) and others who note that the cross-fertilization among previously distinct research traditions offers promising advances in the field.

If you have only one appendix, prepare a title page for the appendix. On that page, include the title *Appendix*, followed by a description of what is contained in the appendix.

Appendix

Survey Questionnaire

Following this title page, place the document that belongs in the appendix. It will usually have its own format and numbering, and that is fine. You do not need to renumber or reformat the pages.

You may create as many appendices as needed. If you have more than one, the preferred method is to assign each a letter, with no period following the letter.

Appendix B
Initial Cover Letter Accompanying Survey Questionnaire

Appendix C
Follow-up Cover Letter Accompanying Survey Questionnaire

Tables and Figures

Tables and figures are placed at end of the paper, tables first. Put each table and figure centered on a separate page. Number and title them, but do not number the pages. The title of the table should be descriptive of the variables shown in the table or figure. Usually, the dependent variable is mentioned first, then the word *by*, and then the independent variable. Each column and row in the table or figure should be labeled with a heading. Make sure you have indicated the location for each table's placement in your text with a note (TABLE 4 ABOUT HERE).

Table 1. Voting Behavior by Religion

The Order of a Document

All documents, including research papers and reports, are assembled in the order shown. Your paper need not include every section.

Title Page
Abstract
Text (body)
Endnotes
References
Appendices
Tables
Figures

Submitting Your Paper

Always make a full copy of your paper (with all appendices, tables, etc.) before submitting it. Make a paper (hard) copy in addition to any computer file copy, in case of computer malfunction. Fires and other acts of fate can strike unexpectedly, so always keep multiple copies of major papers, such as dissertations, in separate locations.

Staple your paper in the upper left-hand corner. Do not submit it secured only with a paper clip or loose within a folder.

3 Library and Internet Research

Most sociology papers require you to conduct research at one or more points in the writing process. Research generally is necessary at three main stages in the writing of a paper: (1) to select a topic, (2) to construct a tentative thesis statement, and (3) to collect evidence in support of your thesis statement. At each stage, your research will progress more quickly and successfully if you take the time to plan a strategy. Usually you will find it helpful to start by searching sources with a broader scope, and as you progress to later steps, you will focus on more specialized articles and books. Additionally, in the first step of your research, you most likely will read for general ideas as you select a topic, while in the later stages, detailed note-taking will be essential. Furthermore, various types of sociology papers require different amounts and types of research at each of the three stages. Term papers, for example, require a different research strategy than a paper reporting your original quantitative or qualitative research.

3a Research to Select a Topic

Unless you have been assigned a subject, your research for a paper should begin before you choose a topic. As you begin brainstorming and narrowing your ideas, conduct a brief, preliminary review of the literature—a check of the published scholarly work in sociology—on the topics you are considering. Confirm that sufficient and appropriate research materials are available on your prospective topic for the type, length, and scope of paper you are writing. At this stage, your goal is to obtain a quick overview of what exists and is accessible to you before making a final decision about a topic.

For more information about conducting a literature review, see Chapter 1.

Tip Make a list of the citations for any potentially relevant articles or books you find. Otherwise, they might take hours to locate again. Keep a record of the databases you have searched so you do not search for them a second time by mistake.

3b Research to Construct a Tentative Thesis Statement

Once you have selected a topic, your next step is to devise a tentative thesis statement for your paper. At this stage, you will need to review the literature relevant to your topic again, but in greater detail. This second round of research will help you determine what research already has been done, what materials are actually available or can be obtained in a timely fashion in order to meet the deadlines for your paper, and what reoccurring questions you might profitably explore. Use this information to develop a viable, albeit tentative, thesis statement. As your paper progresses, you may find new sources of information or change your ideas, and you may decide to revise your thesis statement. Even so, since the thesis statement guides and structures the paper that is beginning to take shape, it should be developed as early as possible. Once you have constructed a tentative thesis statement, you can begin collecting evidence and drafting your paper. For additional information, see Chapter 1.

3c Research to Collect Evidence Supporting the Thesis Statement

Once you have constructed your tentative thesis statement, you are ready to begin your in-depth review of the literature. Collect evidence, such as statistics, research findings, or experts' opinions, that provides support for the main point and each of the subpoints in your thesis statement. Unlike your earlier research, which mainly served to sharpen and focus your ideas, the materials you find at this stage actually will be used in your paper.

3d Tracking Your Progress

As you begin your research, you won't know which articles, books, data, and documents you will use in the final version of your paper. It is therefore imperative to keep track of the search terms you used and the sources you find as you proceed. This way, you will be able to find these materials if you need them later (perhaps unexpectedly!), and you won't find yourself repeating searches because you have forgotten what you already did.

For every possibly relevant article or book, take brief notes, either on your computer or on index cards. Be sure to include information on how to find these materials again. Note the call numbers for books. For journal articles, record the volume number, date, and page numbers for journal articles. If you photocopy articles, make sure full citations are noted on the copies.

Establish a research log to track your progress, either electronically on your computer or in print. To set up an electronic tracking system, try the following suggestions:

1. Create a new folder on your computer and label it with a name that is easy to remember, such as *Research Log for Paper on Juvenile Delinquency.*

2. Within this folder, create subfolders to help you manage your paper. Here are some examples:

Background
Correspondence (e-mails to and from your instructor or others about your paper)
Research Strategy
Outline
Ideas for Research Question and Thesis Statement
Evidence and Sources for Research Question and Thesis Statement
General Ideas
References
Draft 1
Draft 2, and so on
Trash (Instead of deleting information you have collected and then chose not to use, cut and paste it into *Trash*. You may find you can use the information later.)

3. Within each subfolder, create documents for the information you want to save.

If you don't keep an electronic log, you can use a loose-leaf binder for the same purpose. Set up dividers with the same labels as for the subfolders.

Once you identify the materials you want to use for your paper, take detailed notes, or copy them and highlight the relevant sections. Be sure to record the full citation for any quoted or paraphrased words taken from another person.

3e Locating Sources of Information

How do you get started doing research? First of all, use your campus library. Public libraries do not subscribe to the academic databases you will need for sociological research (such as *CSA Sociological Abstracts* and *Social Sciences Index*), nor do they have the necessary specialized reference books covering general sociology and sociological subfields (see the reference books listed in the following sections).

Luckily, most campus libraries have made access to their collections available to students online 24 hours a day, seven days a week. Library research today, therefore, typically involves both print and online materials. More than ever, reference tools are being issued in both formats, and journal articles and books are being converted and stored for access via various databases.

Be aware that most of the online materials available through your library rarely are available for free on the Internet. The various Web sites that offer access to the kind of scholarly articles and books required for college sociology papers will charge you for their services. It is not as though you can sit at home the night before a paper is due and access all the articles, books, and other information needed for a well-researched article (not to mention the time required to write and revise your paper!). Your library purchased these materials. Usually, access to the library's online and print collection is restricted to members of the campus community, and requires you to identify yourself by establishing an account or user ID. Needless to say, it is wise to set up any required account or password and become familiar with your library's online resources before your first paper is assigned.

Where should you begin your research? It depends on what you are trying to find. Are you looking for facts, current statistics, theories, or opinions of experts? Information about a sociological concept? A historical overview of an issue? Basic information on a new subject? You will need to search in different categories of source materials to find each of these types of information.

The guide in Table 3.1 will direct you to categories of sources where you can search for the information you need.

Where you begin searching will also depend on how much you already know about the topic. If you know a great deal, you may decide to go directly to journal articles and books. If you know very little, you probably will want to consult a sociological encyclopedia for a general overview of the topic.

Sociological Dictionaries and Encyclopedias

It is difficult to know which material will be best suited to your needs until you begin your search. To get started, try consulting a sociological dictionary and encyclopedia. Unlike general reference works, these tools provide an in-depth background discussion of major concepts and issues identified with a topic, using the vocabulary of the scholars who wrote about these issues. A sociological dictionary and encyclopedia can help you place your topic in context, so you determine how

TABLE 3.1 Guide to Sources of Information

Information Needed	Where to Search
Factual References	
definition of a sociological term	sociological dictionary
overview of a basic sociological concept	sociological encyclopedia
well-established fact that doesn't need updating	handbook
fact (statistic) that needs frequent updating	statistical yearbook, online database, reputable Web site
historical overview of a recent event	newspaper, magazine article
organizations' names and addresses	directory
Theories and Experts' Opinions	
theories, research findings	book, monograph, journal article, subject yearbook
summary essays	*Annual Review of Sociology*
background information	sociological encyclopedia

relevant your ideas may be and how they fit with research in the field. They also will aid you in learning the vocabulary that sociologists use to discuss your topic, thereby enabling you to recognize subject headings and keywords that you will need later in your research. Lastly, they often include a valuable bibliography that includes many foundational articles on your topic. You can use these bibliographies to initiate your research. Keep in mind, however, that reference books are not revised frequently, and therefore may not be as current as other sources. The *Annual Review of Sociology*, on the other hand, provides the most current reviews of the literature on the major subfields within sociology and is a very useful resource for students.

Most professors will not want you directly incorporating material from a sociological dictionary or encyclopedia into your paper, no matter if it is quoted or paraphrased. Use these tools for "deep background" (your personal information) only.

Each discipline has at least one major dictionary and encyclopedia, and often subfields will have their own reference volumes. Here are few of the many excellent research tools.

Dictionaries—General Sociology

Jary, David and Julia Jary. 2006. *Sociology: Web-Linked Dictionary.* New York: Collins.
Johnson, Allan G. 2000. *The Blackwell Dictionary of Sociology: A User's Guide to Sociological Language.* Malden, MA: Blackwell.
Marshall, Gordon, ed. 1994. *The Concise Oxford Dictionary of Sociology.* New York: Oxford University Press.
Online Dictionary of the Social Sciences.
http://socialsciencedictionary.nelson.com/ssd/main.html.

Dictionaries—Sociology Subfields

Boudon, Raymond and Francois Bourricaud. 1990. *A Critical Dictionary of Sociology.* Translated by P. Hamilton. Chicago, IL: University of Chicago Press.
McLaughlin, Eugene and John Muncie, eds. 2005. *The Sage Dictionary of Criminology.* 2nd ed. London, England: Sage.
Schwandt, Thomas A. 2007. *The Sage Dictionary of Qualitative Inquiry.* 3rd ed. Thousand Oaks, CA: Sage.
Upton, Graham and Ian Cook. 2006. *A Dictionary of Statistics.* New York: Oxford University Press.
Vogt, W. Paul. 2005. *Dictionary of Statistics and Methodology: A Nontechnical Guide for the Social Sciences.* 3rd ed. Thousand Oaks, CA: Sage.

Encyclopedias—General Sociology

Borgatta, Edgar F. and Rhonda J. V. Montgomery, eds. 2000. *Encyclopedia of Sociology.* New York: Macmillan.
Encyclopedia of World Cultures. 1995. New York: Macmillan Library Reference.
International Encyclopedia of the Social Sciences. 2007. 2nd ed. New York: Macmillan.
Ritzer, George, ed. 2007. *Blackwell Encyclopedia of Sociology.* Malden, MA: Blackwell.

Encyclopedias—Sociology Subfields

Clark, Robin E. and Judith Freeman Clark with Christine Adamec. 2007. *The Encyclopedia of Child Abuse*. New York: Facts on File.

Finley, Laura, ed. 2006. *Encyclopedia of Juvenile Violence*. Westport, CT: Greenwood Press.

Lerner, Richard M., Anne C. Petersen, and Jeanne Brooks-Gunn. 1991. *Encyclopedia of Adolescence*. New York: Garland.

Lewis-Beck, Michael S., Alan Bryman, and Tim Futing Liao, eds. 2003. *The Sage Encyclopedia of Social Science Research Methods*. Thousand Oaks, CA: Sage.

Mathison, Sandra, ed. 2004. *Encyclopedia of Evaluation*. Thousand Oaks, CA: Sage.

Saha, Lawrence J., ed. 1997. *International Encyclopedia of Sociology of Education*. New York: Pergamon.

Schulz, Richard, Linda Noelker, Kenneth Rockwood, and Richard Sprott, eds. 2006. *The Encyclopedia of Aging*. New York: Springer.

Handbooks

Handbooks provide facts for quick reference. They are usually organized by subject, and include generally accepted information, not recent statistics. Sociology students will find two types of handbooks helpful: (1) statistical handbooks and (2) subject handbooks.

1. **Statistical Handbooks**

   These handbooks contain statistics useful in describing and analyzing social trends and the demographic and social characteristics of various subgroups in the population.

   > Carter, Susan B., Scott Sigmund Gartner, Michael R. Haines, Alan L. Olmstead, Richard Sutch, and Gavin Wright, eds. 2006. *The Historical Statistics of the United States: Millennium Edition*. New York: Cambridge University Press.
   >
   > Gutierrez, Lynda, Andrea Yurasits, and Angela Hurdle, eds. 1999. *Demographics USA 1999: County Addition*. New York: Market Statistics.
   >
   > U.S. Bureau of the Census. 2000. *County and City Data Book*. Washington, DC: U.S. Government Printing Office.

2. **Subject Handbooks**

   Subject handbooks are useful for focused research in a particular subject area. They present a broad summary of concepts, research, and theory.

   > Adler, Lenore Loeb, ed. 1993. *International Handbook on Gender Roles*. Westport, CT: Greenwood Press.
   >
   > Binstock, Robert, Linda George, Stephen Cutler, Jon Hendricks, and James Schulz, eds. 2005. *Handbook of Aging and the Social Sciences*. 6th ed. San Diego, CA: Academic Press.
   >
   > Bryant, Clifton D. and Dennis L. Peck, eds. 2006. *21st Century Sociology: A Reference Handbook*. Thousand Oaks, CA: Sage.

Hawes, Joseph M. and Elizabeth I. Nybakken, eds. 1991. *American Families: A Research Guide and Historical Handbook.* New York: Greenwood Press.

Hurrelmann, Klaus, ed. 1994. *International Handbook of Adolescence.* Westport, CT: Greenwood Press.

Miller, Delbert and Neil J. Salkind. 2002. *Handbook of Research Design and Social Measurement.* 6th ed. Thousand Oaks: CA: Sage.

Rebach, Howard M. and John G. Bruhn, eds. 2001. *The Clinical Sociology Handbook.* 2nd ed. New York: Springer.

Smelser, Neil J., ed. 1988. *Handbook of Sociology.* Newbury Park, CA: Sage.

Smelser, Neil J. and Richard Swedberg, eds. 2005. *The Handbook of Economic Sociology.* 2nd ed. Princeton, NJ: Princeton University Press.

Sussman, Marvin B., Suzanne K. Steinmetz, and Gary W. Peterson, eds. 1999. *Handbook of Marriage and the Family.* 2nd ed. New York: Springer.

Yearbooks

As the name indicates, yearbooks present information about the trends or events for one year only. Sociology students will find two types of yearbooks most useful in their research: (1) statistical yearbooks and (2) subject yearbooks.

1. Statistical Yearbooks

These yearbooks provide the most current data in print on topics relating to demographic patterns and population trends, such as group size, fertility, economic and political activity, and health.

Morgan, Kathleen O'Leary, ed. 2007. *Health Care State Rankings 2007: Health Care in the 50 United States.* 15th ed. Lawrence, KS: Morgan Quitno Press.

Morgan, Kathleen O'Leary and Scott Morgan, eds. 2007. *State Rankings 2007: A Statistical View of the 50 United States.* 18th ed. Lawrence, KS: Morgan Quitno Press.

Stanley, Harold W. and Richard G. Niemi, eds. 2007. *Vital Statistics on American Politics: 2007–2008.* Washington, DC: CQ Press.

The United Nations. *Statistical Yearbook.* New York: United Nations/ Statistical Office.

Vital Statistics of the United States. Hyattsville, MD: U.S. Department of Health and Human Services.

World Statistics Pocketbook. New York: United Nations/Statistical Office.

2. Subject Yearbooks

The subject yearbook for sociology is the *Annual Review of Sociology.* Each volume features articles that summarize new directions in research in the major subfields within sociology and cite to key recent publications. Students will find this a very valuable resource.

Books and Monographs

Books and monographs (shorter books on an academic topic) have limited use in sociological research. By their nature, books take time to research, write, publish, and reach your library bookshelf, and therefore are not a good source for the most recent theories or research findings. If, however, you are studying a historical topic, or theories that are over 10 years old, you will probably find books useful in your research.

To find books or monographs, search your library's catalog or WorldCat.

Sociology Journals

In every discipline, there is considerable consensus among scholars about the main journals in their fields. There is always contention as to whether the research published in these journals represents the best work of these disciplines, but there is little doubt that scholars in a particular field are looking at, if not reading, the articles published in the journals of their field.

Table 3.2 on page 62 lists the major journals read and cited by sociologists. Most of these journals are peer-reviewed. In a peer-reviewed journal, before a submitted article is accepted for publication, it is sent "out for review" to several experts on the topic of the article who decide whether to publish the article. Several of the journals are official publications of the major association of the discipline, the American Sociological Association.

> **Tip** Researchers generally only cite to articles published in the journals of their own field. Occasionally, they will refer to the literature of closely allied disciplines. For example, sociologists cite to the sociological literature and, less commonly, to the related disciplines of anthropology or psychology. Student should do the same, unless otherwise instructed.

3f Conducting Effective Research

Given the enormous amount of information available today, how can you conduct effective research that is focused and controlled? This is not a big problem when searching for factual references—you simply look up the facts in the appropriate source (dictionary, encyclopedia, handbook, yearbook, etc.). However, when searching for information about theories, experts' opinions, overviews, and analyses, you can't simply look up a "fact," and there is no single source that has all the information. So, how do you find the information you need?

TABLE 3.2 Major Journals Used by Sociologists

American Journal of Sociology
American Sociological Review
British Journal of Sociology
Contemporary Sociology
Criminology
Demography
Gender and Society
Journal of Aging Studies
Journal of Contemporary Ethnography
The Journal of Gerontology
Journal of Health and Social Behavior
Journal of Marriage and Family
Journal of Personality and Social Psychology
Qualitative Sociology
Sex Roles: A Journal of Research
Social Forces
Social Problems
Social Psychology Quarterly
Sociological Focus
Sociological Forum
Sociological Inquiry
Sociological Methods and Research
Sociological Perspectives
Sociological Quarterly
Sociological Review
Sociological Theory
Sociology
Sociology of Education
Symbolic Interaction

The answer is that you need to take control of your research. You need to make decisions about what sources to check for information, and which should be your first source. Once you identify an appropriate starting point, you need to decide which of the many articles and books listed in that source you actually will obtain and consult.

How do you decide which articles and books are useful enough to find and read? If you are an effective researcher, you will *not* take the first 10 books that you can reach off the library shelf. Rather, you will select articles and books that give you the information you have determined you need based on your outline and thesis statement.

But which ones?

To help in locating and previewing articles and books, two important research tools have been developed. If you are not yet familiar with these tools, take a few minutes to make their acquaintance—they will save you a lot of time going forward.

3g Using Research Tools: Indices and Abstracts

Wouldn't it be helpful to know whether an article was actually relevant to your topic before spending time trying to find it? Abstracts supply that overview, giving a one- or two-paragraph summary of the article or book. Reading an abstract will tell you *exactly* what is covered, so you can make thoughtful choices about which materials to obtain and read.

The two main research tools used by sociologists are *CSA Sociological Abstracts* and *Social Sciences Index*. *CSA Sociological Abstracts* indexes and lists abstracts for books and journal articles in sociology and closely allied fields. *Social Sciences Index* lists abstracts for journal articles in sociology and the other social sciences. An index (plural, *indices*) lists articles and books by various keywords so items can be located, for example, by author or topic. These two research tools are available in print, but they are more popular today as searchable databases that can be accessed through your college or university library.

3h Pursuing a Search Strategy

When sociologists start new research, they begin with *CSA Sociological Abstracts*, and only if they find little or nothing there, will move on to search *Social Sciences Index*. Some subfields are not well represented in *Sociological Abstracts* (for example, social psychology), or may have more comprehensive coverage in *Social Sciences Index* (for example, criminology).

To be effective, follow this strategy in your own research. Usually, a good idea is to start your search with *Sociological Abstracts*. If necessary, broaden your scope to include *Social Sciences Index*. Only these two databases, available through your campus library, will help you locate the articles and books that comprise the sociological literature. Sometimes your library will offer these databases as part of a larger social science database, so be sure to check, and ask your instructor or a reference librarian if you need assistance. Searching other databases in your library's list of choices will send you to articles in magazines and newspapers that are not appropriate sources for sociological research.

Do not use Google, Google Scholar, or other Internet search engines to search for journal articles or books. The works you locate through a Google search will not represent the best, most comprehensive, most current, or most relevant sociological information, and what is worse, you won't be able to tell from the huge amount of "hits" you get. There is no context for the entries found in a Google search except quantity, which is not a measure of quality of a source.

Using a sociological database, the keywords or search terms you use will determine what is searched. You need to use the correct keywords or you may miss the majority of works on a subject. For example, if you were interested in female delinquency, you would want to search various combinations and synonyms, since each pair could yield different articles and books.

delinquency + girls

delinquency + females

delinquents + girls

delinquents + females

One way to locate keywords for searching is to note the terms used in the articles you have already found, if any. Keywords may also be listed in the article's abstract in *CSA Sociological Abstracts*. If there are synonyms for keywords, be sure to try each alternative. Additionally, research tools are available to help you identify keywords for searching your topic in your campus library or through your library online resources. Consult your reference librarian if you need assistance.

Tip Here is another way to find the most relevant articles on your topic. Take your best article so far. Look at the reference list at the end of the article, and check out each article by reading its abstract in *CSA Sociological Abstracts*. Chances are you will find some helpful leads.

3i Using the Internet for Research

The Internet has evolved into an indispensable communication and research tool. Using it effectively for research, however, presents a challenge. The sheer quantity of information, coupled with its uneven quality, requires that the researcher exercise great caution in selecting materials to use and cite.

To evaluate information obtained on the Internet, consider these factors:

1. **Authority**

   Who is responsible for posting the information? A government agency? A well-known expert? A self-proclaimed expert? Your neighbor? The Web sites of government agencies (that end in *.gov*) and educational institutions (that end in *.edu*) are more credible and reliable than organizational sites (ending in *.org*) or commercial sites (ending in *.com*). Be selective in your choice of sites to choose dependable sources of information.

✓ Only use materials posted by a recognized authority on the subject.

2. Content

What is the nature of the information posted? What is its scope and source? Is it presented as fact or opinion? Is it directly relevant to your research?

✓ Only use materials when you have a high degree of confidence about the quality of information.

3. Accuracy

Is the information posted accurate? What reasons do you have for believing it may or not be accurate? Can you corroborate the information using authoritative print sources?

✓ Only use materials with a high degree of accuracy.

4. Objectivity

Is the information objective or biased? How can you tell?

✓ Only use materials that are objective.

5. Timeliness

Has the information been updated recently? Is the information still current? (The date of the last update usually is listed at the bottom of the Web site's home page.) If there is no date, look for clues that information may not be current, such as reports of "recent" news and dates of upcoming events.

✓ Only use materials that are updated frequently.

(Note: Thanks to California State University-Northridge, Oviatt Library for the preceding infomation.)

3j   Online Databases And Web Sites

The following topics include many of the content areas discussed in sociology. The Web links shown may provide a place to start your online search process.

Crime and Delinquency

Death Penalty Information Center
http://www.deathpenaltyinfo.org

Federal Bureau of Investigation, Uniform Crime Reports
http://www.fbi.gov/ucr/ucr.htm

National Criminal Justice Reference Service
http://www.ncjrs.gov

Sourcebook of Criminal Justice Statistics
http://www.albany.edu/sourcebook

U.S. Department of Justice
http://www.usdoj.gov

U.S. Bureau of Justice Statistics
http://www.ojp.usdoj.gov/bjs

Culture

Statistical Resources on the Web Sociology
http://www.lib.umich.edu/govdocs/stsoc.html

VCL American Culture Research Guide
http://library.vassar.edu/research/guides/readingrooms/americanculture.html

Demographics

National Opinion Research Center
http://www.norc.org/homepage.htm

U.S. Census Bureau
http://www.census.gov

Education

National Center for Education Research
http://www.ed.gov/about/offices/list/ies/ncer/index.html

National Center for Education Statistics
http://nces.ed.gov

National Center for Educational Evaluation
http://ies.ed.gov/ncee

National Center for Special Education Research
http://ies.ed.gov/ncser

Family

American Statistics Index
http://www.lib.umd.edu/guides/asi.html

Population Index
http://popindex.princeton.edu

U.S. Census Bureau
http://www.census.gov

The White House Economic Statistics Briefing Room
http://www.whitehouse.gov/fsbr/esbr.html

This service provides easy access to current federal social statistics. It provides links to information produced by a number of federal agencies. All of the information included in the Social Statistics Briefing Room is maintained and updated by the statistical units of those agencies. All the estimates for the indicators presented in the Federal Statistics Briefing Rooms are the most currently available values for crime, demography, education, and health.

Gender

Gender Studies Database
http://www.nisc.com/factsheets/qgsd.asp

GenderWatch
http://www.proquest.com

Women's Studies and Feminism Database
http://www.uky.edu/Subject/women.html

Health

Demographic and Health Surveys (DHS)
http://www.measuredhs.com/aboutsurveys/dhs/start.cfm

National Center for Health Statistics (CDC)
http://www.cdc.gov/datastatistics

Immigration

Yearbook of Immigration Statistics (Dept. of Homeland Security)
http://www.dhs.gov/ximgtn/statistics/publications/yearbook.shtm

Methodology

Tests and Measures in the Social Sciences
http://libraries.uta.edu/helen/test&meas/testmainframe.htm

Web Center for Social Research Methods
http://www.socialresearchmethods.net

Race and Ethnicity

Black Studies Center
http://bsc.chadwyck.com/marketing

Chicano Database
http://www.rlg.org

Ethnic NewsWatch
http://www.proquest.com

Social Psychology

PsycExtra
http://www.apa.org/psycinfo

PsycINFO
http://www.apa.org/psycinfo

Sociology as a Discipline

American Sociological Association
http://www.asanet.org

Wealth/Poverty/Social Class

STAT-USA
http://www.stat-usa.gov

Statistical Abstract of the United States
http://www.stat-a.gov/hometest.nsf/ref/vwstatab

U.S. Bureau of Labor Statistics
http://www.bls.gov

U.S. General Accounting Office
http://searching.gao.gov

3k Evaluating the Advantages and Disadvantages of Various Sources

To take control of your research, plan your research trajectory. Consider where you will start (your first source), the categories of material you will search, and the order you will search them.

There are advantages and disadvantages to using various sources of information. The choice of sources is a critically important decision, and you should plan carefully before diving into the process. Consider the following five factors when evaluating sources for use in your research.

1. The Audience

For most students, the audience is the instructor who assigned the paper. Does your instructor prefer print or Internet research? Be aware that many instructors are suspicious of information gleaned from the Internet. It is wise to ask your instructors about their attitude toward Internet research *on your topic*— their response will tell you whether they are enthusiastic supporters, active opponents, or wishy-washy on the issue. It is suggested that Internet sources be used *only* if your instructor is an enthusiastic supporter.

In some academic and work settings, you may find a bias in favor of the Internet, especially where the audience is skewed younger. Courses in media and communications, and businesses specializing in entertainment and telecommunications are examples. If you are preparing research materials in these settings, you will want to use Internet sources for your research, as print sources are viewed as stodgy and out-of-date.

2. The Time Dimension

The Internet's adaptability and the relative ease with which information can be updated make it an excellent source for quickly changing information. Today, current statistics in demography, education, health, and crime can be dependably obtained from government Web sites, as can information about public policy updates and votes in Congress. Using the Internet for the most current statistics on these subjects is widely viewed as appropriate, even by instructors who are not enthusiastic Internet supporters.

If you need to find the most recent studies and articles published on your topic, your search should focus on journals. Books, which take longer to write and publish, are not the best sources for current information. On the other hand, the advantage of books is that they can give complex topics fuller treatment and documentation than is possible in other formats.

If your research involves historical overviews or earlier time periods, plan to use journal articles or books, rather than Internet sources. Data for earlier years are not always available on the Internet, and data for earlier centuries are almost entirely absent.

Tip A research tool such as *Sociological Abstracts* will help you find journal articles, not Internet sources. If you were to use *Sociological Abstracts* to find journal articles that you locate and read online in full-text versions, you still would say that you have researched "journal articles," and not Internet sources. The determining factor is the format in which the original version was published.

3. Complexity

Research topics differ in their level of complexity, and research materials similarly vary. Simple information is more easily searched on the Internet, and more quickly read on a computer screen. Complicated analyses, by contrast, are very difficult to locate on the Internet (if they are present at all!), and are hard to read in their entirety on a computer screen. When you research a complex subject, therefore, plan to use print sources of information.

4. Legitimacy

Today, the ease of duplicating and disseminating printed materials means that anyone can be an author, while YouTube has made Internet fame a possibility for truly anyone (or anything!). In such a world, what information is dependable, accurate, and objective?

In general, print sources tend to be viewed as more legitimate than Internet sources. Print sources, especially those you encounter in a university library, have been screened by a publishing company, which has chosen and edited the work before printing it. The university presses, especially the large ones, are likely to have rigorous standards of scholarship to ensure their publications' content is accurate and carefully researched. Commercial presses, by contrast, tend to adopt less demanding standards in their search for potential bestsellers. Of the books published by commercial presses, those written by academics are viewed as somewhat more reliable than those published by journalists.

The print sources you find in a library also have survived selection by librarians and library committees, who choose which books and journals to buy, and which not to purchase. Works chosen by both major university presses (as opposed to self-published works, small publishers, or conference papers) and librarians tend to be the most credible.

Internet sources are generally viewed as less legitimate than print sources because usually there is no one "vetting" the information, and the information is easily altered, making it difficult for users to verify the information on repeated visits to the Web site. Individual Web sites must establish a reputation for accuracy before the information they post is judged to be credible. U.S. government agencies' Web sites are an example of Internet sources that have established legitimacy, and today the information posted there is generally accepted as credible.

5. Quality

When you review information to determine if it is appropriate for use in your research, consider the quality of the information. High-quality information (1) is produced by an acknowledged expert on the subject; (2) uses an accepted methodology and research tools; (3) cites other experts' works in footnotes, text citations, and reference lists; and (4) is usually published by a publisher with high standards of scholarship.

Use these criteria when evaluating books, journal articles, and other information. Electronic books and e-journals do not have the same legitimacy and credibility as print books and print journals.

4 Citations and References

CHAPTER

Whenever you take another person's words or ideas and place them in your own work, you must state, or *cite*, the source from which you obtained them. *For both quotes and paraphrases, the source of the material must be cited.*

A **quote** is a word or series of words crafted by another person that is placed into your paper inside quotation marks. A **paraphrase** is the unique idea or words of another person that is restated in your own words and placed into your paper without quotation marks. A **citation** is a statement about the source of the quote or paraphrase arranged according to the rules of a particular documentation style.

In most cases, you should paraphrase, and not quote, your sources. Paraphrased information fits into your paper more smoothly and allows you to retain your own voice, pace, and style. A quote should be used only when the original wording is unusually distinctive or powerful, and cannot be adequately captured in a paraphrase. Use quotes sparingly, and when you do, make sure you faithfully reproduce the wording in your text and correctly cite the sources where you found the quotes.

Remember, using the words or ideas of other people without giving them credit is plagiarism, and plagiarism is theft.

4a Doesn't Every Sentence in My Paper Need a Citation?

No. Some information does not require a citation. Statements based on knowledge acquired from your own experiences or observations do not need to be documented, although you should describe the context in which you acquired this knowledge in your paper.

> "In the two years that I have worked as a volunteer for NightAngels, I have never encountered a runaway who reported being happy living on the street."

Another type of information that does not require a citation is **common knowledge,** such as the following:

- Historical facts that can be found in more than one reference book ("Maya Angelou was born in St. Louis as Marguerite Johnson").
- Sociological facts that can be found in more than one reference book ("Reference groups exert great influence over people's lives").
- Common sociological vocabulary ("Anomie is a feeling of alienation or not belonging").
- Familiar truisms ("Writing improves with practice").
- Common maxims ("Birds of a feather flock together").

71

However, using someone else's words or ideas as if they were your own is plagiarism, so you must cite the source if you

- quote from another person's work.
- paraphrase an idea that is uniquely another person's.
- quote or paraphrase another person's opinion.
- quote or paraphrase the facts resulting from another person's research.

How do you know if an idea is common knowledge? The best way to decide is by checking if the idea has been discussed in other books or articles without a citation given. Still, when in doubt, cite!

Sometimes an author employs a commonly used term in sociology (for example, *anomie*), but uses it in a unique way. If you used that source in your paper, you would need to cite it because you are using an idea that is distinctly the author's.

Keep in mind that, in general, the more citations the better—as long as they are relevant and provide appropriate supporting evidence for your paper. Often, students think that when they cite many sources in a paper, they appear lacking in creativity. Quite the contrary! Precise citations are a mark of excellence in a paper, and many citations to a variety of sources indicate to your instructor that your paper is well researched. Table 4.1 contains a quick quiz to test your knowledge on citing sources.

TABLE 4.1 Self-Test: Do You Need to Cite These Statements?

Common knowledge does not need to be cited. Which statements are common knowledge? Take this quick test. Circle *True* or *False* for each statement.

1. World War II began in 1939 and ended in 1945.	True	False
2. An average tuna salad sandwich has 610 calories.	True	False
3. The teen pregnancy rate declined by 2 percent between 1999 and 2000.	True	False
4. At the autumn solstice, the hours of day and night are equal.	True	False
5. The freezing point of water is 32 degrees Fahrenheit, or 0 degrees Centigrade.	True	False
6. Lincoln was the 16th president of the United States.	True	False
7. The critic Stephen Greenblatt argues that the religious conflicts of his period, especially those that occurred during his youth, had an effect on Shakespeare's work.	True	False
8. Hurricanes come in varying degrees of strength, rated from Category 1 to Category 5.	True	False
9. There are 5,283 hospice programs in the United States.	True	False
10. Aluminum cans make up less than 1 percent of solid waste in the United States.	True	False

Answers: (1)T, (2)F, (3)F, (4)T, (5)T, (6)T, (7)F, (8)T, (9)F, (10)F

(*Source:* From Allyn & Bacon's Online My Soc Lab Published by Allyn and Bacon, Boston, MA. Copyright © 1995-2008 by Pearson Education. Reprinted by permission of the publisher.)

4b ASA Documentation Style for Sociology

Each discipline has developed its own guidelines for citing sources. The documentation style for sociological writing has been established by the American Sociological Association (ASA). This book shows you how to cite your sources and prepare your reference list following ASA format. In situations not covered by the *ASA Style Guide* (2007), examples are drawn from *The Chicago Manual of Style* (2003), on which the ASA documentation style is based.

For additional reference, see the following sources: The *ASA Style Guide* (2007), the "Chicago-Style Citation Quick Guide," available online at http://www.chicagomanualofstyle.org/tools_citationguide.html, and the "Electronic Manuscript Preparation Guidelines for Authors" at http://www.press.uchicago.edu/Misc/Chicago/emsguide.html. The 15th edition of *The Chicago Manual of Style (CMOS)* can be found in the reference section of your local or campus library.

4c Citing Your Sources—Text Citations and the Reference List

In ASA documentation style, citations are placed within parentheses "running" in the text. These author-date **parenthetical citations** provide just enough information so that the reader can locate a full description of the source in the **reference list** at the end of the paper.

The following example shows a sample text citation in ASA documentation style.

"Vertical mobility is the decisive factor in making persons uncertain and sceptical of their traditional view of the world" (Mannheim 1936:7).

The citation (*Mannheim 1936:7*) informs you that this quotation was found on page 7 of a work by an author with the last name of *Mannheim*. If you wanted more information, you could turn to the paper's reference list and look for the name *Mannheim* in the alphabetical list. If more than one work was listed by Mannheim, the date of the work (1936) would guide you to the source of the quote, which would include the following information in the reference list entry:

Mannheim, Karl. 1936. *Ideology and Utopia: An Introduction to the Sociology of Knowledge*. Translated by L. Wirth and E. Shils. New York: Harcourt, Brace and World.

This reference list entry states that Karl Mannheim is the author, and the title of the work is *Ideology and Utopia: An Introduction to the Sociology of Knowledge*. Additional information is provided about the work, including the names of its translators (L. Wirth and E. Shils), the place of publication (New York), and the publisher (Harcourt, Brace and World). The italicized title, coupled with the publisher's name, indicates that *Ideology and Utopia* is a book.

Text citations are brief and contain just enough information to enable readers to find the work in the reference list. Therefore, if you mention the author's name or the date of publication in your text, do not repeat that information in the parenthetical citation for the quote or paraphrase that follows. For most sources, the date of publication is the year. For books, the date of publication is the year of the most recent printing on the copy you are using. There is no space between the year, the colon, and the page number. Page numbers are typed in brief form (for examples, see 9–10, 132–35, and 1190–1200).

> **Tip** Make sure you have correctly identified *who* is the author of the material you cite. In an edited volume in which various chapters are written by different people, the author is the person listed at the beginning of the particular chapter you are citing. In a journal article, the author is the person(s) listed at the start of the article under the title. In a book review, the author of the review is the reviewer. In works of corporate authorship, there is no named author, so list the corporate entity (the committee, agency, or department) instead of the author. Occasionally, the author is anonymous.

4d   Text Citations in Footnotes and Endnotes

Citations are placed parenthetically in the text, and therefore are not placed as the sole information within a footnote or endnote. Footnotes (located at the bottom of the page) or endnotes (placed at the end of the text) are used only for substantive information that does not exactly fit in the text, but is relevant enough that you want to include it. If information requiring a citation is placed within a footnote or endnote, cite the source in parentheses in the footnote or endnote, just as you would within the text. List the sources in your reference list together with the other entries.

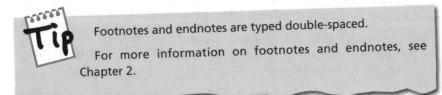

> **Tip** Footnotes and endnotes are typed double-spaced.
>
> For more information on footnotes and endnotes, see Chapter 2.

4e   Handling Quotations in Your Text

A short quotation of five lines or less is placed in the text enclosed in quotation marks. A long quote of about 50 or more words (more than five lines) should be aligned in block form. The block is indented from both sides to set it off from the remainder of the text, and it is typed left-justified and may be single-spaced. The first line of the block paragraph is not additionally indented. No quotation marks are placed around the block as the block indenting indicates it is a quote. Both types of quotes need citations, which are described in the next section.

4f Creating Text Citations

A text citation includes the last name(s) of the author(s), the date of publication, and the page number(s) where the quoted material can be found. This information is placed within parentheses in your text. Generally, citations are placed after the quotation.

> "Vertical mobility is the decisive factor in making persons uncertain and sceptical of their traditional view of the world" (Mannheim 1936:7).

However, if you put some information about the source into the text itself, the remaining information is placed parenthetically. The page number for the quoted material follows the quotation. When the last name of the author is located in the text *after the quote*, follow it with the date of publication and page number within parentheses. If the last name of the author is used in the text *before the quote*, follow it with the date of publication within parentheses. Then, place the page number in parentheses after the quote.

4g Text Citations for Nonblock and Block Quotes

If you put some information about your source into the text—such as the author's name and date of publication—the remaining information, the page number, still needs to be supplied. How and where the page number standing alone is located differs in nonblock and block quotes.

For a short quote of less than five lines (nonblock), when the page number appears alone, use a lowercase *p* for *page*, followed by the page number, as shown. The page number is placed within parentheses at the end of the quote, after the quote mark and preceding the final period of the sentence.

> Mannheim (1936) noted that "vertical mobility is the decisive factor in making persons uncertain and sceptical of their traditional view of the world" (p. 7).

For a long quote of more than 5 lines or 50 words (a block quote), place a full citation after the final period of the quoted material, as shown in the first example on p. 76. When the page number appears alone, use an uppercase *P* for *page* followed by the page number, as displayed in the second example. The page number is placed within parentheses at the end of the quote, after the quote mark and the final period of the sentence.

Full citation after block quote

As noted previously:

> In a basic sense, sociology has always been a historically grounded and oriented enterprise. As wise commentators have pointed out again and again, all of the modern social sciences, and especially sociology, were originally efforts to come to grips with the roots and unprecedented effects of capitalist commercialization and industrialization in Europe. (Skocpol 1984:1)

Page number only after block quote

As Skocpol (1984) noted:

> In a basic sense, sociology has always been a historically grounded and oriented enterprise. As wise commentators have pointed out again and again, all of the modern social sciences, and especially sociology, were originally efforts to come to grips with the roots and unprecedented effects of capitalist commercialization and industrialization in Europe. (P. 1)

4h Text Citations for Quotes

Book with One Author

In a citation or the text itself, generally only the author's last name is used.

• Author's Name Not in Text

When the author's name is *not* used in the text, the citation includes the author's last name, the date of publication, and the page number of the quote. (Note: The citation is placed after the quote and after the quotation mark, but before the period.)

> "Vertical mobility is the decisive factor in making persons uncertain and sceptical of their traditional view of the world" (Mannheim 1936:7).

• Author's Name in Text

When the author's name is used in the text, the citation includes the date of publication, and the page number of the quote.

> "Vertical mobility is the decisive factor in making persons uncertain and sceptical of their traditional view of the world," according to Mannheim (1936:7).

Or

> Mannheim (1936) noted that "vertical mobility is the decisive factor in making persons uncertain and sceptical of their traditional view of the world" (p. 7).

- ## Subsequent Citations to the Same Book

Subsequent citations to the same work follow the format for the first citation.

Book with Two Authors

For a work with two authors, list the authors' last names in citations and text in the order they appear on the work's title page.

- ## Authors' Names Not in Text

When the authors' names are not used in the text, the citation includes the authors' last names, the date of publication, and the page number of the quote. (Note: The citation is placed after the quote and after the quotation mark, but before the period.)

> "With no understanding of ritual, they have no way to create sacred space" (Bly and Woodman 1998:182).

- ## Authors' Names in Text

When the authors' names are used in the text, the citation includes the date of publication and the page number of the quote.

> "With no understanding of ritual, they have no way to create sacred space," noted Bly and Woodman (1998:182).

Or

> Bly and Woodman (1998) noted that "with no understanding of ritual, they have no way to create sacred space" (p. 182).

- ## Subsequent Citations to the Same Book

Subsequent citations to the same work follow the format for the first citation.

Book with Three Authors

For a work with three authors, list the authors' last names in citations and text in the order they appear on the work's title page.

- ## Authors' Names Not in Text

When the authors' names are not used in the text, the first citation for the work includes all the authors' last names, the date of publication, and the page number of the quote. (Note: The citation is placed after the quote and after the quotation mark, but before the period.)

First citation	"Because we have shared symbols, we are able to take the role of the other" (Robboy, Greenblatt, and Clark 1979:192).
Later citations	"Waiting is closely related to power, because those who have power can impose waiting on those who don't" (Robboy et al. 1979:193).

• Authors' Names in Text

When the authors' names are used in the text, the citation includes the date of publication of the source and the page number of the quote.

First citation	"Because we have shared symbols, we are able to take the role of the other," observed Robboy, Greenblatt, and Clark (1979:192).
Or	Robboy, Greenblatt, and Clark (1979) observed that "because we have shared symbols, we are able to take the role of the other" (p. 192).
Later citations	"Waiting is closely related to power, because those who have power can impose waiting on those who don't," noted Robboy et al. (1979:193).
Or	Robboy et al. (1979) noted that "waiting is closely related to power, because those who have power can impose waiting on those who don't" (p. 193).

Book with More Than Three Authors

For a work with more than three authors, list the first author's last name only followed by *et al.* in citations and text. The words et al. are not italicized.

• Authors' Names Not in Text

When the work's authors are not mentioned in the text, the first citation for the work includes the first author's last name only followed by *et al.*, the date of publication, and the page number of the quote. The words *et al.* are not italicized. (Note: the citation is placed after the quote and after the quotation mark, but before the period.)

"Superiors in an organization control the behavior of their subordinates in part because the subordinates consent to having their behavior controlled" (Becker et al. 1961:438).

• Authors' Names in Text

When a work has three or more authors, use the first author's last name only followed by *et al.* in the text. Do not italicize the words *et al.* The citation for the work includes the date of publication and the page number of the quote. (Note: the citation is placed after the quote and after the quotation mark, but before the period.)

> "Superiors in an organization control the behavior of their subordinates in part because the subordinates consent to having their behavior controlled," according to Becker et al. (1961:438).

Or

> As Becker et al. (1961) noted, "superiors in an organization control the behavior of their subordinates in part because the subordinates consent to having their behavior controlled" (p. 438).

• Subsequent Citations to the Same Book

Subsequent citations to the same work follow the format for the first citation.

4i Text Citations for Paraphrases

The parenthetical citation for a paraphrase includes the author's last name and date of publication. With paraphrased material, usually the idea cannot be traced to one or two particular pages, but rather is a broad theme throughout a chapter, article, or book. As a result, the practice of citing to the entire work has developed.

Book with One Author

In citations, and text, generally only the author's last name is used.

• Author's Name Not in Text

When the author's name is not used in the text, the citation includes the author's last name and date of publication. (Note: The citation is placed after the paraphrase, but before the period.)

> Ideologies may be used to stabilize a social order (Mannheim 1936).

• Author's Name in Text

When the author's name is used in the text, the citation includes the date of publication of the source only. The citation is placed immediately after the author's name.

> Mannheim (1936) noted that ideologies may be used to stabilize a social order.

• Subsequent Citations to the Same Source

Subsequent citations to the same work follow the format for the first citation.

Book with Two Authors

For a work with two authors, list the authors' last names in citations and text in the order they appear on the work's title page.

• Authors' Names Not in Text

When the authors' names are not used in the text, the citation includes all the authors' last names and the date of publication. (Note: The citation is placed after the paraphrase, but before the period.)

> Ritual is connected to the creation of sacred space (Bly and Woodman 1998:182).

• Authors' Names in Text

When the authors' names are used in the text, the citation includes the date of publication only. The citation is placed immediately after the authors' names.

> Bly and Woodman (1998) have suggested that ritual is connected to the creation of sacred space.

• Subsequent Citations to the Same Source

Subsequent citations to the same work follow the format for the first citation.

Book with Three Authors

For a work with three authors, list the authors' last names in citations and text in the order they appear on the work's title page.

• Authors' Names Not in Text

When the authors' names are not used in the text, the *first* citation for the work includes all the authors' last names and the date of publication. (Note: The citation is placed after the paraphrase, but before the period.)

First citation	Symbols enable role taking (Robboy, Greenblatt, and Clark 1979).
Later citations	Making others wait can be viewed as a form of power (Robboy et al. 1979).

• Authors' Names in Text

When the authors' names are used in the text, the citation includes the date of publication only. The citation is placed immediately after the authors' names.

First citation	Robboy, Greenblatt, and Clark (1979) pointed out that symbols enable role taking.
Later citations	Robboy et al. (1979) have suggested that making others wait can be viewed as a form of power.

Book with More Than Three Authors

For a work with more than three authors, list the first author's last name only followed by *et al.* in citations and text.

• Authors' Names Not in Text

When the work's authors are not mentioned in the text, the first citation for the work includes the first author's last name only followed by *et al.* and the date of publication. The words *et al.* are not italicized. (Note: The citation is placed after the paraphrase, but the before the period.)

> The control of subordinates depends in part upon their consent (Becker et al. 1961:438).

• Authors' Names in Text

When a work has three or more authors, use the first author's last name followed by *et al.* in the text. Do not italicize the words *et al.* The citation includes the date of publication only. The citation is placed as shown.

> According to Becker et al. (1961), the control of subordinates depends in part upon their consent.

• Subsequent Citations to the Same Source

Subsequent citations to the same work follow the format for the first citation.

4j Other Citations

Book citations are the templates for citations to all other sources. The previous section showed you how to integrate quotes and paraphrases from books into your text and then cite them correctly. This section simplifies the handling of other citations. Remember, a citation is arranged differently depending on the number of authors of the work cited and whether you quote or paraphrase the "borrowed" information.

Handling Multiple Citations in a Series

When you list several citations for one idea or statement, separate them with semicolons and place them within one set of parentheses. You may organize them either in alphabetical order or date order. Whichever system you choose, be consistent throughout your document.

Alphabetical order	Role acquisition has been studied as a function of early childhood socialization (Cooley 1922; Erikson 1950; Mead 1934; Thomas and Znaniecki 1927) and from a role theory perspective (Linton 1936; Merton 1957b; Sherif 1936).
Date order	Role acquisition has been studied as a function of early childhood socialization (Cooley 1922; Thomas and Znaniecki 1927; Mead 1934; Erikson 1950) and from a role theory perspective (Linton 1936; Sherif 1936; Merton 1957b).

Citing Two or More Works by the Same Author

Within a single text citation, if you cite two or more works by the same author, separate the years of publication with a comma. If the works are located in different sets of parentheses, treat them as you would any other cited source.

. . . examined social discontinuity (Wallerstein 1980, 1988).

. . . examined social discontinuity (Wallerstein 1980) and the emergence of modern capitalism (Braverman 1974; Wallerstein 1988).

Citing Two or More Works by the Same Author Published the Same Year

When an author or editor has two or more works published the same year and you cite more than one in your paper, differentiate the works by adding letters immediately following the dates (1961a, 1961b, 1961c). The alphabetical order of the titles determines the letter assigned to the date. The first work is designated *a*, the second *b*, and so forth.

If you edit your paper and eliminate your citations to one for the works, remember to revise or remove the letters from the dates of the remaining works.

. . . develops a vocabulary to study the presentation of self (Goffman 1959, 1961a, 1961b).

. . . in mental institutions (Goffman 1961a) and other social situations (Goffman 1959, 1961b).

Citation for a Book in a Series

Follow the format for a book citation.

(Aron 1998:10)

Citation for an Edited Book

In a book with one or more editors but no author, the editor is treated as the author for the parts of the book that are not attributed to authors of individual chapters. Notice that this citation looks just like the citation for a book with one author.

(Bereday 1969:43)

Citation for a Translated Book

Follow the format for a book citation.

(Foucalt 1977)

Citation for an Edition Other Than the First

Follow the format for a book citation.

(Merton 1968:75)

Citation for a Chapter in an Edited Book or Collected Work

When you cite to the chapter in an edited volume or other collected work, list the work by the author of the chapter, not the editor of the volume. Follow the format for a book citation.

(Kanter 1979)

Citation for an Article in a Scholarly Journal

A citation for an article in a scholarly journal includes the last name of the author, the date of publication (the year only), and the page number (for a quote). For an article with more than one author or paraphrased information, refer to the earlier section on quotes and paraphrases for books.

(Rossi 1968:26)

Citation for a Reprint of a Version Published Earlier

When citing a source that was reprinted from an earlier version of the work, give the earliest date of publication in brackets first, and then state the publication date of the version you actually consulted. All the information is enclosed in parentheses.

As Weber ([1946] 1971:416) noted, many . . .

Citation for a Table and an Appendix

(Blau 1977, table 1:35)

(Jencks et al. 1972, appendix B:349–50)

Citation for a Book Review

When citing to a published book review, give the reviewer's last name and the date the review was published. If you paraphrase the review as a whole, do not list a specific page number. In this example, Garfinkel published a review of Jencks's book.

. . . are not universally accepted (Garfinkel 1994:687).

Citation for an Article in a Popular Magazine or Newpaper

If the author of the article is named, give the name and date of publication (including month, day, and year). If no author is named, the newspaper or magazine is considered the author.

(*Harper's Magazine*, July 2007:51–52)

(*Wall Street Journal*, March 6, 1998:1)

Citation for a Government Document

Unless an author is named on a report, list the government agency as the author of the document.

(U.S. Dept. of Health 1990:121)

Citation for a Report or Newsletter (No Author Named)

If no author is named on reports issued by consulting firms, research agencies, cities, or other corporate bodies, list the institution or corporate body as the author. State its name in brief form.

(American Federation of Teachers 1998)

Citation for a Working or Discussion Paper

If the author is named, use the last name(s) and date of publication or distribution in the citation. If no author is named, list the issuing agency as author.

(Blau and Kahn 1992:12–13)

Citation for a Dissertation or Thesis

Cite an unpublished dissertation or thesis by the author's name and the date listed on the title page.

(Epstein 1968:15)

Citation for a Conference Paper or Presented Paper

List the author's last name and the date of presentation. For a quote, list the page number(s).

(Blau 1972)

Citation for Forthcoming or Undated Material

For a citation to material that is scheduled for publication, use the word *forthcoming*. If no date is given, use *N.d.* (*no date*) in place of the date. (Note: *N.d.* and *forthcoming* are not italicized when used in a citation.)

Recent studies by Johnson (forthcoming) and Peterson (N.d.) found . . .

Some recent studies (Johnson forthcoming; Peterson N.d.) have found . . .

Citation for Machine-Readable Data Files

Citations for machine-readable data files include the name of the author (an organization, institutional producer or person) and the date.

(American Institute of Public Opinion 1976)

Citation for an Archival Source

Use abbreviated information in the citation.

. . . (NA, RG 382, Box 880, June 22, 1966; Tamiment 273, Box 1, April 12, 1937).

Citation for an Interview

If you quote or paraphrase material from an unpublished interview in your paper, place information about the interview (the author, date, and name of the interview subject) directly in the text and in a parenthetical citation. For interviews you conducted, identify yourself as the author. The date should include the month, day, and year.

When you refer to a subject by name, also give his or her title, if any, the first time the name is mentioned. Do not use *Mr., Mrs.,* or *Ms.* In repeated references, generally the subject's last name only is used.

In an interview with the author on December 13, 2007, Warden John Peterson explained his interpretation of "cruel and unusual punishment." Peterson noted that . . .

Citations to material from interviews you conducted in the course of a quantitative or qualitative study are treated differently. The author and date of the interview need not be included in the text together with the cited material, since that information should be discussed at length in the methods section of your paper. Also, you may have guaranteed your interview subjects anonymity and confidentiality, in which case you cannot use the subjects' real names. In citing, you may choose either to assign pseudonyms or labels to subjects as shown in the example. (Note: If you guaranteed anonymity and confidentiality, no label should identify any particular individual to your audience.)

> For some of the occupational exiters, the final decision to resign was a gradual one that occurred over many months or, in some cases, over many years. As one ex-school teacher said, "Those little things got to me, a little nick here and a little nick there, and a griping here and somebody eats you out there. And my wife griped at me because I didn't make enough money and we can't get this or that. It all built up and built up. And finally I said, 'Hey, I've had enough of it and I'm tired of it.' I handed in my resignation the next day." Likewise a hospital administrator simply "ran out" of reasons not to leave and knew that if he was really serious about giving up his job he no longer had any good reasons to stay. He felt that if he didn't make the decision soon, he probably never would. (Ebaugh 1988:124)

Citation for Personal Communication

To cite a letter, phone call, or e-mail message that you receive from another person, place the information within the text itself and not in a text citation. Locate the reference information in a footnote or endnote. Identify yourself as *author*. Personal communications are generally not included in a reference list. The *ASA Style Guide* states that permission must be obtained from the owner of the e-mail prior to use. Do not list the email address.

Text   In an e-mail to the author, Smith indicated that he had completed his field work and he would soon return home.[3]

Footnote [3]Edward Smith, e-mail message to author, June 22, 2006.

Citation for a Source with an Anonymous Author

If the author of an anonymous work is not known, use the title of the work within the citation.

Book   (*ASA Style Guide* 2007:46)

Newspaper article   ("What's Up Doc?" 1999:12)

If the author of an anonymous work is known, the name is placed in brackets within the parentheses.

([Klein, Joe] 1996)

Citation to a Classic Text

For a citation to classic texts, including the Bible, the Apocrypha, translations of ancient Greek texts, and the Federalist Papers, use the standard subdivisions. This reference method allows a passage to be found easily in all published editions of the works.

Cite a passage from the Bible and other classic texts parenthetically, and list (1) the book of the Bible, (2) the chapter, (3) the verse(s), and (4) the translation. Do not italicize. Check with your instructor as to whether names of books and the translation should be abbreviated. You do not need to include a classic text in the reference list.

(Genesis 4:1–4 King James Version)

The Federalist Papers are numbered.

(Federalist 8)

Citation for a CD-ROM and DVD-ROM

A citation to material on CD-ROM and DVD-ROM includes the name(s) of the author(s) and the date of publication.

(Henslin 2005)

Citations for Electronic Resources (E-Resources)

E-books and online periodicals (including online journals, magazines, and newspapers) are cited following the same format as print books and periodicals. For **documents** retrieved from an institution, organization, or corporation with a known Web site, the citation includes the name of the group and the date of the document. A citation to a **blog** includes the name of the author and the date of the entry. For information or **statistics** retrieved from an online database, give the name of the database and the date of access.

Web site	As noted previously (Assn. of Religion Data Archives 2006), the primary connection . . .
Document	A new initiative launched to revamp schools (Microsoft 2005). . .
Blog	This theme was reiterated in a blog (Etzioni 2007).
Statistics	A change in family size and composition has been noted (U.S. Census Bureau 2001).

4k The Reference List

The reference list is an alphabetical listing of all works cited in your paper. All sources cited in the text must appear on the reference list and all entries in the reference list must actually appear in the text. References are typed on a separate page or pages and are placed following the text of your paper. Reference pages are numbered and have headers with your name in the upper left-hand corner. (Table 4.3 presented at the end of this chapter shows a sample reference list.)

Preparing the Reference List

The title REFERENCES is capitalized at the top of the page. This title is not underlined. Triple-space between REFERENCES and the first entry listed. Begin the first entry flush with the left margin. List works in the reference list alphabetically by the author's last name. Where there are two or more authors with the same last name, list them alphabetically by the first author's last name. Double-space within and between entries. When an entry is long enough to continue onto the next line, indent the second line five or eight spaces, consistent with the number of spaces you indented in the body of your document. Do not use the ampersand (&) in place of the word *and*. Use the ampersand only when it is an integral part of a corporate name.

A Sample Reference List Entry

The following example shows a sample reference list entry in ASA documentation style.

Goffman, Erving. 1961. *Encounters*. Indianapolis, IN: Bobbs-Merrill.

This reference list entry states that Erving Goffman is the author, and the title of the work is *Encounters*. Additional information is provided about the work, including the place of publication (Indianapolis, Indiana), and the publisher (Bobbs-Merrill). The italicized title, together with the publisher's name, indicates that *Encounters* is a book.

Creating An Entry

• Author's Name

An entry begins with the author's name (last name first). Type the author's name exactly the way it appears in the publication. If the author uses two initials, add a space between the initials. Do not replace the author's first or middle name with an initial.

Billings, C. Robert

Fischer, Y. J.

Galbraith, John Kenneth

For multiple authors, invert only the first author's last name. All other authors are listed with first name and then last name. List all authors. When there are two authors, do not place a comma after the first author's name. (Note: When a name is followed by the abbreviation *Jr.* or *Sr.*, a comma should precede the abbreviation.)

Featherman, David and Robert Hauser

Brim, Orville G., Jr. and Stanton Wheeler

Hurtado, Aida, David E. Hayes-Bautista, R. Burciaga Valdez, and Anthony C. R. Hernandez

• Author with Multiple Publications

Where one author or editor has two or more publications, order them by the year of publication, beginning with the earliest date. For repeated authorship, use *six hyphens and a period* (or three em dashes and a period) in place of the name. Both original and edited works are considered in the determination of repeated authorship. (Note: The author's name must be identical in two or more entries to be handled in this way, as illustrated in the example.)

Merton, Robert K. 1957a. *Social Theory and Social Structure*. New York: Free Press.

————. 1976. *Sociological Ambivalence and Other Essays*. New York: Free Press.

Merton, Robert K., Marjorie Fiske, and Patricia L. Kendall. 1990. *The Focused Interview: A Manual of Problems and Procedures*. 2nd ed. New York: Free Press.

• Author with Multiple Publications in the Same Year

Where an author or editor has two or more works with the same year of publication, add letters to the date to differentiate them. The works are listed in alphabetical order by title.

Goffman, Erving. 1961a. *Asylums*. New York: Doubleday.

————. 1961b. *Encounters*. Indianapolis, IN: Bobbs-Merrill.

• Date

In a reference list entry, the year of publication follows the name of the author(s). If the work has no date, put *N.d.* in place of the date. If the work is about to be published, use the word *Forthcoming* in place of the date and supply the name of the publisher or journal which will publish the work. If a work is reprinted from an earlier publication, list the earlier date in brackets, followed by the date of the version you used.

• Title

Use headline style capitalization for titles of works in the reference list. In this style, capitalize the first letters of the first word, the last word, and all other words except articles (*a, an, the*), conjunctions (*and, or, but, for, nor*), and prepositions (*by, for, of, to, through*, etc.).

• Subtitle

Often, a work has a main title and a subtitle, or additional title shown below the main title. When preparing an entry with a title and subtitle, separate the two titles with a colon. Treat both as one extended title.

Middletown: A Study in American Culture

• Place of Publication

For the place of publication, include the city and state. Use the U.S. Postal Code abbreviations for states in the United States (see Table 4.2). New York is treated as an exception. For publishers located in New York City, do not list the state.

For publishers located outside the United States, list the city and the country. Do not abbreviate the name of the country. Country abbreviations may be used in text citations or addresses.

London, England: Oxford University Press

TABLE 4.2 List of Geographic Names and Abbreviations

In your text, spell out the names of states, countries, and territories, with a few exceptions (for example, USSR). In citations, abbreviate the names of U.S. states, provinces, and countries.

Africa	Afr.	England	Eng.	Massachusetts	MA
Alabama	AL	Europe	Eur.	Mexico	Mex.
Alaska	AK	Florida	FL	Michigan	MI
Albania	Alb.	France	Fr.	Minnesota	MN
Alberta	AB	Georgia	GA	Mississippi	MS
American Samoa	AS	Germany	Ger.	Missouri	MO
Antarctica	Ant.	Great Britain	Gt. Brit.	Montana	MT
Argentina	Arg.	Greece	Gr.	Nebraska	NE
Arizona	AZ	Guam	GU	Netherlands	Neth.
Arkansas	AR	Hawaii	HI	Nevada	NV
Armenia	Arm.	Hungary	Hung.	New Brunswick	NB
Australia	Austral.	Idaho	ID	Newfoundland and Labrador	NL
Austria	Aus.	Illinois	IL	New Hampshire	NH
Belgium	Belg.	Indiana	IN		
Brazil	Braz.	Iowa	IA	New Jersey	NJ
British Columbia	BC	Ireland	Ire.	New Mexico	NM
Bulgaria	Bulg.	Israel	Isr.	New York	NY
California	CA	Italy	It.	New Zealand	NZ
Canada	Can.	Japan	Jpn.	North America	No. Amer.
Colorado	CO	Kansas	KS	North Carolina	NC
Connecticut	CT	Kentucky	KY	North Dakota	ND
Delaware	DE	Lebanon	Leb.		
Denmark	Den.	Louisiana	LA	Northwest Territories	NT
District of Columbia	DC	Maine	ME		
Ecuador	Ecua.	Manitoba	MB	Norway	Norw.
		Maryland	MD		

Nova Scotia	NS	Saskatchewan	SK	United Kingdom	UK
Ohio	OH	Scotland	Scot.		
Oklahoma	OK	South America	So. Amer.	United States	US, USA
Ontario	ON				
Oregon	OR	South Carolina	SC	Utah	UT
Panama	Pan.			Vermont	VT
Pennsylvania	PA	South Dakota	SD	Virginia	VA
People's Republic of China	PRC	Spain	Sp.	Virgin Island	VI
		Sweden	Swed.		
Poland	Pol.	Switzerland	Switz.	Washington	WA
Portugal	Port.	Tennessee	TN	West Virginia	WV
Prince Edward Island	PE	Texas	TX		
		Turkey	Turk.	Wisconsin	WI
Puerto Rico	PR	Union of Soviet Socialist Republics	USSR	Wyoming	WY
Quebec	QC			Yukon Territory	YT
Rhode Island	RI				

41 References for Books

A reference entry begins with the author's name (last name first) flush against the left margin. Type the author's name exactly the way it appears in the publication. If the author uses two initials, add a space between the initials. Do not replace the author's middle name with an initial. Note the punctuation that separates the information in the entry. The title of a book is italicized. The place of publication is usually a city, followed by a comma, and then the state (a two-letter abbreviation). New York is an exception and needs no state listed. The name of the publisher comes last.

Book with a Single Author

A reference entry for a book with one author includes (1) the name of the author, last name listed first; (2) the date of publication; (3) the title of the book (italicized); (4) the place of publication; and (5) the name of the publisher.

> Mills, C. Wright. 1951. *White Collar: The American Middle Classes*. London, England: Oxford University Press.

Book with Two Authors

A reference for a book with two authors includes (1) the first author's last name inverted. The second author is listed with first name, then last name. Do not place a comma after the first author's name. Then list (2) the date of publication; (3) the title of the book (italicized); (4) the place of publication; and (5) the name of the publisher.

> Lynd, Robert S. and Helen Merrell Lynd. 1959. *Middletown: A Study in American Culture*. New York: Harcourt, Brace and World.

Book with Three or More Authors

A reference for a book with three or more authors includes (1) the first author's last name inverted. The other authors are listed with first name, then last name. Place commas between the authors' names. The word *and* is placed before the last author's name. Then list (2) the date of publication; (3) the title of the book (italicized); (4) the place of publication; and (5) the name of the publisher. (Note: When a name is followed by the abbreviation *Jr.* or *Sr.*, a comma should precede the abbreviation.)

> Singleton, Royce A., Jr., Bruce C. Straits, and Margaret Miller Straits. 1993. *Approaches to Social Research*. New York: Oxford University Press.

> Bellah, Robert N., Richard Madsen, William M. Sullivan, Ann Swidler, and Steven M. Tipton. 1986. *Habits of the Heart: Individualism and Commitment in American Life*. New York: Harper and Row.

Edited Book (Editor as Author)

In a reference for a book with one or more editors but no author, the editor is treated as the author: (1) list the name of the editor; (2) place a comma, followed by *ed.* signifying *editor*. If there are two or more editors, handle the names as you would multiple authors. After all the editors are listed, place a comma and then *eds.* signifying *editors*. Continue listing (3) the date of publication; (4) the title of the book; (5) the place of publication; and (6) the name of the publisher.

If you cite to the introduction or other material written by the editor, list the work by the editor. However, if you cite to a chapter in an edited volume or other collected work, list the work by the author of the chapter, not the editor.

> Bereday, George Z. F., ed. 1969. *Essays on World Education: The Crisis of Supply and Demand*. New York: Oxford University Press.

> Brim, Orville G., Jr. and Stanton Wheeler, eds. 1966. *Socialization after Childhood*. New York: John Wiley.

Book in a Series

A reference for a book in a series with a volume number lists (1) the name(s) of the author(s); (2) the date of publication; (3) the title of the series (italicized); (4) the volume number; (5) the title of the volume or book (italicized); (6) the place of publication; and (7) the name of the publisher.

> Aron, Raymond. 1998. *Main Currents in Sociological Thought*. Vol. 2, *Durkheim, Pareto, Weber*. New Brunswick, NJ: Transaction.

Translated Book

A reference for a translated book includes (1) the name(s) of the author(s); (2) the date of publication; (3) the title of the book (italicized); (4) the name(s) of the translator(s), with a first initial and last name only; (5) the place of publication; and (6) the name of the publisher. If there are two translators, list both names as shown in the example.

> Foucault, Michel. 1977. *Discipline and Punish: The Birth of Prison.* Translated by A. Sheridan. New York: Vintage Books.
>
> Mannheim, Karl. 1936. *Ideology and Utopia: An Introduction to the Sociology of Knowledge.* Translated by L. Wirth and E. Shils. New York: Harcourt, Brace and World.

Edition Other Than the First

In a reference to a later edition of a work, indicate the edition after the title. Use abbreviations for revised edition (*Rev. ed.*), second edition (*2nd ed.*), third edition (*3rd ed.*), and so forth.

> Merton, Robert K. 1968. *Social Theory and Social Structure.* Rev. ed. New York: Free Press.
>
> Kuhn, Thomas. 1970. *The Structure of Scientific Revolutions.* 2nd ed. Chicago, IL: University of Chicago Press.
>
> Hewitt, John, P. 1984. *Self and Society: A Symbolic Interactionist Social Psychology.* 3rd ed. Boston, MA: Allyn & Bacon.

Dictionary

A reference for a dictionary uses the title of the work in place of the author's name.

> *American Heritage Dictionary of the English Language.* 1992. 3rd ed. Boston, MA: Houghton Mifflin.

4m Chapters in an Edited Book or Collected Work

In an edited book or other collected work, usually each chapter is written by a different author. The editor of the volume generally writes a lengthy, substantive introduction and a few shorter pieces, often introducing sections or specific chapters.

When you cite to a chapter in an edited volume or other collected work, list the work by the author of the chapter, not the editor.

Often, the editor of the book will write a chapter for the book (you will know because the title of the chapter and the author's name will be listed at the start of the chapter). If you cite to a chapter written by the editor with the editor's name as author of the chapter, list the same person as author and editor as shown in the following examples. (Note: If you are citing the introduction or introductory material in various sections of the book, prepare the reference entry as you would for an edited book (see the previous section for an Edited Book).

In the reference for an edited book, list (1) the name(s) of the author(s); (2) the date of publication (the date of the book in which the chapter is published); (3) the title of the chapter in quotation marks; (4) *Pp.* followed by the page numbers of the chapter (the number of the chapter's first page, an en dash, and the number of the chapter's last page); (5) the word *in* (not italicized); (6) the title of the edited book (italicized); (7) the words *edited by*; (8) the first initial and last name of the editor(s) as shown on the title page of the book; (9) the place of publication; (10) a colon; and (11) the name of the publisher.

Kanter, Rosabeth Moss. 1979. "Women and the Structure of Organizations: Explorations in Theory and Behavior." Pp. 166–190 in *Social Interaction: Introductory Readings in Sociology*, edited by H. Robboy, S. L. Greenblatt, and C. Clark. New York: St. Martin's Press.

Elder, Glen H. 1977. "Age Differentiation and the Life Course." Pp. 165–90 in *Annual Review of Sociology*, Vol. 1, edited by A. Inkeles. Palo Alto, CA: Annual Reviews.

Shibutani, Tamotsu. 1970. "On the Personification of Adversaries." Pp. 223–233 in *Human Nature and Collective Behavior*, edited by T. Shibutani. Englewood Cliffs, NJ: Prentice Hall.

4n Articles

Article in a Scholarly Journal

A reference for a journal article includes (1) the name(s) of the author(s); (2) the date of publication, which is the year of the journal issue in which the article appears, unless contrary information is given on the first page of the article; (3) the title of the article, unabbreviated and placed in quotation marks, followed by a period inside the final quotation mark; (4) the journal name, unabbreviated and italicized; (5) the volume number; (6) the issue number, placed in parentheses and followed by a colon; and (7) the page numbers of the entire article (ie., the article's first page number, an en dash, and the article's last page number).

Rossi, Alice S. 1968. "Transition to Parenthood." *Journal of Marriage and Family* 30(1): 26–39.

Thornton, Russell and Peter Nardi. 1975. "The Dynamics of Role Acquisition." *American Journal of Sociology* 80(4):870–885.

Emerson, Robert M., Kerry O. Ferris, and Carol Brooks Gardner. 1998. "On Being Stalked." *Social Problems* 45(3):289–314.

Book Review

In a reference for a published book review, list (1) the name of the reviewer; (2) the year the review was published; (3) the name of the review, if any; (4) the words *review of* (not italicized); (5) the name of the reviewed work (italicized), followed by a comma and the word *by* (not italicized); (6) the name of the author of the reviewed work; (7) the name of the journal, magazine, or newspaper in which the review appears (italicized); and (8) the volume, issue, and page numbers of the journal.

> Garfinkel, Irv. 1994. Review of *The Homeless,* by Christopher Jencks. *Contemporary Sociology* 23(5):687–689.

Article in a Popular Magazine

A reference for an article in a popular weekly or monthly magazine lists (1) the author, or if no author is given, the title of the article; (2) the date of publication; (3) the title of the article (in quotation marks, comma inside the parenthesis), if not previously stated; (4) the name of the magazine (italicized); and (5) the month and day of the magazine issue. Page numbers are not listed, as an article often starts at the beginning of the magazine and continues in the back.

> Cose, Ellis. 2000. "What's White Anyways?" *Newsweek,* September 18.
>
> Silverstein, Ken. 2007. "Their Men in Washington." *Harper's Magazine,* July 2007.

Article in a Newspaper or Press Service

A reference for an article in a newspaper includes the section of newspaper and the page numbers, as shown. For an article from a press service, such as AP or Reuters, list the name of the service.

> Felsenthal, Edward. 1998. "Justices' Ruling Further Defines Sex Harassment." *Wall Street Journal,* March 5, pp. B1–B2.
>
> Passell, Peter. 1996. "Race, Mortgages and Statistics." *New York Times,* May 10, pp. D1, D4.
>
> "Americans Work More." Associated Press, September 1, 2001.

4o Other Sources

Government Document

In a reference for a government document, unless an author is named on a report, list the government agency as the author of the document.

> U.S. Department of Health and Human Services, Public Health Service. 1990. *Healthy People 2000.* Washington, DC: U.S. Government Printing Office.
>
> U.S. Bureau of the Census. *Statistical Abstract of the United States: The National Data Book.* Washington, DC: U.S. Government Printing Office. Published annually.

Report or Newsletter (No Author Named)

Consulting firms, research agencies, cities, or other corporate bodies often issue reports on which no author is named. If no publisher is named, assume the corporate body is the publisher.

American Federation of Teachers. 1998. *Survey and Analysis of Teacher Salary Trends 1998.* Washington, DC: American Federation of Teachers.

Working or Discussion Paper

In a reference for a working or discussion paper, give the number of the document, the issuing agency, and its location.

Blau, Francine D. and Lawrence M. Kahn. 1992. "The Gender Earnings Gap: Some International Evidence." Working Paper No. 4224, National Bureau of Economic Research, Chicago, IL.

Dissertation or Thesis

A reference for an unpublished dissertation or thesis states the degree, name of the department, name of the university, and location of the university.

Epstein, Cynthia Fuchs. 1968. "Women and Professional Careers: The Case of the Woman Lawyer." PhD dissertation, Department of Sociology, Columbia University, New York.

Conference Paper or Presented Paper

A reference for an unpublished conference paper and other presented paper lists a description of the conference or event, the location, and the date of the paper presentation or where it is available for viewing.

Blau, Zena Smith. 1972. "Role Exit and Identity." Paper presented at the annual meeting of the American Sociological Asssociation, August 28, New Orleans, LA.

Forthcoming or Undated Material

For a reference to material that is scheduled for publication, use the word *Forthcoming*. If no date is given, use *N.d.* (no date) in place of the date. (Note: *N.d.* and *forthcoming* are not italicized when used in a citation.)

Johnson, John. Forthcoming. *New Currents in Sociological Theory.* New York: HarperCollins.
Peterson, Pat. N.d. *Fighting Smog.* Aurora, IL: Home Press.

Machine-Readable Data Files

For a reference to machine-readable data files, name the individual(s) responsible for data collection. If no one is named, list the institutional producer of the file. State the title of the data, followed by *[MRDF]*, an abbreviation for machine-readable data file. In place of the publisher, list the name of the distributor of the file.

Miller, Warren, Arthur Miller, and Gerald Klein. 1975. *The CPS 1974 American National Election Study* [MRDF]. Ann Arbor, MI: Center for Political Studies, University of Michigan [producer]. Ann Arbor: Inter-University Consortium [distributor].

American Institute of Public Opinion. 1976. *Gallup Public Opinion Poll # 965* [MRDF]. Princeton, NJ: American Institute of Public Opinion [producer]. New Haven, CT: Roper Public Opinion Research Center, Yale University [distributor].

Archival Material

A reference entry for material from an archive gives enough information so the information can be found again by another researcher.

New York Public Library, Manuscripts and Archives Division, Robert Moses Papers, Box 116. August 16, 1957. File: Committee on Slum Clearance 1957. Letter to Moses on the Development of the Polo Grounds, Dunbar McLaurin.

Columbia University Archives, Morningside Heights Area Alliance Archives, Box 32. April 29, 1966. File: 6. Report of the Community Programs Committee to the Annual Meeting of the Board of Directors, Morningside Heights, Inc.

Unpublished Interview

A reference for an unpublished interview lists (1) the name of the subject of the interview; (2) the year of the interview; (3) the name of the interviewer; (4) the month and day of the interview; and (5) the location of the interview. If you conducted the interview, identify yourself as "author."

Bush, William. 2005. Interview by author. Tape recording. Los Angeles, CA, July 31.

Personal Communication

Personal communications are generally handled within the text of the paper, and the reference is placed in a footnote or endnote. See the previous section "Citation for Personal Communication" for an example. In the rare case that personal communications are included in the reference list, the following format may be used. Check with your instructor regarding format guidelines for your paper.

Doe, Adam. 2001. Letter to author, April 1.

Doe, Allison. 2002. Telephone conversation with the author, May 3.

Doe, Karen. 2000. E-mail to author, March 22.

Anonymous Source

Where the author of a work is not known and there is no editor or compiler, the title of the work is used in place of the author's name. Alphabetize the title by the first word, or if the title begins with an article (*a, an, the*), by the second word. Do not use the word *anonymous* in the reference. Where the author of an anonymous work has been established, the author's name is placed in brackets before the date and title.

[Klein, Joe]. 1996. *Primary Colors: A Novel of Politics.* New York: Grand Central Publishing.

CD-ROM and DVD-ROM

A reference to material on CD-ROM and DVD-ROM, namely that is "published" and protected on a CD or DVD, includes (1) the name of the author; (2) the date of publication; (3) the title of the CD or DVD, italicized; (4) the edition, if any; (5) the publisher; and (6) the date you accessed the information. The place of publication is omitted unless relevant.

> Henslin, James M. 2005. *Instructor's Resource CD-ROM for Sociology: A Down-to-Earth Approach.* 8th ed. Allyn & Bacon (November 28, 2007).

4p Electronic Resources (E-Resources)

Book—Available Both in Print and Online

A reference for a book that is available in print, but that you viewed online, is prepared like an entry for a print book, with the addition of the date you accessed the book and the URL.

> Adamson, Walter L. 1993. *Avant-Garde Florence: From Modernism to Fascism.* Cambridge, MA: Harvard University Press. Retrieved June 15, 2007 (http://name.umdl.umich.edu/HEB00462).

Book—Available Online Only

A reference to an e-book that has been published digitally and has never been published in print uses the following format:

> Trochim, William and Sarita Davis. 1996. *Computer Simulations for Research Design.* Retrieved June 17, 2007 http://www.socialresearchmethods.net/simul/simul.htm).

Journal Article—Available Both in Print and Online

A reference for an online journal article follows the format for print articles of the same type. If a print journal article was accessed online as part of a database such as JSTOR, indicate the name of the database and the date of retrieval.

> Tilly, Charles. 2004. "Observations of Social Processes and Their Formal Representations." *Sociological Theory* 22(4):595–602. (Retrieved from JSTOR on July 10, 2007.)

Journal Article—Available Online Only

A reference for an article in an electronic journal lists the name of the author, the date of publication, the title of the article, the name of the journal, the volume and issue number, the retrieval date, and the URL.

> Caplan, Priscilla. 1997. "Will the Real Internet Please Stand Up?" The Public-Access Computer Systems Review 8(2). Retrieved June 12, 2007 (http://epress.lib.uh.edu/pr/v8/n2/capl8n2.html).

Report—Available Both in Print and Online (Author Named)

A reference for an online report lists the name(s) of the author(s), the date of publication, the title of the report, the place of publication, the publishing or distributing organization, the date you accessed the document, and the URL.

> Peter, Katharin and Laura Horn. 2005. *Gender Differences in Participation and Completion of Undergraduate Education and How They Have Changed Over Time*. National Center for Education Statistics: Report. Washington, DC: U.S. Department of Education. Retrieved June 15, 2007 (http://nces.ed.gov/das/epubs/2005169/ references.asp).

Report—Available Online Only (No Author Named)

A reference for an online report with no author(s) named lists the institutional producer as the author. State the date of publication, the title of the report, the date you accessed the document, and the URL.

> World Energy Council. 2004. *Survey of Energy Resources 2004*. Retrieved June 15, 2007 (http://www.worldenergy.org/wecgeis/publications/default/ launches/ser04/ser04.asp).
> U.S. Department of Justice. Federal Bureau of Investigation. 2005. *Hate Crime Statistics, 2005*. Retrieved June 15, 2007 (http://www.fbi.gov/ucr/ hc2005/index.html).

Fact Sheet—Online

A reference for information obtained from online databases lists the source of information, the date posted on the Internet (the date is usually located at the bottom of the home page), the title, the date you retrieved it, and the URL.

> National Center for Education Statistics. 2006. "Fast Facts." Retrieved June 15, 2007 (http://nces.ed.gov/fastfacts/display.asp?id=16).

Article in a Newsletter—Available Both in Print and Online (Author Named)

A reference for an article, item, or announcement in a newsletter available both in print and online with the author named includes (1) the name(s) of the author(s); (2) the date of publication; (3) the title of the article; (4) the name of the newsletter; (5) the issue—month or number; (6) the date you retrieved it; and (7) the URL.

> Sager, Rebecca. 2007. "The Faith-Based Initiative." *Footnotes*, April. Retrieved June 15, 2007 (http://www2.asanet.org/footnotes/ ap07/fn4.html).

Article in a Newsletter—Available Online Only (No Author Named)

A reference for an article, item, or announcement in a newsletter available online only with no author named lists (1) the institutional producer as author; (2) the date of publication; (3) the title of the article; (4) the newsletter's name; (5) the issue—month or number; (6) the date you retrieved it; and (7) the URL.

> Association of Public Data Users. 2005. "Daytime Population." *APDU Newsletter*, December. Retrieved June 15, 2007 (http://www.apdu.org/resources/samplenewsletter.pdf).

Article in a Newspaper or Magazine—Accessed Online

A reference for an online newspaper or magazine article lists the name of the author, the date of publication, the title of the article, the name of the newspaper or magazine, the date of the article, the retrieved date, and the URL.

> Sengupta, Somini. 2007. "Indian Officials to Rule How 'Backward' Group Is." *New York Times*, June 5. Retrieved June 17, 2007 (http://www.nytimes.com).

Web Site

If you use data or evidence from a Web site (as opposed to reading a report or fact sheet available on the site), cite it using the following format. Some Web sites have a "suggested" citation already prepared for the site, which can be found at the bottom of the Web site's home page. In the reference entry, list (1) the author(s); (2) the date information was posted or most recently updated; (3) the title of the Web site; (4) the location of the sponsoring organization, if known; (5) the name of the sponsoring organization, if any (omit the name here if the organization is listed as the author); (6) the date you accessed page; and (7) the URL.

• Document Accessed on a Web Site Sponsored by an Organization with a Location Named

> Association of Religion Data Archives. 2006. "Denominational Family Trees." University Park, PA: Association of Religion Data Archives. Retrieved June 16, 2007 (http://www.thearda.com/Denoms/Families/).

• Document Accessed on a Web Site Sponsored by an Organization with No Location Named

> Microsoft Corporation. 2005. "School of the Future: Understand the Vision." Retrieved December 12, 2007 (http://www.microsoft.com/Education/SchoolofFutureVision.mspx).

• **Blog Entry**

Etzioni, Amitai. 2007. "Basic Security Comes First." Amitai Etzioni Notes, November 19, 2007. Retrieved December 20, 2007 (http://blog.amitaietzioni. org/2007/11/basic-security.html).

FIGURE 4.1 Sample Reference List (Example from Student Paper)

Smith

REFERENCES

Bereday, George Z. F., ed. 1969. *Essays on World Education: The Crisis of Supply and Demand.* New York: Oxford University Press.

Blau, Zena Smith. 1972. "Role Exit and Identity." Paper presented at the annual meeting of the American Sociological Asssociation, August 28, New Orleans, LA.

Cooley, Charles H. 1922. *Human Nature and the Social Order.* New York: Scribner's.

Erikson, Erik. 1950. *Childhood and Society.* New York: Norton.

Goffman, Erving. 1961a. *Asylums.* New York: Doubleday.

————. 1961b. *Encounters.* Indianapolis, IN: Bobbs-Merrill.

Hurtado, Aida, David E. Hayes-Bautista, R. Burciaga Valdez, and Anthony C. R. Hernandez. 1992. *Redefining California: Latino Social Engagement in a Multicultural Society.* Los Angeles, CA: UCLA Chicano Studies Research Center.

Kuhn, Thomas. 1970. *The Structure of Scientific Revolutions.* 2nd ed. Chicago, IL: University of Chicago Press.

Mannheim, Karl. 1936. *Ideology and Utopia: An Introduction to the Sociology of Knowledge.* Translated by L. Wirth and E. Shils. New York: Harcourt, Brace and World.

Miller, Warren, Arthur Miller, and Gerald Klein. 1975. *The CPS 1974 American National Election Study* [MRDF]. Ann Arbor, MI: Center for Political Studies, University of Michigan [producer]. Ann Arbor: Inter-University Consortium [distributor].

Rossi, Alice S. 1968. "Transition to Parenthood." *Journal of Marriage and Family* 30(1):26–39.

Sager, Rebecca. 2007. "The Faith-Based Initiative." *Footnotes,* April. Retrieved June 15, 2007 (http://www2.asanet.org/footnotes/ap07/fn4.html).

Sengupta, Somini. 2007. "Indian Officials to Rule How 'Backward' Group Is." *New York Times,* June 5. Retrieved June 17, 2007 (http://www.nytimes.com).

5

Writing a Library Research Paper or Term Paper

Library research papers, also called term papers, are based mainly on **secondary-source materials:** books, articles, research reports, observations, and analyses written by others. By contrast, papers that rely on **primary-source materials** report data from (1) your personally conducted field research, such as your own survey, observational study, or experiment; or (2) your firsthand analysis of original documents, interview transcripts, or computer data files. (Papers based on primary-source materials are discussed in Chapters 6 and 7.) Exceptional term papers might use both primary and secondary sources, and such papers are much loved by instructors!

Writing a term paper is a form of scientific research. You collect data (evidence) derived from secondary sources obtained through the library or the Internet (methodology) to test your thesis statement (hypothesis).

This chapter will assist you in writing your paper. It discusses selecting an appropriate topic for a term paper, defining it as a sociological question, planning a research strategy, locating information, and structuring your paper. For additional help in getting started, see Chapter 1. For aid in locating and evaluating sources, pursuing a search strategy, and using research tools, see Chapter 3.

5a Selecting a Topic

A term paper generally is written to fulfill course requirements, and it should be written with the class subject matter in mind. Check your assignment for topic suggestions. Review the course syllabus and table of contents of your textbook, including subjects not yet covered in class, to brainstorm for ideas.

As stated in Chapter 1, two additional sources you may draw on in thinking of topic ideas are personal concerns and social problems. When you find a general subject that interests you, think about the aspect you find most curious. What exactly would you like to know? What would you like to devote time to investigating in this particular assignment? Personal interest often will lead to a good research question. (For more help, see Chapter 1.)

5b Defining a Sociological Question

Once you have a general subject in mind, refine it into a precise, researchable sociological question. This question is very important because *your proposed answer is your thesis statement.* The research question and your thesis statement are placed in the paper's introduction. Usually, the research question is not explicitly stated, but is discussed as an issue that is debatable, controversial, or unresolved.

Keep in mind that a sociology term paper is *not* an informative report about your topic, but a carefully argued and well-documented effort to prove your thesis statement. As such, if you cannot state your narrowed topic as a researchable question—one that can be "answered" in a one- or two-sentence thesis statement—you haven't refined your topic enough. Also, make sure you can competently argue your thesis and present sufficient supporting evidence. Limit the scope of the topic so it can be addressed within the page and time limits set by your instructor. (For more information, see Chapter 1.)

Also, as you probably noticed in the title of this section, your research question needs to be "sociological." When you write a paper for a sociology course, you must *write from a sociological viewpoint.* Sociology focuses on group behavior and interaction. Some subjects fall within the scope of sociology by definition of the discipline (for example, *delinquency, family,* and *gender roles*). Other subjects have been studied by a subfield within sociology, thus gaining legitimacy as subjects of sociological interest (for example, *civil inattention, technology,* and *time*). Your paper will be sociological *only* if you frame your research question in sociological terms, and if you use the sociological literature for your research.

Suppose you are enrolled in a sociology course and are asked to write an 8- to 10-page paper about some topic listed on the syllabus. In this case, if you find the subject of *time* interesting, you may consider writing about the *sociology of time.* These subjects, however, are both too broad in themselves to serve as the topic of your paper (in fact, an entire journal is devoted to the subject). To narrow your focus, you would do a brief overview of the published scholarly work on *time* in sociology. You quickly would discover that when sociologists think about *time,* they view it as a product of the social construction of reality. You therefore would need to use this theoretical viewpoint in framing your research question.

In such a case, you should consider taking one the following approaches to your topic:

1. How a theory can be applied to a particular case

   the development of daylight savings time

2. How a theory has developed and been applied over time

   an analysis of the ideas of the main scholars who developed and extended the theory

3. The implications of a theory

   collective memory and the effect of time

Note that if a subject has not been studied by sociologists, it probably is not appropriate for a paper topic, unless you are told otherwise. The groundbreaking work of applying existing theory to a new content area is best left to a master's thesis or doctoral dissertation.

5c Getting Feedback

When you have developed a list of your top choices for a paper topic, it is wise to schedule a meeting with your instructor to discuss your list and get feedback. Do this soon after receiving the assignment; your instructor will view it as a sign of your motivation and competence. For a paper with a due date two months away, it is best to set the meeting for one to two weeks after the assignment is distributed. Be sure to go to the meeting prepared, having preliminarily researched each topic on your list.

When you arrive at your instructor's office, have your list handy. Be ready to take lengthy notes, as your instructor is likely to suggest sources, authors, and theories to consult. Jot down every idea, because at this early phase it will be difficult to judge which information you will want to use. Many students have been surprised to discover that a seemingly obscure comment by their instructor turned out to be the missing puzzle piece in their research. Don't hesitate to seek help. If you are genuinely interested, most instructors will be delighted to be of assistance.

5d Planning a Research Strategy

As noted in Chapter 3, you will need to do research at three stages in the writing of your paper: (1) to select a topic, (2) to construct a tentative thesis statement, and (3) to collect information supporting your thesis statement. To use your time effectively, consider the following points in planning your search strategy.

Research to Select a Topic

Unless you have been assigned a subject, begin your research before selecting a topic. Preliminary research will help you narrow and refine your topic ideas. Do a cursory **review of the literature**—check of published scholarly work—on your preferred topic to confirm that enough appropriate research materials are available for the length and scope of the paper you are writing. If not, begin researching your second choice, and if that doesn't pan out, move on to your third. At this stage, your goal is to find a topic with plenty of available research materials. (For more information, see Chapters 1 and 3.)

 Record the citations of any potentially relevant sources you find.

They might take hours to locate again.

Research to Construct a Tentative Thesis Statement

Once you have selected a topic, you need to define your research question and construct your proposed answer (your paper's thesis statement). At this stage, review the sociological literature in greater detail than before to determine the following:

1. Which research questions are discussed extensively?

   * Avoid these subjects, as your instructor will think them unoriginal.

2. Which research questions are discussed, but not extensively?

   * You will find good topic choices in this category.

3. Which research questions are discussed in books and journal articles actually available to you?

   * You need available research materials that relate, at least tangentially, to your research question. Otherwise, you will have no evidence to cite in support of your thesis statement. A topic with insufficient literature will lead to a poor paper.

Use this information to develop a tentative thesis statement. Keep in mind that as your paper progresses, you may discover information that influences you to change your ideas and revise your thesis statement. (For more information, see "Constructing a Thesis Statement" in Chapter 1.)

Research to Locate Information That Supports Your Thesis Statement

Once you have constructed your thesis statement, you are ready to conduct an in-depth review of the literature. Collect evidence, such as facts, theories, and experts' opinions, that provides support for the main point and each of the subpoints in your thesis statement. Unlike your earlier research, which mainly served to sharpen and focus your ideas, the materials you find at this stage actually will be used in your paper. If you revise your thesis statement at this stage, additional research usually will be needed to locate supporting evidence for the changed thesis.

5e Honoring the Creative Rhythm of Research

As straightforward as the research process may seem, it is rarely linear. Research is a creative undertaking and, like other such endeavors, progresses discontinuously. Your search is likely to lurch forward at a stop-and-go pace, frequently backtracking and branching in ways you could not have anticipated. Honor the creative rhythm of research by acknowledging it and allotting time to engage in its unpredictability.

More often than not, research is recurrent, looping back on itself. In practice, you may find a topic of interest, start research to narrow it, realize it won't work, and need to restart preliminary research on a new topic. Or, after selecting a topic, you may begin more focused research to develop a thesis statement, and then discover you can't find materials on the thesis of interest to you. In this case, you would need to either choose another thesis or go back to the beginning and pick a new topic. Or, having constructed a thesis statement, you may start in-depth research, only to discover that the materials you find don't support your thesis. Here, you would need to revise your thesis statement, and then start in-depth research again.

 Don't view the need to backtrack as a mistake. Just make sure to begin working on your paper early enough so you will have the time to revise and start again if necessary.

5f Record Keeping

Be sure to keep a record of the search terms you use and the sources you find. You want to be able to locate these materials later if you need them. Take brief notes on each article or book, and include information on how to find these materials again—call numbers for books; volume number, date, and page numbers for journal articles. If you photocopy an article, write the full citation on the copy.

Keep a research log either on your computer or in print. To set up an electronic tracking system on your computer, try the following suggestions:

1. Create a new folder and label it with a name that is easy to remember, such as *Research Log for Paper on Sociology of Time*.

2. Within this folder, create subfolders to help you manage your term paper. Here are some examples:

   Literature review
   Outline
   Evidence and Sources for Thesis Statement
   References
   Draft 1
   Draft 2, and so on
   Trash (Instead of deleting information you have collected and then chose not to use, cut and paste it into *Trash*. You may be able to use it later.)

3. Within each subfolder, create documents for your information.

If you don't keep an electronic log, you can use a loose-leaf binder for the same purpose. Set up dividers with the same labels as for the subfolders.

Once you locate the materials you want to use for your paper, take detailed notes, or copy them and highlight the relevant sections. Be sure to record the full citation for any quoted or paraphrased words taken from another person.

5g Locating Information

Term papers report data derived from library sources, and sometimes from the Internet. Use a college or university library for your research. Public libraries do not have the specialized books and reference tools you need for sociological research, nor do they subscribe to the two academic databases sociologists find essential, *CSA Sociological Abstracts* and *Social Sciences Index*. Most campus libraries make resources available online, so you can access them day or night from any location. Library research today usually involves both print and online materials.

Note that online resources are not the same as Internet resources, however. Going to your campus library, you will encounter materials and research tools not available on the Internet. Through your library, for example, you can access online databases for searching academic journals in various disciplines. In some cases, you can locate and read full-text articles. Since your library pays for subscriptions to these databases, access to the collection is usually limited to campus ID holders. By contrast, access to sites on the Internet is largely free, and materials can be posted at little cost. This has led to great differences in the quality, reliability, and authority of information available on the Internet.

Using the Internet to locate research materials has advantages and disadvantages. How do you determine which Internet sites provide reliable and credible information for academic research? You can find guidelines to evaluate Internet materials in Chapter 3. Still, you should be wary of including information from the Internet in your paper, and it is wise to check with your instructor before doing so. Most instructors expect term papers to be based primarily on library sources.

1. Don't quote or paraphrase information from an encyclopedia in your paper.

2. Try to avoid quoting or paraphrasing a dictionary definition in your paper.

3. If you must define a sociological term in your paper, the best approach is to use the definition proposed by either the first or the most important sociologist who employed the term, citing the source.

4. If you must quote or paraphrase a dictionary definition, it is preferable to use and cite to the print version.

5h Structuring the Paper as an Essay

Most sociology term papers are structured as essays. Check your assignment or ask your instructor if you are not sure. An essay includes the following elements: an introduction, body paragraphs, and a conclusion.

The example in Table 5.1 shows the structure of an essay that has a thesis statement with a main point and three supporting subpoints. Note that you can adapt the outline shown here to the actual number of subpoints in your thesis statement. Also, use this outline whether or not you actually list the subpoints in your thesis statement.

Note that in Table 5.1, the matter of length is undetermined. In a short paper, each thesis point can be discussed in *one paragraph that includes three subordinate ideas*. In a longer paper, each thesis point might be treated in *one key and three subordinate paragraphs* or more.

5i Compare/Contrast Papers

Some assignments require that you compare and/or contrast two things—two ideas, two social policies, two social theorists' ideas or works. This type of paper is actually an essay, but you will need to adapt the model shown in Table 5.1. Two outlines for compare/contrast papers and detailed instructions can be found in Chapter 9.

TABLE 5.1 Outline for an Essay, Research Paper, or Term Paper

Introduction (including thesis statement with three supporting points)

I. First subpoint of the thesis
   A. First subordinate idea (supporting evidence 1)
   B. Second subordinate idea (supporting evidence 2)
   C. Third subordinate idea (supporting evidence 3)

II. Second subpoint of the thesis
   A. First subordinate idea (supporting evidence 1)
   B. Second subordinate idea (supporting evidence 2)
   C. Third subordinate idea (supporting evidence 3)

III. Third subpoint of the thesis
   A. First subordinate idea (supporting evidence 1)
   B. Second subordinate idea (supporting evidence 2)
   C. Third subordinate idea (supporting evidence 3)

Conclusion

5j Writing Each Section of the Paper

Each section of an essay, research paper, or term paper contains specific information arranged in a particular order. The three main sections of an essay are the introduction paragraph, body paragraphs (covering your thesis subpoints), and conclusion paragraph. These sections do not begin with headings.

The Introduction Paragraph

The introduction paragraph is usually five to eight sentences long and is a preview of your entire paper. The first sentence is a general introduction of the subject to the reader. Avoid humor, anecdotes, and quotations in your opening sentence in college-level or graduate school sociology papers. The last sentence of the introduction paragraph is the thesis statement.

The three to six sentences between the first sentence and thesis statement build up to the thesis statement by moving from general (the first sentence) to specific (thesis statement). There must be a logical progression in your sentences, and each sentence must move you one step closer to the thesis. The content of these sentences should (1) frame your research question in sociological terms; (2) indicate or lead up to the ideas that will be the major points of your thesis; and (3) indicate the general nature of the sources consulted for the paper (for example, an analysis of two key works by two authors, a sociological literature review, or a personal opinion). Make sure the progression of sentences flows smoothly to culminate in the thesis statement.

The Body Paragraphs

The body of the paper presents a discussion or defense of the thesis statement. Each subpoint in the thesis is treated in one or more paragraphs, following the order of placement in the thesis statement. If the thesis has three subpoints, each point is treated in one or more separate paragraphs. Allot the same number of paragraphs to each thesis subpoint. See Chapter 2 for more information on paragraph structure.

Conclusion Paragraph

The conclusion provides a one-paragraph finale to your paper. Summarize or review the main ideas raised in your paper. You may restate your thesis statement, but this time as an assertion (e.g., "This paper has demonstrated X, Y, and Z"). Then, discuss the implications or broader import of your thesis statement being supported. Emphasize any interesting approach or interpretation you made in your paper. End with a flourish!

No new information should appear in the conclusion paragraph. Do not give examples or introduce new arguments. Do not use quotations or paraphrased material. Do not include citations, footnotes, endnotes, tables, figures, or appendices. Do not refer back to the introduction paragraph in the conclusion.

5k Creating a Term Paper Title

In academic writing, it is important that your title includes the one or two most important keywords from your thesis statement or main finding. If you use a general or catchy title, add a descriptive, substantive subtitle that includes your keywords.

It is wise to avoid humor or puns in your titles unless you know your instructor will appreciate the gesture. If you hope to submit your paper for an application to graduate school or the like, also skip the humor. What seems funny to you as you finish a marathon session writing your third term paper may not appear humorous at all by dawn's early light or to your instructor at grade time. Deeply thoughtful students who ponder great thoughts don't make jokes about their ideas, and neither should you. Leave the trite and tiring puns and clichés for other venues, and stick with clear, straightforward titles.

For more information on formatting for titles and title pages, see Chapter 2.

5l References

The reference list includes only works actually cited in your paper. If you compile your citations as you write your paper, make sure to compare your reference list to the final version of your paper. Citations in footnotes or endnotes, if any, also are placed in the reference list.

References are placed on one or more separate pages, with the heading REFER-ENCES in all capital letters, placed near the top of the page. Triple-space between the heading and the first reference entry. The reference list is placed at the end of the document (following the order of the document shown in Table 6.3 in Chapter 6). The reference pages are numbered. For help in creating reference list entries, see Chapter 4.

5m Revising Your Paper

Once you write a draft of your paper, remember to revise it using the 10 Revision Cycles discussed in Chapter 2.

5n Final Check

Make sure you have . . .

1. an appropriate title.
2. a correct title page.
3. headers with your name in the upper right-hand corner of each page.
4. correctly numbered pages.

5. text citations following ASA documentation style.
6. a reference list following ASA documentation style.
7. spell-checked and personally proofread your document.
8. printed on good-quality, white paper with black ink.
9. stapled your paper in the upper right-hand corner, or placed it in a binder as instructed.

6 Writing a Quantitative Research Paper

A **quantitative research paper** presents and analyzes new data resulting from (1) your personally conducted research, such as your own survey, observational study, or experiment; or (2) your firsthand analysis or reanalysis of a computer data file or other "available data"—including the content analysis of documents, letters, films, television shows, advertisements, and song lyrics. In this type of paper, the main focus is on the data you have collected and analyzed. The published scholarly research of others appearing in the paper is used only to establish the context for your own study. In reporting your original research, a quantitative paper differs in structure and format from a term paper, which is based on secondary sources.

 You will need familiarity with research methods in sociology to write this type of paper.

6a Quantitative versus Qualitative Papers

In quantitative research, data are presented in **numerical form.** By contrast, in qualitative research, data are presented in **nonnumerical form,** such as words, descriptions, narratives, pictures, or symbols. Of the four major research designs preferred by sociologists—surveys, observational studies, experiments, and participant observation—all can be made to yield quantitative data. However, in general, researchers with a quantitative bent tend to choose surveys and experiments as their favored research designs, and researchers with a predilection for observational studies and participant observation tend to use qualitative methods. Keep this in mind when selecting a topic for your paper.

6b "Writing Up" Your Research Study

As you probably know, much of the effort and time involved in writing a quantitative research paper is expended long before you sit down to write. After all, first you need to plan and conduct your research study. Only when you have finished can you write up the results of your research study as a paper.

This chapter addresses the *writing* of a quantitative paper. Research-related decisions and concerns are discussed only as they directly affect your paper. Keep in mind that research methods is an important subfield within sociology, and at the college level, it is treated in semester-long courses and plump textbooks. If you have already completed a research methods course or are currently enrolled in one, you should know how to handle the research design, data collection, and data analysis for your study, or be in the process of learning to do so. If, however, you are considering starting a quantitative research project without having taken at least one research methods course, be forewarned. It is difficult to complete the research and successfully write the paper without adequate knowledge and support. If you are serious about your plan, sign up for a methods course. It will be well worth your effort.

 Leave plenty of time for completing your research study, as well as for writing your paper. Collecting and analyzing quantitative data can take much longer than expected.

6c   Structuring the Paper

A paper reporting original research is structured as a **research article,** not as an essay. A research article has five sections, (Table 6.1), although in short papers (those with fewer than 10 pages), the discussion and conclusion sections frequently are combined into a single section titled discussion/conclusion.

How much detail about your research study should be placed in your paper? The research article structure of the quantitative paper requires you to include information about how you developed and executed your research study, and the ways in which you analyzed your data and reached conclusions. This material is placed in your paper in predetermined sections, and within a section, in a particular order.

To help you organize information about your research study as you begin to outline and draft your paper, consult the Overview of the Research Process (see Table 6.2). Researchers in all branches of science follow the eight steps listed here when they conduct scientific research. You will need to follow them, too, as you carry out your

TABLE 6.1 Outline of a Research Article

Introduction (this section has no heading)

Methods

Results

Discussion

Conclusion

TABLE 6.2 Overview of the Research Process

1. Choose a topic. Define it as a sociological problem.
2. Review the literature.
3. Form a hypothesis and operationalize key variables.
4. Choose a research design (survey, observational study, experiment, or participant observation).
5. Choose a sample.
6. Collect data.
7. Analyze data.
8. Draw a conclusion (was your hypothesis proved, yes or no?).

study, and you will need to discuss them as you write up your paper. Perhaps you recognize the eight steps, collectively known as the Scientific Method. For a research study to be considered "scientific" by the community of scholars in the discipline, the researcher must have followed the Scientific Method; if not, the study is considered "flawed" and its conclusions untrustworthy.

As you start writing your paper, it is helpful to keep the Overview of the Research Process close by for reference, as information about each step must be placed in your paper at a specific location. (Note: The eight steps have been adapted for sociology, but are *not* used as headings or subheadings in your paper.)

6d Developing the Paper

Most quantitative papers reporting original research follow the model of **hypothesis testing.** In conducting your study, you will have chosen a topic and defined it as a sociological question, reviewed the literature, and most likely formulated a hypothesis. Once you arrive at the writing phase, you will need to make explicit the connection between the topic, sociological question, and hypothesis to establish the rationale for your study. This information is placed in the introduction, and is returned to later in the discussion section of your paper.

To understand how these three elements are linked, consider the following example. Imagine you need to choose a topic for a paper, so you begin to brainstorm for ideas. You may start to wonder why some members of your class hold the opinions they do, why some women in your neighborhood enjoy being stay-at-home mothers and some do not, and why some relatives are delighted with their lives in a retirement community in Arizona while others are sorry they have left their old homes in Illinois. Notice that although these ideas may be interesting and they certainly relate to social phenomena, none are (as yet) in the form of a sociological question. Your paper will be sociological only if you frame your research question in sociological terms, and if you use the sociological literature for your literature review.

When you frame a sociological question, you attempt to explain the great variation in social life in terms of some broad, unifying themes. Students' responses to surveys become data for a study of college student attitudes, interviews with stay-at-home mothers inform a study of the multiple roles available to women, and opinions about moving to Arizona shed light on attitudes toward migration among elderly people.

The framing of specific empirical observations (e.g., *Jill Harris lunches with friends twice a week and regularly volunteers in a local hospital*) in terms of a larger question (*How do retired people spend their time?*) leads to the development of a hypothesis (*People who migrate to retirement communities report higher levels of satisfaction than those who do not migrate to retirement communities*). Most quantitative research tests a hypothesis, although there are some exceptions.

6e   Writing the Quantitative Paper

The body or text of the quantitative paper, structured as a research article, has five sections. The sections are written in the order of their position in the paper: introduction, methods, results, discussion, and conclusion. Generally, the first four sections of the paper are roughly equal in length, while the conclusion is shorter. Ask your instructor about the amount of detail and expected length of the sections, and which scholarly journal to use as a guide.

Review the list in Table 6.3 to confirm that your paper is ordered correctly. Some parts are required in all papers, while others are added as needed. If you are unclear as to whether you should include an abstract or appendix, for example, consult your instructor.

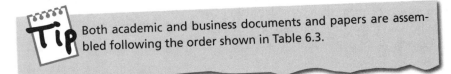

Tip Both academic and business documents and papers are assembled following the order shown in Table 6.3.

TABLE 6.3 The Order of a Document

Title page	Usually required.
Abstract	Check with your instructor. Abstracts are required for conference and journal submissions.
Text (body)	Introduction (no heading), Methods, Results, Discussion, Conclusion.
Endnotes	Optional. May use footnotes instead, or may have no notes in the paper.
References	Required.
Appendices	Use if needed.
Tables	Usually required in a quantitative paper.
Figures	Use if needed.

While a paper is assembled prior to submission in the order shown in Table 6.3, it is rarely written in that sequence. Usually the text or body is written first, with the footnotes/endnotes and references compiled as you go along. The other parts are written later. The remainder of this chapter will guide you through the process of writing your paper, step by step.

6f The Introduction

The introduction creates a context for the rest of your paper by placing your research within a larger sociological framework. The introduction signals how you intend your work to be understood—for example, as following a certain theoretical, methodological, or empirical tradition.

> "This paper maintains that Goffman's work, particularly his treatment of the interaction order and his elucidation of deference and demeanor, can be used to extend the theory of citizenship" (Colomy and Brown 1996:371).

The tradition or framework you choose determines the concepts you will use and the literature you will review in your paper. If you take an interactionist perspective in your paper, make sure to use interactionist terminology (e.g., *deference, demeanor)* and base your literature review on the work of interactionists (e.g., Goffman, Mead). It would be inappropriate to use conflict theory's terminology (e.g., *class, proletariat)* and literature (e.g., Marx, Dahrendorf) in a paper that otherwise uses an interactionist perspective. This is a fundamental aspect of your paper's content, so confirm that your definitions, concepts, sources, and literature all emerge from the same theoretical or sociological perspective.

Tip To cross-check your work, find one or two excellent articles on your topic written from the sociological or theoretical perspective you are taking in your paper (functionalist, conflict, or interactionist). Note the concepts and literature mentioned by the authors of the articles. Pay attention to the way terms are defined and sources are cited for definitions. Then review the articles' references. What journals published the articles in the reference lists? Have you located articles for your literature review in those journals? Get some ideas, remembering to cite your sources where appropriate.

The introduction also includes the hypothesis or thesis statement that will structure the remainder of your paper. The hypothesis or thesis, in stating what you plan to accomplish or demonstrate in the paper, indicates the direction the paper will take and the type of sources and arguments the paper will present.

TABLE 6.4 Writing a Research Article: The Introduction Section

Introduce the topic in a general statement (and define the key terms, if necessary).

Review the literature.

State the problem.

Frame a sociological question.

State your hypothesis or thesis statement.

The goals of the introduction section need to be accomplished in just a few compact, tersely worded paragraphs. It is also important to be very clear and precise, so you may need to define your interpretation of key terms. For example, in sociology papers, the term *schooling* generally does not need to be defined in the introduction, whereas less well-known terms, such as *civil inattention* and *studied nonobservance*, require definitions. Keep in mind that in the methods section, you will need to give operational definitions for your main variables, which must be far more precise.

Most writers find the introduction the most challenging section to write. Once drafted, however, it will speed the writing of the rest of the paper. So, put your ideas on paper following the sequence shown in Table 6.4, and then proceed to the next sections. When you go back to revise your document, you will undoubtedly "tighten" and "tweak" your intro (and later sections, too), but that is to be expected. In the meantime, you will have developed the momentum needed to write and successfully finish your paper.

As you write the introduction section, address each part in order as listed in Table 6.4. No subheadings or separate paragraphs are used, and the introduction section itself has no heading. Depending on the scope of the paper, the introduction section may range from several paragraphs to several pages in length. The overall length of the section determines the amount of space devoted to each step. The opening sentence, definition, and review of the literature usually are combined in one or more paragraphs, and the remaining parts form the rest of the section.

Introduce the Topic

Begin with a general opening statement assessing the history or current state of research devoted to a particular topic. This one-sentence generalization may focus on the type of work that has been done or on the findings from this body of work. Here are some examples.

Gang behavior is a subject that has attracted considerable sociological interest for almost a century.

Social change theorists have long been concerned with the use of violence in social conflict.

Previous research indicates considerable consensus regarding the importance of economic factors in migration decisions.

In the past several decades, the study of juvenile delinquency has increasingly focused on the medicalization of deviance.

After the opening sentence, which introduces your key concept (e.g., *medicalization of deviance*), define the term, if necessary. Generally, only one term is central and unusual enough to require definition at this point, and it is rare to find a paper with multiple definitions placed at the beginning of the introduction section. As mentioned earlier, common sociological terms (e.g., *schooling, socialization, gender roles*) do not require definition. Only more specialized terms that are not widely recognized or agreed on by sociologists need to be defined in the introduction (e.g., *civil inattention, migration decisions, medicalization of deviance*).

How do you determine if there is recognition or agreement about a concept? Look at the recent literature (the published scholarly articles on your topic). Did those articles define the term? If they did, you should, too.

Furthermore, if you define a term, use a sociological definition and not one drawn from a general dictionary. The best place to find a sociological definition is—yes!—in a recent scholarly article on the subject. Paraphrase the definition and cite the source. This is preferable to using a definition drawn from a sociological dictionary, as the citation to a dictionary will make your work appear simplistic. Keep in mind that the primary use of a sociological dictionary is for *deep background* (your personal information), but not for use in your paper.

Review the Literature: Two Approaches

The introduction section often is organized in point–counterpoint fashion. If you take this approach, you would begin with a general statement and definition if necessary, as discussed in the first step. Then you would point out the failings of this opening general statement, using it as a foil against which to present the thesis of your paper. You may (1) call attention to the omission of an important variable from previous research (*but few have been directly concerned with the role of X in this process*); or you may (2) challenge the assumptions of previous research (*but research to date has underestimated Weber's depth of understanding of X*); or you may (3) question the methods employed in previous research (*but comparative analysis based on survey results is necessarily misleading*). The examples you provide to substantiate your claims come from, and comprise, your literature review.

The one danger in using this approach is that you must make sure you are not starting with an invalid criticism of previous research simply to create an argument and justify your thesis. If you write, *Introductory sociology textbooks describe a gang as if it were a closely knit organization controlled by a few powerful individuals. Such a picture misrepresents the current reality*, then you must be able to support your claim that this generalization (1) is true, and (2) holds for *all* introductory textbooks. Consequently, authors often qualify their initial claims to deflect potential criticisms (e.g., Many *introductory texts* or Older *introductory texts*). The reader must agree with your generalization. Otherwise, your introduction will create a hostile audience from the outset.

An alternative approach to starting the introduction is to place your specific topic within a context of similar social phenomena, thereby describing how you will discuss this topic. Here, your "argument" addresses which concepts and literature, or established body of work, are most relevant and useful for understanding your topic. To develop your points, you will need to bring examples from the literature (or from more than one "literature"), citing your sources. This is your literature review.

Imagine you were interested in studying college students' public preening behaviors (i.e., primping or adjustment of hair or clothes). You search *Sociological Abstracts* using the three keywords—*preening, primping,* and *adjustment*—but find few articles, books, or papers. However, once you link this term to the sociological concept of *appearance management,* you suddenly tap into a broader category of literature, although it is small compared to the literature on other topics. Additionally, if the sociological literature has little on your topic, and you have checked for synonyms of your keywords by seeking help from reference materials, you could turn to the literature of other social sciences (e.g., psychology, anthropology), and if that yields little, to the literature of other natural sciences (e.g., zoology, biology) for examples of preening among animals. This would enable you to make the argument that (perhaps) human preening behavior shares common elements with animal behaviors. (Note: This is an effective way of starting your paper if you are writing on a topic about which little research has been done, or if your paper is mainly descriptive.)

In choosing which research studies to include in your review of the literature, be sure to include the major studies most relevant to your topic. How do you determine which studies are *major?* How do you gauge the relative significance of published research? One way is to see whether an article is cited often in the work of others. How many entries are listed below it in the *Social Sciences Citation Index* (available in your campus library's reference department)? How many of the articles you have collected refer to it? Another way of assessing a study's significance is to look at where it was published. Did it appear in one of the leading journals of its discipline or subfield? Keep in mind that, aside from the scholarly significance of the research, your discussion of previous research is guided by its relevance to your specific thesis. Include only those studies that relate to your thesis statement or hypothesis.

How much do you write about each article or book referred to in your review of the literature? Ask your instructor, as expectations differ. In published research articles, like those appearing in major sociology journals, such as the *American Journal of Sociology* or the *American Sociological Review,* you will notice that very little information is given about each cited work. Rather, one key point is made about each— and often, they are grouped so that a single point is made about several works.

Note how the review of the literature is presented in this paragraph, with the focus on the key points.

Small group researchers regularly report that in mixed-sex discussion groups, men talk more, engage in more task behavior, are evaluated as more competent and knowledgeable, and exercise more influence within the group than women, while women tend to accept influence more often and exhibit higher levels of positive socioemotional behavior (e.g., making compliments and showing consideration) than men (Ridgeway and Smith-Lovin 1999;

Wagner and Berger 1997). In addition, men tend to occupy leadership positions more often than women, particularly when the task is "masculine-typed" or gender-neutral (Aries 1996; Eagly and Karau 1991; Ridgeway and Smith-Lovin 1999). The term *leader* often refers to the group member who is the most talkative, task oriented, and influential, and who provides the most guidance in completing the task. (Hysom and Johnson 2006:391–2)

For more information on citation format, see Chapter 4.

The goal in reviewing the literature relevant to your hypothesis/thesis is to demonstrate that while much research has been done by others on your topic (and they have found *X, Y,* and *Z* about it), no research so far has examined *Q,* which—amazingly!—is exactly what your hypothesis or thesis will examine. With this in mind, you can see that it is not important to give a full report on each work cited as part of your literature review. Rather, you must show how the various reviewed works fit together to form a "map" of the research on your topic. In the following step, you will point out where there is a gap (the one you intend to fill!).

Tip Do not point out gaps in the literature that you do not intend to address in this paper. Save those ideas for future assignments.

The literature is reviewed only in the introduction. You generally do not "come back to it" in the discussion or conclusion to compare it with your own research findings unless your paper is a testing of another researcher's work. The sole purpose of the literature review is to provide background for your sociological question and the hypothesis/thesis you develop in response. After the introduction, the remainder of the paper focuses solely on your research. You may cite others' works later in the paper in footnotes or endnotes, and occasionally in the text itself in support of an important point, but do not refer back to the overall literature later in your paper.

State the Problem

In the previous step, you constructed a literature review with the "hidden agenda" of pointing out a gap or problem (the one you intend to fill). Only now, however, do you openly point out this neglected area and elaborate on the existing flaw.

Here, you state what previous research neglected to mention—what important concepts, variables, or theories they failed to study. Depending on the length of your paper, you may treat this in one or two sentences in a short paper, in several sentences in a longer paper, or in a paragraph or two in a master's thesis or doctoral dissertation.

In the following paragraphs, the problem is stated clearly:

> **In contrast to this research on mixed-sex groups, results on same-sex groups are inconsistent** [emphasis added]. While some researchers report that women in all-female groups exhibit lower levels of task behavior than men in all-male groups (e.g., Carli 1989; Piliavin and Martin 1978), others find few gender differences in task behaviors (e.g., Johnson, Clay-Warner, and Funk 1996; Shelly and Munroe 1999). Findings regarding leadership structures in same-sex groups are similarly inconsistent (Walker et al. 1996). (Hysom and Johnson 2006:392)

> Christopherson notwithstanding, **treatment of the family is one topic that has received little attention in studies of romance novels** [emphasis added]. Although romance protagonists are typically (though not always) unmarried and the novels end with the romantic relationship resolving into a "happily ever after" scenario, the novels nonetheless often include visions of the family that will emerge. Many characters have their own children or are responsible for orphaned children, caregiving arrangements that foreshadow marital arrangements as do distributions of other forms of household labor performed even by unmarried people. (Clawson 2005:463)

Frame a Sociological Question

In response to the gap or inconsistency you identified in the previous step, you now need to frame a sociological question that will move your reader one step closer to your thesis statement. To do so, think about the gap and develop a question about it. Then, reword your question to employ sociological concepts and fit within some theoretical framework. Here are some examples.

Gap:	Inconsistent findings exist on leadership in same-sex task groups.
and:	You intend to study an aspect of this issue.
Question:	Does the way in which leadership has been measured in past studies give rise to the inconsistencies in their findings?
Gap:	No research exists on the relationship between family size and migration decisions.
and:	You intend to study an aspect of this issue.
Question:	Is family size related to migration decisions among older people?
Gap:	Inadequate research exists on the relationship between poverty and runaway behavior among urban females.
and:	You intend to study an aspect of this issue.
Question:	Is poverty related to runaway behavior among urban females?

Frequently, questions will address the testing of some new variables, the study of an existing theory as it applies to a new population, or correction of the outdated or faulty methodology in previous research. Note that you do not have to state this as an actual question followed by a question mark, although some papers do. The sociological question, usually one or two sentences in length in a short paper, is developed into the thesis statement/hypothesis. In the following example, the sociological question is developed fully.

> To address these inconsistent findings, and bearing in mind the measurement concerns of Walker et al. (1996), in this article we assess leadership differentiation in same-sex discussion groups, using differentiation measures based on four commonly used, individual-level behavioral measures: procedural acts, influence, task behaviors, and amount of time spent talking. We apply each of these four measures to a single data set gathered from all-male and all-female discussion groups meeting in one of two organizational settings. In one setting, women held the majority of authority positions within the organization; in the other, men held the majority of positions. By taking this approach, we can better assess how the leadership differentiation measures compare with one another, and we are also able to investigate the effect of an organization's authority structure on leadership in small groups meeting with the organization (Ridgeway 1988; Fennell et al. 1978). (Hysom and Johnson 2006:392)

Notice that the authors discuss their methodology very generally in the previous paragraph to provide background for the hypotheses they will present next. A much more detailed review of their methodology is located in their methods section. Here is another example.

> These differing components of masculinity and femininity—gendered division of labor within the family, headship and submission, work, and sexuality—and the differences between how these themes are presented in Christian and secular popular culture are the focus of this article. (Clawson 2005:464)

State a Hypothesis or Thesis Statement

The introduction concludes with a research hypothesis or thesis statement that structures the remainder of your paper. It also organizes your presentation of findings in the results section, and your treatment of subjects in the discussion section. The hypothesis or thesis statement is *your announcement of what your study will do*, thereby indicating what gaps your work will fill and what problems it will try to resolve. In this sense, it is the culmination of the argument you built up in the introduction, which can be summarized as follows:

- Make a generalization.
- Review the literature.
- Identify a gap (define a problem).
- Restate the problem in sociological terms (frame a question).
- Propose a tentative answer to the question (offer a hypothesis or thesis statement).

Generally, quantitative papers test one or more hypotheses, and these are stated at the end of the introduction section, sometimes followed by a sentence or two elaborating on the relationship you expect to find. Note that the terms *hypothesis* or *prediction* can be used interchangeably.

Here is the end of the introduction section from the article by Hysom and Johnson.

Thus, we offer the following predictions:

Prediction 1: The difference between all-male and all-female groups' average level of leadership differentiation in a male-dominated organization will be greater for a procedural-based indicator than for an influence-based indicator.

Prediction 2: The difference between all-female groups' average level of leadership differentiation in a female-dominated organization and all-female group's average level of leadership differentiation in a male-dominated organization will be greater for a procedural-based indicator than for an influence-based indicator. (Hysom and Johnson 2006:396)

In descriptive or exploratory research, you do not have enough information to develop a hypothesis. In these cases, use a thesis statement to indicate what you plan to study.

This article examines how romance novels differently construct gender and family roles for Christian and secular readerships, and finds that the most striking differences between the books lie in the heroes. Although the heroes of secular romances are more stereotypically masculine in a number of ways, they are also more likely to be in some way changed or "tamed" by the heroine. Christian heroes, by contrast, are never as hyper-masculine, but their masculine authority is ultimately more stable, vulnerable to taming only by God. (Clawson 2005:461)

6g The Methods Section

The methods section describes how you measured, collected, and analyzed the data presented in your paper. Do not describe your research project chronologically ("First, I did this, and then I did that"). Instead, you should precisely and tersely state how you handled steps 3 to 7 in Table 6.2. Namely, how did you operationalize key variables; what research design did you choose; what sampling technique did you use to select the sample; how and when were data collected; and what techniques were used in data analysis, thereby indicating that your study met the standards of scientific research? Make certain that you fully describe any aspects of your methodology that would lead a critical reader to raise questions.

The methods section is introduced with the heading METHODS capitalized and centered. The length of this section varies. In a short paper, the methods section may run two or three paragraphs in length. In a longer paper, the section may be divided into subsections with the subheadings *Sample, Measures,* and *Procedures* italicized and placed at the left margin. Other subheadings are used only when the paper's methodology is very complex. In a master's thesis or doctoral dissertation, a full chapter is

TABLE 6.5 Writing a Research Article: The Methods Section

Sample
>What data were used in this study?
>Where was the sample studied?
>When was the sample studied?

Measures
>How were the data collected?
>How were the key variables measured?

Procedures
>How were the data analyzed?

---

devoted to methodology. Note that this section should be worded in past tense since your research is already completed at the time of writing.

While no formal order has been established for the methods section (as opposed to the introduction section, for example) the following information must be included. Many papers use the sequence shown in Table 6.5.

Sample

• *What* Data Were Utilized in This Study?

To craft the sentences to address this question, you need to identify information about your sample, sampling technique, and research design (e.g., survey, observational study, experiment). Take a look at this first sentence from a methods section.

>The data utilized in this study were drawn from a survey of 500 randomly selected undergraduates at a major metropolitan public university in the Midwest.

Notice that you need certain information to compose this sentence. First, you need to describe the **units of analysis** in your study. Did you study individuals? Groups (families, peer groups, clubs)? Organizations (businesses, schools)? Programs (tutoring, counseling)? Social artifacts (movies, newspapers, books, magazines, documents)? How many subjects did you study?

Next, describe your sampling procedures. How did you select your specific sample from the larger population of people, groups, organizations, programs, or social artifacts you chose to study? If you chose a **random sample,** describe the sampling frame from which you sampled (e.g., city directory, block maps, court dockets, class rosters).

Then, discuss how you selected the sample from this list. Did you use **simple random sampling** (numbering each case and selecting cases using a table of random numbers) or **systematic sampling** (beginning with a random start, and selecting every Xth case)? If you divided your list into two or more groups before sampling (what social scientists refer to as a **stratified sample**), then state your reason for doing so. For example, if you are interested in an issue on which you expect men and women to hold different opinions, but your list of potential respondents contains many more men than women, you many want to use a stratified sample based on sex. In this case, using a simple random sample may not yield enough women to allow for a meaningful analysis employing sex as an independent variable.

If you do not or cannot use a random sampling technique (i.e., **probability sampling**), explain why. Systematic sampling cannot be used, for example, when the list that comprises the **sampling frame**—the list from which you choose elements for inclusion in your sample—is ordered by a variable relevant to your research (e.g., students are listed by class). Randomness in sample selection is more important in quantitative than in qualitative studies because it is a prerequisite for the tests of statistical significance used in quantitative analysis.

However, even when randomness is not essential to the goals of your research, you should address the **representativeness** of your sample. You might claim that you selected a particular college class for your study of teacher–student interaction because it appeared typical of other classes taught at this school in size and distribution of gender, age, racial/ethnic, and other variables relevant to your study.

Next, state the total sample size and the response rate, as well as how the researcher obtained the sample (Note: Specify the research design here!) Problems encountered in selecting the sample should be discussed, and you should indicate whether these lowered the **response rate.** For example, did people refuse to fill out the questionnaire or give interviews? Were documents in the sample found to be incomplete? How did you handle missing data?

Finally, describe the characteristics of the sample relevant to your study. It is appropriate to compose a one-paragraph profile of your sample, giving numbers and percentages for the total sample, supplemented with a graphic presentation summarizing the information. Today, sociologists generally describe their sample in terms of the breakdown by gender, age, and race/ethnicity, in addition to the one or two key variables being studied.

In the following example, the size and industry of companies are important variables, so the author describes the way in which businesses in the sample are distributed among the categories of these two variables (size and type of company):

To investigate the diffusion and determination of company job-training programs, I use the 1997 National Organizations Survey of Human Resources Policies. The principal investigators for this survey are. . . . The sampling frame was from the well-known Dun and Bradstreet Market Identifier data set. Dun and Bradstreet initially provided 1,714 organizations, of which 1,478 establishments with at least fifty employees were declared eligible for the study. This list of 1,478 establishments was stratified by size and industry prior to random sampling selection, which later yielded 695 randomly selected establishments. Interviewers sent letters to the 695 establishments and followed up with telephone interviews. A total of 389 establishments completed the telephone interviews, yielding a response rate of 56 percent. (Yang 2006:330)

The following example illustrates a sample profile:

A profile of the respondents whose documents comprise data set II (n = 110) indicates the following composition: 50% white, 8% black, 31% Hispanic, and 11% Asian; 45% male and 55% female. Data set II includes 47 achieved statuses, representing a variety of situations about which respondents provide role information: the family, workplace, school, and friendship groups. (Yellin 1999:241)

• *Where* Was the Sample Studied?

Researchers identify the location of the sample and data collection in order to demonstrate that their research is comparable to other studies conducted in similar settings. To protect its anonymity, the name of the location should not be disclosed (otherwise researchers may be barred entry in the future). Instead, describe the location(s) in terms commonly used in the sociological literature. You may get some ideas from the journal articles in your literature review. For course papers and assignments, consult your instructor, as more details may be required.

. . . at a large, metropolitan public university in the Midwest

. . . at two small rural community colleges

. . . at a large indoor shopping mall in a middle-class community

• *When* Was the Sample Studied?

State the date(s) of data collection and, if relevant, the times of day. For a survey, dates are sufficient.

The research team collected data February 1–7, 2008.

If the time element in your method is likely to be questioned by a critical reader, anticipate the questions and address the issue directly. In the following example, the authors responded to a concern they expected to be raised by giving additional explanation:

. . . Respondents completed a self-administered questionnaire in the beginning of spring semester 1994 and again two months later. While a two-month period between waves is not ideal for assessing major changes in identity, stress, or mental health outcomes, a problem with previous research in this area has been the inability to assess whether identity characteristics moderate the effect of strain on mental health or whether, to some extent, characteristics of the identity change as a function of strain (Thoits 1992). (Marcussen, Ritter, and Safron 2004:294)

Measures

• *How* Were the Data Collected?

Describe the tools used to observe and record your data. Did you conduct a survey? If you administered a questionnaire to respondents, describe the process of distribution and collection. For mailed questionnaires, describe the mailing procedures, identifying information, and the number and timing of follow-up mailings. If you conducted interviews, describe your procedures (e.g., phone, face-to-face) and techniques. Were interviews **structured** (did you ask each subject the same questions in the same order) or **unstructured** (did you allow the subjects' answers to determine the course of the interview)?

For all surveys, describe the type of questions you asked. Were both **open-ended** and **closed-ended** questions included? How long did it take to complete a typical questionnaire or interview? Were there follow-up visits for interview subjects? Remember to place a copy of the questionnaire and cover letter(s) or interview schedule in appropriately labeled appendices.

For other research designs, such as observational studies, experiments, and content analysis, describe the tools and procedures used for data collection, coding, and other aspects of the study's methodology that may need clarification.

> To code the books, I created a questionnaire containing eighty-six primary questions—many with follow-up secondary questions—on a range of issues including professions, family status and childcare roles, appearance and sexuality, household labor, and leisure activities, as well as on aspects of the romantic relationship, including economic exchanges. (Clawson 2005:466)

• *How* Were The Key Variables Measured?

Indicate how you measured, or operationalized, the main variable in your study. Usually, this is your **dependent variable,** the variable you are attempting to explain or predict. Also, operationalize any other important variables in the study.

> We operationalize geographic mobility as living in a U.S. state different from the state of one's birth. Our analyses of geographic mobility include only individuals who were born in the 50 U.S. states, because all others are geographic movers by definition. (Rosenfield and Kim 2005:545)

For a survey, state the actual questions used to operationalize each variable. If several questions were combined in an index or scale, describe the scale and give an example of the questions. Place the full list of questions in the index or scale in an appendix to your paper. If you use an index or scale created by someone else, refer to it by name in your description and provide a full citation.

Variables may be operationalized with behaviors (in an experiment), observations by the researcher (in an observational study), or documentary evidence (in content analysis).

> Our measures of group-level leadership differentiation were created using four different individual-level behavioral indicators. The first individual-level measure, *time talked*, is the time in seconds that a given group member spoke, divided by the total time in seconds that his or her group met.
>
> The second individual-level measure, *task behavior*. . . .
>
> Finally, we developed a measure of each member's level of *influence*. . . . (Hysom and Johnson 2006:398)

Procedures

• *How* Were the Data Analyzed?

Describe how the data were analyzed. Explain what you did to handle your data and collapse (combine and change) categories during data analysis.

> We used multiple regression to examine the relationship between stress and well-being. Our focus is primarily on the moderating effects of identity meaning on the relationship among role strain, self-evaluation, and depression. Specifically, for each dependent variable we examined twelve interactions between three types of stressors in the student role and four measures of identity meaning. (Marcussen et al. 2004:295)

6h The Results Section

When you present your findings, you are answering the questions posed by your hypothesis or thesis statement. The results section should build a strong case in support of the hypothesis (or alternatively, show why it was not proved) using quantitative data (numbers and percentages), and setting the stage for the interpretations of the data you provide in the discussion section that follows.

The results section is organized around the research hypothesis/thesis statement presented in your introduction, and discusses the variables in the order in which they appear there. For example, if your hypothesis is "Career aspirations are a function of socioeconomic status (SES), race, and sex," you would relate the results of your analysis in the same order. Thus, you would first describe the effects of SES on career aspirations; next, describe the effects of race on career aspirations; and lastly, describe the effects of sex on career aspirations.

The results section in a quantitative paper generally includes tables or, less commonly, figures summarizing your main findings, particularly the relationship between variables you indicated you were seeking in your research hypothesis/thesis statement. All important findings are summarized in tables. Additional tables should be included to display other important bivariate or multivariate relationships. If you use statistical measures, such as correlations and multiple regression analysis, discuss the results of the relationship between the variables separately for each statistical measure.

The results section is introduced with the heading RESULTS capitalized and centered.

6i   Constructing Tables and Figures

Tables and figures are valuable tools for conveying a large amount of information visually. They must be able to be read on their own, apart from the text. Follow these general points as you construct any kind of table.

1. Tables are numbered consecutively throughout the text (e.g., Table 1, Table 2). The table number and table title are left-justified above the table.

2. Figures are numbered consecutively throughout the text (Figure 1, Figure 2). Figures are treated separately from tables. The figure number and figure title or caption are left-justified below the figure.

3. Each table and figure must have a descriptive title. The title should mention the variables that appear in the table, and the type of data that are being presented (percentages, coefficients, means). If applicable, include information about the data file, data set, and time period covered. Here are some examples.

Table 1.   Degree of Financial Satisfaction by Gross Annual Income

Table 2.   Age at First Marriage by Level of Educational Achievement

Table 3.   Marital Status of Respondents in the Sample

Table 4.   Standardized and Unstandardized Regression Coefficients for Workplace Characteristics in an Equation Estimating Worker Alienation

Table 5.   Mean Levels of Education for Respondents Stratified by Sex and Hours Worked per Week

Figure 1.   Women's and Men's Proportion of the U.S. Labor Force, 1980 and 2000

Notice that in the examples of Tables 1 and 2, the word *by* indicates the cross tabulation of two variables. Table 1 displays the cross tabulation of two variables *degree of financial satisfaction* and *gross annual income*. Table 2 shows the cross tabulation of *age at first marriage* and *level of educational achievement*. When you name a contingency table showing a cross tabulation, the title is constructed as follows:

Dependent variable *by* Independent variable

Do not use computer or SPSS lingo in naming the variables used in your table. It makes far more sense to the reader to see "Attitudes toward Racial Integration by Residential Neighborhood by Race" than to read "RACEINT by NEIGH by RACE."

4. Provide headings for all columns and rows in a table. Do not abbreviate headings. The word *percent* is spelled out in headings. Use subheadings to separate categories of a variable or sections of a table.

5. Print each table and figure on a separate page. All tables and figures are placed at the end of the document. The pages are not numbered, but are ordered by the number of the table or figure (Table 1, Table 2, Figure 1). The tables are placed first, and are ordered sequentially starting with Table 1. The figures, if any, follow, and are ordered sequentially starting with Figure 1.

6. Explain anything that could be difficult to understand in the tables or figures. Use footnotes to explain how variables were measured or how indexes were constructed, if such matters are unclear from the title (for example, if they were not operationalized in the methods section). If the source of the data is not your own (e.g., survey data collected by your entire class, census data from the U.S. Bureau of the Census), you should provide the name of the source of the data on a line at the bottom of the table.

7. Standardize the appearance of all tables and figures. Use the same size fonts for headings and subheadings, the same overall table size, and location for titles and footnotes, if any. Present all frequency distributions using the same format, all cross tabulations using the same format, and so forth.

8. In your text, indicate the location where each table and figure should be placed, by placing a note in the text, as illustrated. The note should be all-capital letters and placed in parentheses at the end of the paragraph that discusses the table.

(TABLE 1 ABOUT HERE)

9. Discuss each table and figure in your text, but do not simply repeat the information contained in them. For example, if you write, "the sample was 55 percent female and 45 percent male," do not also include a table displaying the frequency distribution of sex in your sample. That is simply repetitive.

So what should you mention when you discuss a table? Your text should guide the reader through the table. You might wish to point out **trends** in the table. As you move across categories of the independent variables, what happens to the dependent variable? What are the modal categories (i.e., the ones with the greatest frequencies, or highest numbers) in the table?

Alternatively, you may wish to **highlight** the most interesting findings in the table. Why are some variables in the table statistically significant and others not? Why are most of the cases concentrated in the extreme diagonal corners of the table? What additional information or insight does the table provide about the variables?

For figures, guide the reader through the diagram. Point out trends or other interesting aspects. After all, why did you think the figure important enough to include? Convey that sense of importance to the reader.

10. Be selective in choosing which tables and figures to include in your paper. You don't have to discuss everything that appears in a table, but you need to have enough to say about it to warrant including it in your paper at all. While you should avoid repeating information from a table or figure directly in your text, on the other hand, if you include a table or figure, don't forget to mention it in your text. Including too many tables, or tables that are inadequately discussed in your text, will confuse your reader.

Be picky. A few carefully chosen and well-constructed tables will strengthen your presentation and contribute toward a thoughtful and effective research paper (see Table 6.6).

TABLE 6.6 Number of Marriages and Median Age at First Marriage: Various Years, 1950 to 2003

Year	Number of Marriages[1] [in thousands]	Median Age at First Marriage	
		Male	Female
1950	1,667	22.8	20.3
1955	1,531	22.6	20.2
1960	1,523	22.8	20.3
1965	1,800	22.8	20.6
1970	2,159	23.2	20.8
1975	2,153	23.5	21.1
1980	2,390	24.7	22.0
1985	2,413	25.5	23.3
1986	2,407	25.7	23.1
1987	2,403	25.8	23.6
1988	2,396	25.9	23.6
1989	2,403	26.2	23.8
1990	2,443	26.1	23.9
1991	2,371	26.3	24.1
1992	2,362	26.5	24.4
1993	2,334	26.5	24.5
1994	2,362	26.7	24.5
1995	2,336	26.9	24.5
1996	2,344	27.1	24.8
1997	2,384	26.8	25.0
1998	2,244	26.7	25.0
1999	2,358	26.9	25.1
2000	2,329	26.8	25.1
2001	2,345	26.9	25.1
2002	2,254	26.9	25.3
2003	—	27.1	25.3

— Not available.

[1]Includes remarriages.

NOTE: Some data have been revised from previously published figures.

SOURCE: U.S. Department of Commerce, Census Bureau, *Statistical Abstract of the United States, 2004*; Current Population Reports, Series P-20, *Household and Family Characteristics, Marital Status and Living Arrangements, and America's Families and Living Arrangements,* nos. 468, 478, 491, and 553; Table MS-1: Marital Status of the Population 15 Years Old and Over, by Sex and Race: 1950 to Present; and *Marital Status Historical Time Series Table MS-2: Estimated Median Age at First Marriage, by Sex: 1890 to the Present,* 2004. U.S. Department of Health and Human Services, National Center for Health Statistics, *Monthly Vital Statistics Report,* various years; *National Vital Statistics Reports,* various years; and *Vital Statistics of the United States,* various years.

TABLE 6.7 Writing a Research Article: The Discussion Section

TABLE 6.7 Writing a Research Article: The Discussion Section

Restate the hypothesis or thesis statement.

State whether the hypothesis or thesis statement was confirmed.

Summarize the major ideas developed in the paper. What are your findings an example of?

Discuss the broader significance of your findings.

6j   The Discussion Section

The discussion section answers the question(s) posed at the beginning of your paper, and goes beyond the details of your study to address the broader significance of your research. Usually, the discussion is the longest section of the paper, ranging from three to four paragraphs in a short paper to a full chapter or more in a thesis. This discussion section is introduced with the heading DISCUSSION capitalized and centered. Subheadings aren't used in this section. In writing the discussion section, follow the order shown in Table 6.7.

Restate the Hypothesis or Thesis Statement

Begin the discussion section by formally reasserting the hypothesis or thesis statement that began your paper. Usually this sentence starts, "This paper examined . . ."

State Whether the Hypothesis or Thesis Statement Was Confirmed

Indicate whether your data supported your hypothesis or thesis statement. Frequently, results will be ambiguous, and you should report that, too. Simply state "the sample data did not support the hypothesis" or "the sample data yielded ambiguous results."

Summarize the Major Ideas Developed in the Paper

Relate the statistical significance of your findings to the theoretical issues with which you began your paper. Go back to the sociological problem and question you described in the introduction section. What new knowledge or perspective do your findings offer?

Discuss the Broader Significance of Your Findings

Think beyond your data to consider the insight they provide. What has your study contributed to the broader body of literature on this subject? What are the implications of your research? For example, what does the research on runaway delinquent females say about the continued importance of the family as an agency of socialization? Of what significance are women's choices to be full-time stay-at-home mothers? How do the migration patterns of older individuals affect larger economic and social trends nationally?

This point comprises the heart of the discussion section. Approach it thoughtfully.

6k The Conclusion Section

In a paper reporting original research, the conclusion is formally structured and generally runs one or two paragraphs in length. It sums up the paper and asks "where do we go from here?" Whether the conclusion section stands alone or is combined with the discussion section, it addresses the four points shown in Table 6.8. In a short paper, the conclusion runs one paragraph in length. In a longer paper, plan on writing two paragraphs, and for a thesis or dissertation, the conclusion will comprise a full chapter.

The conclusion section is introduced with the heading CONCLUSION capitalized and centered. In writing the conclusion, discuss the information in the order that follows. Keep in mind for a short paper, each point may be treated in two or three sentences at most.

Writing a Joint Discussion/Conclusion Section

In a short paper, the discussion section is frequently combined with the conclusion to create one longer section. This section should have a minimum of three paragraphs: two for discussion and one for conclusion. Keep in mind that all the points required for each section still must be covered in the combined entity. The main advantage of the joint section is to improve the appearance of your paper by eliminating two very short sections, one after the other. The section is introduced with the heading DISCUSSION/CONCLUSION capitalized and centered.

What Questions Have Been Addressed?

Begin by restating your hypothesis or thesis statement in slightly different words, as an assertion (for example, "this paper has demonstrated X, Y, and Z"). Review the main ideas developed in your paper. What are the implications or the broader import of your thesis statement being proved? Emphasize any interesting approach or interpretation you made in your paper.

TABLE 6.8 Writing a Research Article: The Conclusion Section

What questions have been addressed?

What questions have been left unanswered?

What are the limitations on the generalizability of your findings?

What is the next step?

What Questions Have Been Left Unanswered?

Point out one or two questions that remain unanswered by your analysis. This gesture of humility is expected in scientific research, and even the most prestigious sociologists are not exempt.

What Are the Limitations on the Generalizability of Your Findings?

Scientific work is by its nature tentative. Mention how your research methodology—the sample you drew, the questionnaire design, the interviewing techniques, the limitations imposed by time or budgetary constraints—affected your findings. If the measures or operational definitions used were altered, would the results differ? Indicate any other limitations on your analysis. What are the implications of these limitations for your conclusions?

What Is the Next Step?

You have already addressed the way in which your research furthers sociological knowledge in the discussion section. Now, you need to show how your study serves as a stepping-stone on which future researchers can build.

Indicate what constitutes the next logical step in studying this topic. Where should researchers go from here? Emphasize the new approach or interpretation you have made. Point out any type of research that now appears more important in retrospect. What other variables might profitably be studied? Perhaps it would be fruitful to test your hypothesis in other settings or with different samples to see whether the results of this research can be replicated? End the conclusion with a final sentence stating that future research is needed to further examine this question.

No new information should appear in the conclusion section. Do not give examples or introduce new arguments. Do not use quotations or paraphrased material. Do not include citations, footnotes, endnotes, tables, figures, or appendices. Do not refer back to the introduction section in the conclusion.

61 Handling Headings and Spacing

Each section begins with a heading, all uppercase, except for the introduction which has no heading. Leave a double double-space (four single lines) between the end of a section and the heading of the next section. After a section heading, double-space once and begin the paragraph.

6m Writing an Abstract

Abstracts found at the beginning of papers, articles, and books present an overview, or the essential elements, of a work. On the basis of the abstract alone, a sociologist often decides whether to read the abstracted article or book. You probably will prepare an abstract of a paper reporting your original research if you submit a proposal to present your paper at a conference. If you submit a paper for publication, you will be required to include an abstract. Usually, abstracts are not prepared for undergraduate papers. Check with your instructor to be sure. For more information about writing an abstract, as well as a sample outline for an abstract and an example of an abstract for a quantitative paper, see Chapter 8.

6n Creating a Title for a Quantitative Paper

In academic writing, it is important that your title is brief and mentions (1) the two variables examined in your hypothesis, or the main point of your thesis statement, or most important finding; and (2) the population surveyed (remember, this can include documents or other social artifacts). Make certain the title contains the keywords that would be used to classify your paper were it to be published in a sociology journal.

Keep in mind that the keywords you choose will depend on the literature that provides a context for your paper. For example, imagine you were studying delinquent girls. If most of the recent studies you found in your literature review referred to the girls as female delinquents, then you should, too, and that would be an important keyword to place in your title.

Keywords link your work with a particular literature within sociology, so it is essential to include at least two or three in your title—one for each of the two variables in your hypothesis (or thesis or main finding) and one for your population. You may also want to include a keyword linked to your setting if it is specialized and therefore constitutes a special case (e.g., *college campus, high school, daycare center*). If you want to use a general or catchy title, add a descriptive, substantive subtitle that includes your keywords.

Poor:	Dating in College
Better:	Ethnic Differences in the Dating Expectations of College Students
Poor:	The Earnings Gap between Men and Women
Better:	The Gender Earnings Gap: A Statistical Review and Analysis 1970–2000
Poor:	Who's White Anyway?
Better:	Determinants of Racial Identity among Children of Biracial Parents
Poor:	Role Exit among Nuns in Three Convents in Chicago in 1970
Better:	The Crafting of Identity: Role Exit among Nuns in Three Convents

Notice that in the first three examples, the *poor* examples are so general that it is difficult to guess what the paper actually discusses. The *better* versions add variables to the title so that the paper's focus and scope is clear. The last example illustrates the opposite problem. In this case, the *poor* title is too detailed, and needs to be made more general to arrive at the *better* example.

Finally, it is wise to leave out humor or puns from your title. You may wish to show off your cleverness, but your reader may find the humor tiring or trite, and your work may be viewed as less serious and thoughtful. You can't go wrong with a straightforward, practical, hardworking title.

For help with the format for titles, see Chapter 2.

6o Preparing the Reference List

The reference list includes only those sources actually cited in your paper. If you compile your citations as you write your paper, make sure to compare your reference list to the final version of your paper. Citations in footnotes or endnotes also are placed in the reference list.

References are placed on one or more separate pages, with the heading REFERENCES capitalized and centered at the top of the page. Triple-space between the heading and the first reference entry. The reference list is placed at the end of the document (following the order of the document shown in Table 6.3). The reference pages are numbered. For help in creating reference list entries, see Chapter 4.

6p Adding an Appendix

In a paper reporting original research, items such as survey questionnaires, interview schedules, raw data, statistical calculations, and scales and indices are usually placed in appendices at the end of the document. As a general rule, if you are using any of these items, it is wise to attach them in appendices. Note that each separate item is placed in its own appendix, and each appendix is preceded by a title page with the name of the appendix and a descriptive title. More information about the format for an appendix can be found in Chapter 2.

6q Revising Your Paper

Once you have written a draft of your paper, revise it using the 10 Revision Cycles discussed in Chapter 2.

6r Final Check

Make sure you have . . .

1. an appropriate title.
2. a correct title page.
3. headers with your name in the upper right-hand corner of each page.
4. correctly numbered pages.
5. text citations following ASA documentation style.

6. a reference list following ASA documentation style.
7. spell-checked and personally proofread your document.
8. printed on good-quality, white paper with black ink.
9. stapled your paper in the upper right-hand corner, or placed it in a binder as instructed.
10. tables and figures prepared correctly.
11. an appendix or appendices prepared correctly, if needed.

7

Writing a Qualitative Research Paper

A **qualitative research paper** presents and analyzes data resulting from research you personally conduct, such as your own observational, ethnographic, or participant observation study. In a qualitative research paper, like the quantitative paper, the main focus is on the data you personally have collected. The published scholarly research of others appearing in the paper is used only to establish the context for your own observations. In reporting your original research, a qualitative paper differs in structure and format from a term paper, which is based on secondary sources.

Qualitative research presents a rich, vivid description of social behavior in everyday life. It pays careful attention to the details of individual and group behavior, giving the reader empathy for the study's subjects and a chance to see the world from their point of view. Usually, qualitative papers do not focus on the frequency of behaviors and do not express data in numbers and percentages. As a result, qualitative methods are often used to examine research questions that involve

1. identifying the variation in response to some phenomenon.
2. identifying the stages in a process.
3. identifying the social organization of a particular group or setting.

 A familiarity with qualitative research methods in sociology is necessary when you write this type of paper.

7a Qualitative versus Quantitative Research

In qualitative research, data are presented in nonnumerical form, such as words, descriptions, narratives, images, or symbols. By contrast, in quantitative research, data are presented in numerical form, with raw numbers and percentages. Of the four major research designs preferred by sociologists—surveys, observational studies, experiments, and participant observation—all can be manipulated to yield qualitative data. However, researchers with a qualitative bent tend to choose observational studies, ethnography, and participant observation as their preferred research designs, and researchers with a predilection for surveys and experiments largely use quantitative methods. Other qualitative methods used less commonly by sociologists include discourse and conversational analysis, ethnomethodology, narrative analysis, and comparative historical analysis. These latter methods should not be undertaken by undergraduates without adequate preparation and supervision.

Qualitative research is distinctive in that it usually does not test hypotheses, use survey instruments, or employ other measurement tools. Rather, it examines *what* happens, *how* it happens, and *what it means* for the individuals involved. Qualitative research typically requires the recording and analyzing of lengthy, detailed field notes, which can be very time-consuming. Once data collection is completed, the researcher reviews the field notes to identify patterns in the data and propose categories and labels to make sense of findings.

7b Qualitative Methods: Observation, Ethnography, and Participant Observation

What is the difference between observation, ethnography, and participant observation? In an observational study, the researcher observes and records aspects of the subjects' behavior in field notes without talking to them or interacting with them. Ideally, the researcher should be "invisible" to the subjects in an observational study. This may be accomplished either by literally staying out of sight (for example, by sitting and recording data from behind a big, potted fern) or by not being identifiable as a researcher (for example, by dressing up and "passing" as a high school student). The goal of observational research is to see and record subjects' actual behavior in everyday life uninfluenced by the presence of the researcher. Of course, the ethics of social research permit only the public behavior of subjects to be studied this way, as it is presumed they know their acts in public places may be seen by others. No peeping Toms are allowed.

Ethnography, also known as field research, differs from observational studies in that the researcher is visible to the subjects, interacts with them, and talks to them. The researcher may even conduct short informal interviews with subjects (for example, by asking where subjects eat lunch and with whom, in order to identify friendship networks and peer cliques). The ethnographer studies the everyday life of their subjects, often focusing on communities or other groups. Since the researcher is recognized by subjects as a nongroup member, interesting problems sometimes can arise as various factions of subjects attempt to manipulate or co-opt the researcher. The longer the study continues, the more the researcher must maintain vigilance to minimize **reactivity** (the effect the presence of the researcher has on the subjects). When it occurs, as it inevitably will, it is the researcher's duty to document what happens in field notes. Furthermore, the researcher will develop **biases** toward subjects, either positive or negative, and these reactions, too, and their implications must be discussed in field notes. Lastly, photographs and audio and video recordings may be placed in the ethnographic record to complement the researcher's direct observations.

In participant observation, the researcher joins the group being studied and records field notes describing experiences, observations, conversations, impressions, and interpretations. Typically, students do not undertake participant observation research because it usually requires a lengthy time commitment. Participant observation is fraught with difficulties, including the need to remain as unbiased as possible, to document every experience in great detail, to defend your work against the critiques of other sociologists who view participant observation as "unscientific," not to mention the occasional death threat by members of the group who discover your true identity (imagine doing participant observation in a gang or secret religious cult, for instance). The ethics of social research permits the researcher to not reveal his or her true identity, but on the other, the researcher may not lie. Needless to say, one enters the field to conduct participant observation research only with great preparation and trepidation.

7c "Writing Up" Your Research Study

As you undoubtedly know by now, much of the time involved in writing a paper reporting original research is expended long before you sit down to write. After all, first you need to plan and conduct your study, and qualitative research takes time. Only when you have finished your research can you write up your results as a paper.

This chapter focuses on the writing of a qualitative paper. Research-related decisions and concerns are discussed only as they directly affect your paper, and therefore a course in qualitative methods will help you greatly. Research methods is an important subfield within sociology, and at the college level, it is treated in in-depth courses. If you are interested in this area, you should plan to take at least one course in qualitative research methods.

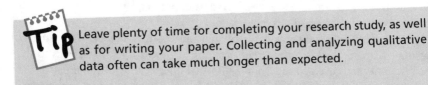

Leave plenty of time for completing your research study, as well as for writing your paper. Collecting and analyzing qualitative data often can take much longer than expected.

7d Structuring the Paper

A paper reporting original research is structured as a research article, not as an essay. A research article has five sections, although in short papers (those with fewer than 10 pages), the discussion and conclusion frequently are combined into a single section titled discussion/conclusion. Unlike quantitative papers, generally qualitative papers have a more flexible structure adapted to their subject matter. As a student, however, you would be wise to review an outline of your paper with your instructor before proceeding to the writing stage (see Table 7.1).

TABLE 7.1 Outline of a Research Article (Adapted for a Qualitative Paper)

Introduction (this section has no heading)

Methods

Results (this section is not headed RESULTS, but is divided by subheadings)

    Subheading A

    Subheading B

    Subheading C

Discussion

Conclusion

How much information about your research study should be placed in your paper? The qualitative paper's research article structure requires details about how you designed and executed your research study, and how you analyzed your data and reached conclusions. This material is placed in your paper in predetermined sections, and within each section, in a particular order.

For help in organizing information about your research study as you begin to outline and draft your paper, consult Table 7.2. Researchers in all branches of science follow a version of these eight steps, also known as the Scientific Method, when they conduct scientific research (for the original version, see Table 6.2). Qualitative research, which usually employs inductive reasoning, generally does not test a hypothesis or use sampling techniques for choosing subjects. A version of the Overview of the Research Process adapted for the qualitative paper is displayed in Table 7.2.

You must follow these steps as you carry out your study, and then discuss them as you write up your paper. For a research study to be considered "scientific" by the community of scholars in the discipline, the researcher must have followed the Scientific Method. If not, the study is considered flawed and its conclusions

TABLE 7.2 Overview of the Research Process (Adapted for a Qualitative Paper)

1. Choose a topic. Define it as a sociological problem.
2. Review the literature.
3. Decide what you will investigate.
4. Choose a research design (observational study, ethnography, or participant observation).
5. Choose subjects to be studied (a community? a group?).
6. Collect data.
7. Analyze data.
8. Draw conclusions.

untrustworthy. Qualitative research continues to be viewed as "less scientific" than quantitative research by some sociologists, and therefore the need and expectations for careful adherence to scientific standards in writing the qualitative paper is very high. Also, because it is so tempting to lapse into broad generalities and casual description when writing up qualitative research, you must remain extra vigilant to maintain your scientific approach and attention to precise detail.

If qualitative research's downside is its use of inductive reasoning, and not deductive reasoning based on hypothesis testing, its strength is its thickly detailed and life-like description of social scenes and everyday life. The best qualitative research makes the reader feel he or she is fully present at the scene with the researcher. The researcher conducting qualitative research should try to approximate the mindset of a Martian, newly dropped to Earth and observing everything afresh, in great detail and without prior assumptions about the meanings of particular actions.

7e Developing the Paper

In conducting your qualitative research study, you will have chosen a topic and defined it as a sociological question; reviewed the literature; decided on a problem, issue, or group to study; and chosen a research design. Once you arrive at the writing phase, you will need to make explicit the connection between the topic, the sociological question, the problem, and the research design to establish the rationale for your study. This information is placed in the introduction, and is returned to later in the discussion section of your paper.

To understand how these four elements are linked, consider the following example. Imagine you need to choose a topic for a paper, so you begin to brainstorm for ideas. Perhaps you start to wonder why some members of your class act the way they do, why some women in your neighborhood enjoy being stay-at-home mothers more than others, and why some relatives are delighted with their lives in a retirement community while others are sorry they have left their old homes. Now, these ideas may be interesting and they certainly relate to social phenomena; however, none are in the form of a sociological question as yet. Your paper will be viewed as "sociological" only if you frame your research question in sociological terminology, and if you use the sociological literature for your review of the literature.

By the way, if you have read Chapter 6 these examples should look familiar. To clarify the difference between qualitative and quantitative research, the same subjects will be used to demonstrate how an idea that worked well for a quantitative study can be shaped into an appropriate topic for a qualitative study.

When you frame a sociological question, you attempt to explain the great variation in social life in terms of some broad, unifying themes. Your observation of students' behaviors become data for a study of college student roles, participant observation with stay-at-home mothers inform a study of the process of leaving the workforce to become stay-at-home mothers, and an ethnography of a retirement home sheds light on the social organization of the facility.

The framing of specific empirical observations (*e.g., Susan Johnson meets her friends every morning at the playground and they talk while their children play*) in terms of some larger question (*how do stay-at-home mothers spend their time?*) leads to the development of a problem for study (*how do employed mothers who leave the workforce and become stay-at-home mothers form new social networks and identities that help them adapt to their new situation?*).

Most qualitative research does not test a hypothesis, although there are some exceptions. Usually, qualitative research is used to study subjects for which there is little theory or previous research. Qualitative findings identify relevant variables and note patterns, laying the groundwork for quantitative researchers to begin studying the subject by forming hypotheses and testing them with precise measurement tools.

7f Handling Your Data

Qualitative data typically consist of field notes or quotations from interviews with subjects. Your research design may specify you use one or both methods of data collection. If you collected field notes for a class paper, usually you will be required to submit your field notes with your paper. For interview data, usually placing a number of direct quotes in your paper is sufficient. Check with your instructor about the format and placement of field notes and interview quotations.

7g Field Notes

Field notes are literally your notes, taken in the "field" (or everyday life, as opposed to the "lab"), which are recorded in your field journal (your notebook for keeping field notes). Field notes are used in observational studies, ethnography, and participant observation to record what you see and hear, as well as your interpretation of events.

Field notes should be dictated or transcribed as soon as possible after your observation. If possible, take your field journal with you to jot down notes as they occur. In some situations, it may be possible to set up a file called "field journal" on a laptop computer, assuming the nature of your study allowed you to take notes on your computer unnoticed. Usually, however, that will not be possible, and you will need to rely on an old-fashioned notebook and pen. In that case, as soon as you are able, type them up on your computer while they are fresh in your mind, adding every detail you can remember. It is not possible to know what will prove to be important at this stage, so record everything you see and hear.

If your instructor does not provide guidelines, you may find the outline for field notes in Table 7.3 works well in most settings. This outline is for a single field note documenting a single observation or act. Feel free to adapt the format shown here to fit your individualized needs. Keep in mind that you may collect 50 to 100 field notes or many more before your data collection is finished. Often, your field notes will be placed in an appendix to your paper (see Figure 7.1a and b on p. 157–158). Individual notes are placed in the body of your paper as you would a quote and then are discussed in your text.

TABLE 7.3 Outline for a Field Note

For each observed act, record the following information.

Case 1

1. Date and time of the observation
2. Location where the observation occurred
3. Visible characteristics of the individual(s) involved in the act (i.e., the researcher's evaluation of subject's sex, age, race/ethnicity, other?)
4. What was said and done
5. Your interpretation—how you understood the observed behavior as it related to the problem you are investigating

7h Writing a Short Paper Based on Field Notes from Observation or Participant Observation

You may be assigned a short paper where you simply need to submit your field notes from an observational study or a participant observation study. Often, this entails your recording field notes during a single long event, such as a police "ride along" or a visit to a prison, where observations are difficult to neatly subdivide as shown in the outline in Table 7.3. For such single, lengthy observations, the outline shown in Table 7.4 may be used for the paper.

7i Writing a Full-Length Qualitative Paper

A qualitative paper is structured as a research article, not an essay, and in this respect is similar to the quantitative papers discussed in Chapter 6, but with some important differences.

7j The Introduction Section

The introduction creates a context for the rest of your paper by placing your research within a larger sociological framework. The introduction signals how you intend your work to be understood—in this case, as a qualitative study. Your review of the literature should cite only the results of qualitative studies on your topic. If there are few such studies, you may discuss trends in the quantitative research on the subject, but distinguish those works from the qualitative work on the same subject. Make sure to use qualitative terminology when discussing the literature, as this is an integral aspect of your paper's content. Confirm that your definitions, concepts, sources, and literature all emerge from the same methodological approach.

TABLE 7.4 Outline for a Short Observation or Participant Observation Paper Based on Field Notes

1. **The Setting**
   A description of the general physical and social setting being observed: Where specifically were you observing?

2. **The People**
   A description of the people in the setting: How many people were there? How were they dressed? What were their sex, age, race/ethnicity, socioeconomic status, other?

3. **Their Behavior**
   A description of what happened: How did people behave? How did you feel as you began the experience and during your interaction with the other people in the setting? How did people relate to one another? Who talked to or interacted with whom, and in what fashion? What was the approximate duration and frequency of the interactions? How did you know how to behave? Was your behavior appropriate? How did you figure out the norms/values of the situation?

4. **Analytical Ideas and Inferences**
   Looking back on the experience, how did you feel about what you were experiencing? How did you find yourself acting? What other factors (variables) may have affected your behavior?

5. **Personal Impressions and Biases**
   Note any negative or positive feelings that may alert you to biases in your observations: Did you find yourself liking or disliking the people with whom you interacted?

The introduction also includes a thesis statement that will structure the remainder of your paper. The thesis, in stating what you will examine and how, indicates the direction the paper will take. In a qualitative paper, you do not propose a hypothesis, but rather state the problem, group, or setting you will study, using terms such as *what, how,* and *what does it mean for the subjects* (see Table 7.5).

As you write the introduction, address each of these parts in order. No subheadings introduce the parts, and the introduction section itself has no heading.

TABLE 7.5 Writing a Research Article: The Introduction Section (Adapted for a Qualitative Paper)

Introduce the topic in a general statement (and define the key terms if necessary).

Review the literature.

State the problem.

Frame a sociological question.

State what you will examine and how.

Depending on the length of the paper, this section may run from several paragraphs to several pages. The overall length and complexity of the section determines the amount of space devoted to each step. The opening sentence, definition, and review of the literature are usually combined in one or more paragraphs, and the remaining parts form the rest of the section.

Introduce the Topic

Start with a general opening statement that addresses the history or current state of research on your topic. This one-sentence generalization may focus on the type of work that has been done or on the findings from this body of work. Here are some examples.

> Gang behavior is a subject that has attracted considerable sociological interest over the past century.

> Runaways continue to be an ever-present phenomenon both in the United States and abroad.

> High school peer groups have been linked to a variety of educational accomplishments and social ills.

After the opening sentence, which introduces your key concept (e.g., *peer group*), define that term, if necessary. Generally, only one or two terms are central and unusual enough to require definition at this point, and it is rare to find a paper with multiple definitions placed at the beginning of the introduction section. As mentioned earlier, common sociological terms (e.g., *schooling, socialization, gender roles*) do not require definition. Only more specialized terms that are not widely recognized or agreed on by sociologists need to be defined in the introduction.

How do you determine if there is recognition or agreement about a concept? Look at the recent literature (the published scholarly articles on your topic). Did those articles define the term? If they did, you should, too. If you define a term, be sure to use a sociological definition and not one drawn from a general dictionary. The best place to find a sociological definition is in a recent scholarly article on the subject. Paraphrase the definition and cite your source. This is better than using a definition drawn from a sociological dictionary, as the citation to a dictionary will make your work appear juvenile. In general, the main use of a sociological dictionary is for "your eyes only background," but not for use in your paper.

Review the Literature: Two Approaches

The introduction often is organized in point–counterpoint fashion. If you take this approach, you would begin with a general statement and definition if necessary, as discussed previously. Then you would point out the failings of this opening general statement, using it as a foil against which to present the so-called thesis of the paper (what this paper aims to accomplish). In doing so, you may (1) call attention to the omission of an important variable from previous research (*but few have been directly concerned with the role of* X *in this process*); or you may (2) challenge the assumptions of previous research (*but research to date has underestimated Brown's depth of understanding of* X); or you may (3) question the methods employed in previous research (*but comparative analysis based on qualitative results are necessarily misleading*). The examples you provide to substantiate your claims come from, and comprise, your literature review.

The one danger in using this approach in the introduction is that you must make sure you are not starting with an invalid criticism of previous research simply to create an argument and justify your thesis. If you write, *Introductory sociology textbooks describe high school peer groups as if they were a closely knit group controlled by a few powerful individuals. Such a picture misrepresents the current reality,* then you must be able to support your claim that this generalization (1) is true, and (2) holds for *all* introductory textbooks. Consequently, authors often qualify their initial claims to deflect potential criticisms (e.g., Many *introductory texts . . .* or Older *introductory texts . . .*). The reader must agree with your generalization. Otherwise, your introduction will create a hostile audience from the outset.

An alternative approach to starting the introduction is to place your specific topic within a context of similar social phenomena, thereby describing how you will discuss this topic. Here, your "argument" addresses which concepts and literature, or established body of work, are most relevant and useful for understanding your topic. To develop your points, you will bring examples from the literature (or from more than one "literature"), citing your sources. This is your literature review.

Imagine you were interested in studying high school students' peer groups. You search *Sociological Abstracts* using the keywords *high school, friends*, and *clique*, but find few articles, books, or papers. However, once you link this term to the sociological concept of *peer culture*, you suddenly tap into a broader category of literature, although it is small compared to the literature on other topics. Additionally, if the sociological literature has little on your topic, and you have checked for synonyms of your keywords by seeking help from reference materials, you could turn to the literature of other social sciences (e.g., psychology, anthropology). If that yields little, you could search the literature of other natural sciences (e.g., zoology, biology) for examples of groupings among animals. This would enable you to make the argument that (perhaps) human grouping behavior shares common elements with animal behaviors. (Note: This is an effective way of starting your paper if you are writing on a topic about which little work has been done, or if your paper is mainly descriptive.)

In choosing which research studies to include in your review of the literature, be sure to include the major studies most relevant to your topic. How do you determine which studies are "major"? How do you gauge the relative significance of published research? One way is to see whether an article is often cited in the work of others. How many entries are listed below it in the *Social Sciences Citation Index* (available in your campus library's reference department)? How many of the articles you have collected refer to it? Another way of assessing a study's significance is to look at where it was published. Did it appear in one of the leading journals of its discipline or subfield? Keep in mind that, aside from the scholarly significance of the research, your discussion of previous research is guided by its relevance to your specific thesis. Include only those studies that relate to your study.

How much should you write about each article or book mentioned in your review of the literature? Ask your instructor, as expectations differ. In published research articles, like those appearing in major sociology journals, such as the *American Sociological Review,* you will notice that very little information is given about each cited work. Rather, one key point is made about each—and often, they are grouped so that a single point is made about several works.

Note how the review of the literature is presented in this article by Adler and Adler (1984):

> Empirical studies and conceptual explorations of the socialization process can be grouped into two camps: the normative school and the interpretive school. The former perspective emphasizes the way children internalize society's norms and values and learn roles for future use (Bandura 1971; Brim 1960; Inkeles 1966; Merton 1957[b]; Parsons and Bales 1955; Watson 1970). In contrast, interpretive sociologists focus on the active interpersonal processes by which children develop interactional competence (Cicourel 1970; Garfinkel 1967; Mead 1934; Rose 1962; Shibutani 1962; Speier 1970). These forms of socialization are usually treated as mutually exclusive; but we will show how carpool interaction encompasses biomodal forms of socialization. (P. 200)

For more information on citation format, see Chapter 4.

The goal in reviewing the literature relevant to your topic or thesis statement is to demonstrate that while research has been done on your general topic, and those researchers have found X, Y, and Z to be true, no studies have researched Q, which—amazingly enough!—is exactly what your study will examine. With this in mind, you can see that it isn't important to give a full report on each work cited as part of your literature review. Rather, you must show how the various reviewed works fit together to form a "map" of the research on your topic, because in the following step, you will point out where there is a gap (in fact, the one you intend to fill!).

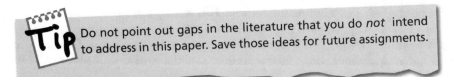

Tip Do not point out gaps in the literature that you do *not* intend to address in this paper. Save those ideas for future assignments.

The literature is reviewed only in the introduction. You generally do not return to the literature in the discussion or conclusion to compare it with your own research findings unless your paper is a test of another researcher's work. The sole purpose of the literature review is to provide background for your sociological question and the thesis statement you developed in response. After the introduction, the remainder of the paper focuses solely on your research. You may cite others researchers' works later in the paper in footnotes or endnotes, and occasionally in the text itself in support of an important point, but do not refer back to the overall literature later in your paper.

State the Problem

In the previous step, you constructed a literature review with the "hidden agenda" of pointing out a gap or problem (the one you intend to fill). Only now, however, do you openly indicate where there is a vacuum and elaborate on the existing flaw.

Here, you state what previous research neglected to mention—what important concepts, variables, problems, groups, or settings they failed to study. Depending on the length of your paper, you may treat this in one or two sentences in a short paper, in several sentences in a longer paper, or a paragraph or two in a master's thesis or doctoral dissertation.

Adler and Adler (1984) state the problem straight out:

> "Numerous childhood activities and relationships have been studied within the context of socialization, but one experience remains uninvestigated by social researchers: *the carpool.*" (p. 200)

Frame a Sociological Question

In response to the gap or inconsistency you identified, you now need to frame a sociological question that will move your reader one step closer to your thesis statement. To do so, think about the gap and develop a question about it. Then, reword your question to employ sociological concepts and fit within some theoretical framework.

Here is Adler and Adler's (1984) recasting of the topic into a sociological question—and note that it need not literally be phrased as a question. After discussing the literature review and stating that they intend to show how carpooling encompasses both forms of socialization, they go on to ask an unstated question: How can carpooling be viewed as a form of socialization? They then discuss that unstated question. Here is part of that paragraph:

> Carpooling falls within a critical overlap of three predominate socializing agents: the peer group, the family, and the school. First, children who carpool together form a peer primary group because of their closeness in age and the regularity of their contact. The encapsulated (Zurcher 1979) nature of the automobile setting intensifies their relationships and reciprocal influence on each other. Thus, although carpool peer associations are involuntary, members come to know each other well and serve as both a social base and a reference group for each other. (Adler and Adler 1984:200–201)

State a General Thesis Statement

The introduction of a qualitative paper concludes with a broad thesis statement that helps structure the remainder of your paper. The thesis statement indicates what you intend to study. In this sense, it is the culmination of the argument you built up in the introduction that can be summarized as follows:

- Make a generalization
- Review the literature

- Identify a gap (define a problem)
- Restate the problem in sociological terms (frame a question)
- Propose a game plan for discovering a tentative answer to the question (the thesis statement)

Generally, quantitative papers test a highly-defined thesis statement or one or more hypotheses. These are stated at the end of the introduction section. Qualitative studies, however, often do not begin with a hypothesis. Indeed, one key reason researchers undertake qualitative research is because the information needed to develop a hypothesis is not yet available. Frequently, after several qualitative studies have been done, enough data are gathered to generate workable hypotheses, which then can be tested quantitatively with more controlled sampling and measurement techniques.

Here is the thesis from "The Carpool":

In this study, we investigate the types of interaction that take place within the carpool setting both between children and adults and among peer group members. We discuss the behavioral patterns and roles that commonly emerge in this setting and analyze their impact on the developing child. We identify and describe three carpool-generated relationships: intimate, combatant, and obligatory. We conclude by extracting the features of carpool interaction that correspond to both the normative and interpretive models of socialization and show how the two can coexist rather than compete. (Adler and Adler 1984:201)

7k The Methods Section

The methods section describes how you collected and analyzed the data for your research paper. In a paper reporting qualitative research, this section usually is quite short and is not as rigidly structured as in a quantitative paper (see Table 7.6).

The methods section is introduced with the heading METHODS capitalized and centered. The information in the section is worded in the past tense since your research is completed at the time of writing.

TABLE 7.6 Writing a Research Article: The Methods Section (Adapted for a Qualitative Paper)

Where were the data collected?

When were the data collected?

What were the relevant social characteristics of the researcher?

How were the data collected?

How were the data analyzed?

Where Were the Data Collected?

Identify the location of data collection to show that your research is comparable to other studies done in similar settings. The name of the location should not be disclosed to protect its anonymity (otherwise researchers may be barred entry in the future). If you can't give its name, what information can you give about the location? Describe the location in terms commonly used in the sociological literature. You may get some ideas from the articles in your literature review. For course papers and assignments, consult your instructor as more details may be required.

> . . . at a major suburban public university
>
> . . . at a small rural community
>
> . . . at a large outdoor shopping area in a working-class community

When Were the Data Collected?

State the date(s) of data collection and, if relevant, the time(s) of day.

> The research team collected data September 1–7, 2008.

What Were the Relevant Social Characteristics of the Researcher?

You, like every researcher, have your own set of social characteristics which may influence your perceptions, as well as other people's reactions toward you. Your gender, race/ethnicity, disabilities, social class, marital status, parenting status, religion, and other characteristics may make you particularly aware or sensitive to the plight of others, influencing the quality of your observations and insights. Moreover, these characteristics may wrap you in a "cloak of invisibility" if your subjects possess the same traits themselves, or expose you as an outsider if you differ.

The social characteristics of the researcher, therefore, may have a profound influence on a study's outcome. When writing up your research, you need to indicate how you attempted to reduce **reactivity,** the reaction of subjects being studied (e.g., by sitting at a dark corner table or by dressing to blend in with the study subjects).

How Were the Data Collected?

Describe the process by which you collected your data. How did you identify the location, get set up, find your subjects, and begin taking field notes? Were you seen, challenged, accepted? Did you encounter any unusual problems? (Do not recite a litany of normal occurrences that social researchers encounter, such as electrical storms, police inquiries, strangers asking you for a date, and the like.)

How Were the Data Analyzed?

First, explain how you recorded data. Did you observe subjects and record your observations in field notes? Did you conduct interviews, tape-recording and transcribing them in computer files? Did you videotape interviews? If you conducted interviews, indicate how many and with which subjects. Note any details that may have influenced the data collection process.

Then, describe how you analyzed your data. How did you group your data to find patterns? How did you determine how to categorize behavior and observations? If you collapsed categories, explain what categories you originally set up and why you decided to collapse them. What were the results?

Sometimes you may arrive at a point where you can't figure out just what you have found. If this is a problem, you need help in analyzing your data. A good rule of thumb is "show me the difference." Look for differences among people doing the same thing. Who does it differently, better, or with different attitudes? What meaningful categories can you separate these people into—and keep in mind that you want to set up only a small number of categories (two or three is best). Too many becomes confusing. In the carpool article discussed previously, for example, the authors developed three categories for adult behavior toward the children in their carpools: moderators, interventionists, and laissez-fairists. Note that the names given to the categories you create are very important and leave a lasting impression. Develop labels that are broadly descriptive of behaviors and fit the context of the topic you are studying. Many qualitative studies became famous because of the category names they pioneered.

71 The Results Section

In a qualitative paper, the results section usually is not preceded with a heading indicating the section name, as in a quantitative paper. Rather, immediately following the methods section (or in some cases where methods are interwoven in the introduction, following the introduction section) subheadings introduce a discussion of each of the study's findings. In each subsection, the way in which the finding was discovered is explained and discussed fully, and illustrating examples are provided from excerpted field notes or interview quotes. Create as many subsections as needed. Remember, the strength of a qualitative paper is in the rich detail of its descriptions, so take no shortcuts! In a qualitative paper, the results section is the longest section of the paper (see Table 7.7).

TABLE 7.7 Writing a Research Article: The Results Section (Adapted for a Qualitative Paper)

Subheading A

Subheading B

Subheading C

Subheading D

TABLE 7.8 Writing a Research Article: The Discussion Section (Adapted for a Qualitative Paper)

Restate the thesis statement.

Summarize the major ideas developed in the paper. What are your findings an example of?

Discuss the broader significance of your findings.

7m The Discussion Section

The discussion section answers the question posed at the beginning of your paper, and it should go beyond the details of your study to address the broader significance of your research. In a qualitative paper, the discussion section will be several paragraphs long. It is introduced with the heading DISCUSSION, capitalized and centered. Subheadings aren't used in this section. In writing the discussion section, follow the order shown in Table 7.8.

Restate the Thesis Statement

Begin the discussion section by formally reasserting the thesis statement that began your paper. Usually this sentence starts, "This paper examined . . ."

Summarize the Major Ideas Developed in the Paper

Relate your findings to the issues with which you began your paper. Go back to the sociological problem and question you described in the introduction section. What new knowledge or perspective do your findings offer?

Discuss the Broader Significance of Your Findings

Think beyond your data to consider the insight they provide. What has your study contributed to the broader body of literature on this subject? What are the implications of your research? For example, what does the research on carpooling say about the continued importance of the family as an agency of socialization? Of what significance are women's choices to be full-time stay-at-home mothers in influencing their children's socialization? Are parental choices about children's friends concretized through carpooling available only to middle-class, suburban families, or are they exercised in different ways by urban and working-class families?

7n The Conclusion Section

In a paper reporting original research, the conclusion is formally structured and generally runs one or two paragraphs in length. It sums up the paper and asks "where do we go from here?" Whether the conclusion section stands alone or is combined with the discussion section, it addresses the four points shown in Table 7.9. In a combined

TABLE 7.9 Writing a Research Article: The Conclusion Section (Adapted for the Qualitative Paper)

What questions have been addressed?

What questions have been left unanswered?

What are the limitations on the generalizability of your findings?

What is the next step?

discussion/conclusion, keep the paragraphs for the discussion and conclusion sections separate. In a short paper, the conclusion usually runs one paragraph in length. In a longer paper, plan on writing two paragraphs, and for a thesis or dissertation, the conclusion will comprise a full chapter.

The conclusion section is introduced with the heading CONCLUSION capitalized and centered. In writing the conclusion, discuss the information in the order that follows. Keep in mind that for a short paper, each point may be treated in two or three sentences at most.

Writing a Joint Discussion/Conclusion Section

In a short paper, the discussion section is frequently combined with the conclusion to create one longer section. This section should have a minimum of three paragraphs: two for discussion and one for conclusion. Keep in mind that all the points required for each section still must be covered in the combined entity. The main advantage of the joint section is to improve the appearance of your paper by eliminating two very short sections, one after the other. The section is introduced with the heading DISCUSSION/CONCLUSION capitalized and centered.

What Questions Have Been Addressed?

Begin by restating your thesis statement in slightly different words, as an assertion ("This paper has demonstrated X"). Review the main ideas developed in your paper. What are the implications or the broader import of your thesis statement being examined? Emphasize any interesting approach or interpretation you made in your paper.

What Questions Have Been Left Unanswered?

Point out one or two questions that remain unanswered by your analysis. This gesture of humility is expected in scientific research, and even the most prestigious sociologists are not exempt.

What Are the Limitations on the Generalizability of Your Findings?

Scientific work is by its nature tentative. Mention how your research methodology—the group you studied, the observational or interview techniques used, the limitations imposed by time or budgetary constraints—affected your findings. Was the group you studied different than other similar groups? If you had studied a different group, do you think your results would have differed? Indicate any other limitations on your analysis. What are the implications of these limitations for your conclusions?

What Is the Next Step?

You have already addressed the way in which your research furthers sociological knowledge in the discussion section. Now, you need to show how your study serves as a stepping-stone on which future researchers can build.

Indicate what constitutes the next logical step in studying this topic. Where should researchers go from here? Emphasize the new approach or interpretation you have made. Point out any type of research that now appears more important in retrospect. What other variables might profitably be studied? Perhaps it would be fruitful to study this same question in other settings or with different samples to see whether the results of this research can be replicated. End the conclusion section with a final sentence stating that future research is needed to further examine this question.

Do not put new information in the conclusion section. Do not give examples or introduce new arguments. Do not use quotations or paraphrased material. Do not include citations, footnotes, endnotes, tables, figures, or appendices. Do not refer to the introduction section in the conclusion.

7o   Handling Headings and Spacing

Each section begins with a heading, all uppercase, except for the introduction which has no heading. Leave a double double-space (four single lines) between the end of a section and the heading of the next section. After a section heading, double-space once and begin the paragraph.

7p   Writing an Abstract

Abstracts provide an overview or the essential elements of a work. An abstract often accompanies a proposal to present a paper reporting your original research at a conference. If you submit a paper for publication, you will be required to include an abstract. Abstracts usually are not prepared for college papers. For more information, see Chapter 8, which includes an outline for an abstract and an example of a qualitative paper's abstract.

7q   Creating a Title for a Qualitative Paper

The title of your paper should include (1) the main point of your thesis statement, or your key finding; and (2) the population surveyed. Make certain the title contains the keywords that would be used to classify your paper were it to be published in a sociology journal. The keywords chosen depend on the literature that provides a context for your paper. Your methodology should be one such keyword (for example, *observational study, ethnography, participant observation*). You may also want to include a keyword linked to your setting if it is specialized and therefore constitutes a special case (e.g., *college campus, high school, daycare center*). If you must use a general or catchy title, add a descriptive, substantive subtitle.

Poor:	Dating in College
Better:	Courtship Rituals in a Four-Year College
Poor:	Caution: Children at Play
Better:	Cheating and Fighting at Three Playgrounds: An Observational Study
Poor:	Eye Can't See You
Better:	Participant Observation in a Visually Impaired Group

As you can see, the *poor* examples are so general that it is difficult to guess what the paper actually discusses. The *better* versions add variables to the title so that the paper's focus and scope is clear. The last pair of titles illustrates the value of leaving humor and puns out of your title. You never know what your reader will find boring, trite, or offensive. A humorous title often makes your work seem trivial. Stick with a straightforward title for the best results.

For information about the format for titles, see Chapter 2.

7r   Preparing the Reference List

The reference list includes only those sources actually cited in your paper. If you compile your citations as you write your paper, make sure to compare your reference list to the final version of your paper. Citations in footnotes or endnotes also are placed in the reference list.

References are placed on one or more separate pages, with the heading REFERENCES capitalized and centered at the top of the page. Triple-space between the heading and the first reference entry. The reference list is placed at the end of the document (following the order of the document shown in Table 6.3). The reference pages are numbered. For help in creating reference list entries, see Chapter 4.

7s   Adding an Appendix

In a paper reporting original research, items such as field notes, coding sheets, and interview schedules and transcripts are usually placed in appendices at the end of the document. As a general rule, if you are using any of these items, attach them in appendices. Note that each separate item is placed in its own appendix, and each appendix is preceded by a title page with the name of the appendix and a descriptive title. More information about the format for an appendix can be found in Chapter 2. For an example of an appendix, see Figures 7.1a and b.

FIGURE 7.1a Title Page for Appendix

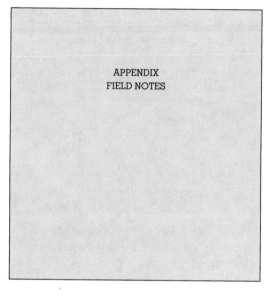

APPENDIX
FIELD NOTES

FIGURE 7.1b An Example of Field Notes

FIELD NOTES

Case 1:

Date/Time:

Monday, March 20, 2008, at 11:20 a.m.

Location:

Fox Hall, hallway near Room 105

Visible Characteristics:

Two apparently white students in
their early 20s

What Was Said or Done?

An apparently male student and
female student had been sitting
next to each other in class, stood up
as class ended, picked up their
belongings, and began to exit

Field Notes, continued

the room. The male student

appeared to wait near his chair for

the female who was slightly slower

in assembling her things. She

walked over to him, and then he put

his arm around her, and they

walked to the door to exit.

Interpretation:

The fact that the woman walked to

him I interpreted as a sign of her

deference to him because her seat

was actually closer to the door than

his was. I interpreted his putting his

arm around her as a signaling his

dominance to her and to others.

Case 2 . . .

Case 3 . . .

7t Revising your Paper

Once you have written a draft of your paper, revise it using the 10 Revision Cycles discussed in Chapter 2.

7u Final Check

Make sure you have . . .
1. an appropriate title.
2. a correct title page.
3. headers with your name in the upper right-hand corner of each page.
4. correctly numbered pages.
5. text citations following ASA documentation style.
6. a reference list following ASA documentation style.
7. spell-checked and personally proofread your document.
8. printed on good-quality, white paper with black ink.
9. stapled your paper in the upper right-hand corner, or placed it in a binder as instructed.

CHAPTER

8 Writing an Abstract

An **abstract**, found at the beginning of a paper or article, presents a brief overview so the reader can decide whether to read the entire abstracted work. When social scientists—and yes, even you!—conduct research, dozens of abstracts may have to be read to find one article with the necessary information. Abstracts help researchers save time by providing a condensed summary of the article's key points, making locating relevant articles easier and faster.

When will you need to write an abstract? Authors are expected to prepare abstracts of their own papers. Let's say you want to present your paper at a conference—a smart idea, especially if you want to upgrade your curriculum vita (or résumé) before applying for graduate school or a job. To submit a proposal, send an abstract of your paper together with a letter of inquiry to the person organizing the conference session most appropriate for your paper. In your letter briefly state your interest in the session, generally describe your paper, and supply a very short "bio" (including the school, department, and degree program in which you are enrolled).

Furthermore, if your paper is accepted for the conference session, consider distributing copies of your abstract at your presentation—with your name and paper title placed at the top of the page, of course, so they will remember you. While not required, it is an opportunity to make an impression and give your audience something to take home with your name on it. Students applying for grad school, grants, or jobs may benefit from the networking that conferences offer. Your instructors or department can help you identify conferences that are suitable for your paper.

Lastly, if you submit a paper for publication, an abstract must be attached as part of your submission. Consult the journal's guidelines for help in preparing your abstract and manuscript.

8a Constructing an Abstract

An abstract is one paragraph long and runs about 100 to 200 words. It presents the main points of the original work in the words and terminology of the author. In an abstract, there should be no "distance" or effort to step back and summarize the work from a different perspective (like in a book review, for example).

Since an abstract is written after the work is finished, it should use the past tense.

This study examined X. . .
Findings included Y. . .

TABLE 8.1 Outline of an Abstract

The problem addressed in the paper

Definition of the key term, if necessary

Research design used

Sample (size, sampling technique, source)

Method of data collection

Method of data analysis

Main findings, in descending order of importance

Abstract are very concise and exclude extraneous words and information, such as failed hypotheses and footnotes. Remember to incorporate into your abstract the keywords that identify your work to other sociologists. Briefly state the problem you examined, your sample size, sampling technique, research design, and method of data collection and analysis. Present your main findings, in descending order of importance. Examples of abstracts for both quantitative and qualitative papers can be found at the end of this chapter.

An abstract is placed on its own page, with the heading ABSTRACT capitalized and centered at the top of the page. Triple-space (three single lines) between the heading and the first line of the abstract paragraph. The paragraph is indented. The abstract is placed immediately after the title page in a document and is not a numbered page.

Abstracts usually include the information listed in Table 8.1 in the order shown. The order of the information is very important, as abstracts have a highly formalized structure. Also, since all the information must be fit into one paragraph, conciseness is essential. There is no introduction, discussion, or conclusion and no extra words.

8b Abstracts for Quantitative and Qualitative Papers

Two sample abstracts are shown in Figures 8.1 and 8.2. The first abstracts a quantitative paper, and the second was prepared for a qualitative paper. Note the differences between the two abstracts, as well as the terse and formal style that characterizes both.

FIGURE 8.1 Abstract for a Quantitative Research Paper

ABSTRACT

This study examines the tendency for there to be similarities between the qualities that initially attract individuals to romantic partners and those they later dislike, that is, "fatal attractions." Approximately 44 percent of the individuals in this sample of 125 dating persons experience fatal attractions. Individual cases illustrate opposing themes, such as "nice to passive," and "strong to stubborn." One-third (33.7%) of the respondents themselves identify similarities between attracting and disliked partner characteristics. This disenchantment occurs in ongoing, as well as previous, relationships, suggesting that it is not simply sour grapes but is associated with the dissipation of infatuation. Dissimilar or extreme qualities in a partner are significantly more likely to become disliked.

Source: Felmlee 2001:263.

FIGURE 8.2 Abstract for a Qualitative Research Paper

ABSTRACT

Exploring Lyng's notion of "edgework," this article draws on ethnographic data to explore the ways skydivers create and sustain the belief that they can maintain control while working the "edge" in this sport. The article focuses on the ways skydivers construct and maintain the "illusion" that they can exercise control as they negotiate their particular edge. It elaborates the ways this sense of control is constructed and the extent to which it informs the ways risk recreators approach the edge. In the choices jumpers make about how they participate in the sport and the ways they interpret the experiences of themselves and other jumpers, they defend the position that their hazardous environments are within their control. When this position becomes untenable, they often draw on the notion of fate to construct certain hazards as outside of the sport, thereby sustaining their sense of control.

Source: Laurendeau 2006:583.

9

Writing a Compare/Contrast Paper

Some papers require that you compare and/or contrast two things—two authors' ideas, two authors' works, two works by the same author, two ideas, or two social policies. This type of paper is best handled as an essay or a term paper, following the guidelines discussed in Chapter 5, but with a twist.

There are two ways of structuring a compare/contrast paper. Version 1 (Table 9.1) is organized by the *items* being compared or contrasted, such as two authors, works, ideas, or policies. Version 2 is organized by the *points* of comparison or contrast, namely the similarities or differences between the items.

For a 10-20 page paper, you typically will be required to compare and/or contrast two items. If you choose three or four points of comparison or contrast—important ways the items are similar or different—you will have plenty of material about which to write.

9a Organizing The Compare/Contrast Paper

To illustrate the two ways of structuring a compare/contrast paper, a hypothetical thesis statement is shown here, followed by outlines for two versions of a paper based on this thesis (Table 9.1). Version 1 is an outline for a paper organized by authors, and Version 2 a paper organized by points of comparison.

Note: Whichever version is used, the order in which the authors, items, or points are listed in your thesis statement must be followed throughout the rest of your paper. Usually, they are listed chronologically, from oldest to most recent.

Thesis Statement:

Karl Marx and Max Weber, while sharing some ideas about society, differed regarding three key concepts: class, culture, and the role of the social scientist.

TABLE 9.1 Outlines for a Compare/Contrast Paper

Version 1	Version 2
Introduction (including a thesis statement with three points of comparison or contrast)	Introduction (including a thesis statement with three points of comparison or contrast)

I. First author (Marx)
  A. First point (class)
  B. Second point (culture)
  C. Third point (role of the social scientist)
	I. First point (class)
	  A. First author (Marx)
	  B. Second author (Weber)

II. Second author (Weber)
  A. First point (class)
  B. Second point (culture)
  C. Third point (role of the social scientist)
	II. Second point (culture)
	  A. First author (Marx)
	  B. Second author (Weber)

	III. Third point (role of the social scientist)
	  A. First author (Marx)
	  B. Second author Weber

Conclusion	Conclusion

Tip Choose only the most important points to compare and contrast.

Sometimes, in an effort to be creative, students are tempted to look for minor points to discuss that no one else has considered. This approach usually will not be appreciated by your instructor who wants to see if you have understood the main points about the subject.

9b Finding Points to Compare or Contrast

To compare or contrast two authors' ideas, two authors' works, two works by the same author, two ideas, or two social policies, you will need to identify two, three, or four important points of similarity (for comparison) or difference (for contrast). The number of points selected will be determined by the complexity of the points and the limitations of time and length on your paper. It is better to treat fewer points fully than more points haphazardly.

How do you choose which points to discuss? If your instructor has assigned a question for you to answer, your job is fairly straightforward. Look over the assignment carefully. The guidelines below may help in focusing your ideas. If you are choosing your own topic, briefly review the literature to see what others have identified as important points about the particular authors, works, ideas, or social policies you are considering as subjects. These insights should help you narrow your ideas. Also, refer to the following guidelines for aid in refining your best idea into a suitable topic. It is wise to check with your instructor to confirm your topic and thesis statement are appropriate before proceeding further. For a compare/contrast paper, your topic and thesis statement will be particularly important in ensuring a successful outcome to your efforts.

9c Some Guidelines for Compare/Contrast Papers

As you think about points to discuss in your paper, consider what you actually are going to compare or contrast. Two authors' ideas? Two authors' works? Two works by the same author? Two ideas? Two social policies?

Two Authors' Ideas

To compare or contrast two authors' ideas, you first need to decide if your main focus is the *people* or the *ideas*. In a short paper, this distinction is crucial. In a long paper, you may need to discuss both the people and the ideas.

If you are writing about the authors as **people**, address the way in which their early life and education may have influenced the later development of the ideas you are discussing. Also, talk about the implications of their work for sociology as a discipline. Was one author's work more influential than the other's? Why or why not?

If you are writing about the authors' **ideas** with a focus on the ideas, explain each author's main ideas one-by-one, and talk about how those ideas were distinctive or original. Were those ideas similar to or different from the other author's ideas? How did the ideas influence sociology as a discipline? Here, notice, there is little or no attention given to the author as person.

In both of these cases, you should use more than a single source by each author for your paper. (Hint: Even if you are told that just one work by each author "is enough," you would be wise to seek out other sources to broaden your paper's perspective.) You can examine more than one work by each author, assessments of the author written by others (including books, journal articles, magazine and newspaper articles, critiques, and book reviews), or comments on the work written by the author. For a longer paper, you should review materials for understanding the context in which the authors lived or the ideas developed.

Two Authors' Works or Two Works by the Same Author

Comparing or contrasting two authors' works or two works by the same author is aided by the use of text analysis. For information about writing a critique or a text analysis paper, see Chapter 11.

Two Ideas

To compare or contrast two ideas, address some or all of the following for each idea separately: What are its main points? What are its underlying assumptions? What are its implications? Who is its audience? In what context did it emerge and thrive or lose ground? Remember, you will need to compare or contrast the two ideas on each of these points that you select. Review the two versions of the compare/contrast paper for help in organizing your ideas.

Two Social Policies

To compare or contrast two social policies, discuss the following for each policy: What are its main points? What are its underlying assumptions? What are its implications for different audiences? When and in what context was it proposed and why? Remember, you will need to compare or contrast the two social policies on each of these points you select. Check the two versions of the compare/contrast paper for help in organizing your ideas.

9d Writing the Compare/Contrast Paper

Write the paper just as you would a term paper. It should have an introduction paragraph, body paragraphs, and a conclusion paragraph. For help in organizing and writing these three sections, see Chapter 5. You also may find it useful to add an additional paragraph before the final conclusion paragraph to serve as a short "discussion" section. In this paragraph, for a "contrast" paper, you could highlight points of comparison and assess the relative importance of the similarities and differences. In a "compare" paper, you similarly could mention the points of contrast or discuss the implications of these similarities and/or differences. Do they matter? What has been their importance? For whom? Then, use the conclusion paragraph to summarize and end with a flourish. Your paper should have a title page and reference list, unless you are instructed otherwise. Don't forget to revise your paper using the 10 Revision Cycles discussed in Chapter 2.

9e Final Check

Make sure you have . . .

1. an appropriate title.
2. a correct title page.
3. headers with your name in the upper right-hand corner of each page.
4. correctly numbered pages.

5. text citations following ASA documentation style.
6. a reference list following ASA documentation style.
7. spell-checked and personally proofread your document.
8. printed on good-quality, white paper with black ink.
9. stapled your paper in the upper right-hand corner, or placed it in a binder as instructed.

10 Writing a Book Review

A book review describes and evaluates a work, assesses its strengths and weaknesses, and places it within an established literature. Book reviews usually are written soon after a book's publication to generate interest or debate and thereby attract an audience to buy the book. However, book reviews also can serve as a valuable research tool when used correctly. Social scientists find that book reviews, because they are brief and include both positive and negative points about the work, provide a useful guide for library research.

10a How to Read and Evaluate a Book Review

How do you use a book review correctly? A book review is not a book report, but an opportunity for the reviewer to express his or her opinion about the work. When reading a review, be cautious about accepting information—especially controversial information—at face value. Remember, a review consists primarily of evaluation, not fact. Check the credentials of the reviewer given at the end of the review. Is the reviewer likely to be objective or an old rival with a score to settle? It may not always be possible to discover the connection between the reviewer and the author, but you would be surprised how much can be discovered in a minute or two by Googling the reviewer and the author.

In a perfect world, a strongly biased reviewer, whether for or against the author, would not be allowed to publish a review of the book in a reputable journal, newspaper, or magazine. Well-established publications are more likely to refuse to publish such a review, and if they do publish it, will usually insert a notation alerting readers, albeit subtly, that something is afoot. Imagine a book review written by the author's spouse or ex-spouse. How objective would we expect either to be? The takeaway point here is to stay alert and use your critical faculties as you read reviews. This is not a perfect world, even reputable publications occasionally print reviews by the author's sworn enemies, and book reviews do not necessarily present facts.

The popular media, in particular, provides many examples of bias in book reviews. Ever striving to attract an audience, popular media thrives on controversy. Blatantly biased reviews may be placed in popular magazines and newspapers and on television and the Internet because they have entertainment value and create "buzz." As a result, social scientists consider book reviews in popular media, and especially on the Internet, as undependable sources of information, since it is difficult to know who is writing (under whose name!), and both praise and criticism often take extreme forms.

Sociologists consult book reviews that appear in sociology journals or journals of related disciplines. They avoid, with rare exceptions, citations to reviews in popular magazines or newspapers or on the Internet. The journal *Contemporary Sociology,* for example, is devoted to publishing only book reviews and review essays (which compare several books on the same topic). This journal is one of the key forums for sociologists to learn about newly released books of interest.

10b Writing a Book Review

A book review is not a book report, nor should it present a play-by-play recital of the plot or chapter headings. If you are assigned a book review, do not just summarize the book's contents. Instead, describe, analyze, and evaluate the work. A good book review provides a brief overview of the book, points out its strengths and weaknesses, and discusses the book in comparison to other works in the same literature.

As you prepare to start writing, remember that a book review is written with an audience in mind. That audience determines the reviewer's assumptions and the aspects of the book to be discussed and evaluated. A review written for sociologists (or your instructor) should employ sociological concepts, theory, and perspective in its analysis of the book, as appropriate. Such a review can discuss well-known theorists and their ideas without a great deal of explanation, confident that the audience will recognize the names and terminology. On the other hand, a review written for a popular audience, such as a magazine or newspaper, must use nonsociological language to be understood. If social theorists are mentioned, they will need to be identified and placed in historical and social context before their ideas can be explained. Often, the latter task is so cumbersome that the reviewer bypasses it, or if undertaken by the reviewer, it is often cut by the editor—thereby yielding a review that is *sociology lite*.

How do you get started writing a thoughtful book review? The next sections will guide you step-by-step through the process.

Select a Book to Review

If you are given a choice of books to review, which should you choose? Pick a book you are passionate about—either because you agree or disagree with some aspect. Alternatively, select a book where your personal experiences or expertise provide background or added insight into the book's subject matter. This doesn't mean you should write about yourself in the review—"showing off" that way is not appreciated. However, it is perfectly appropriate to subtly convey your insider information. Say you were involved in the environmental movement and now you have a chance to review a book on environmentalism. Certainly do the review—just announce your bias by explaining in your first footnote that you were a member of environment group X from Y date to Z date. Your knowledge of the movement may add depth and texture to your review, perhaps through your incisive comments about the leadership structure or your keen grasp of the complex relationships between key players.

The poorest way to choose a book is to make your decision based on the number of pages. Students who deliberately pick short books fail to realize that they will have to dig deeper to find enough material for their reviews. Important books that are short, to be reviewed properly, need the reviewer to provide a great deal of background in the review—either by reading and discussing other works that may have contributed to the writing of the little book, or by bringing historical or statistical data to discuss the book's impact.

Long books have disadvantages, too. Very long books are hard to handle because of the large quantity of material and the increased reading time. Your best choice is the middle path. A book in the 200- to 300- page range should give you plenty to discuss, assuming the topic is appropriate for your interests.

Review the Literature

Read the book. Depending on the assignment, you also may wish to read other books on the same topic, or other reviews of your book. Don't skim-read the book. Pay attention to content, tone, the author's assumptions and conclusions, and your reaction to the book. If you have a strong reaction, think about why. You will want to address your reaction in your review.

Construct a Thesis Statement

Like all papers, a book review must have a thesis statement. The thesis statement presents the reviewer's position on the book, or what will be argued in the review. Usually subpoints of the thesis are not explicitly stated. Keep in mind that the thesis statement of the review is not the same as the book's thesis statement. Your thesis statement will indicate the major point *you* intend to make in your review.

The following example illustrates the difference between the reviewer's thesis and the author's purpose, as both are included in the first paragraph of this review of Christopher Jencks's 1994 book *The Homeless* (Cambridge, MA: Harvard University Press):

> In eleven short, crisp chapters, Christopher Jencks examines the nature, causes and some partial cures of homelessness. The book began as a review essay of eight books. As Jencks dug deeper into the academic literature and conducted his own reanalyses and new analyses of data, a new book emerged. It is vintage Jencks: pungent and witty, insightful and debunking, full of numbers, and mostly right. (Garfinkel 1994:687)

How do you find a thesis statement?

1. Think about what is distinctive about the book you have chosen, and focus on this uniqueness in your review. The subject matter does not make a book distinctive. Rather, the author's innovative ideas or unusual point of view sets the work apart from others.

2. How is the subject matter treated by the author? Who the author is will influence the background, approach, knowledge, and style he or she brings to the topic.

3. Does the author accomplish his or her stated purpose in the book? Why or why not?

Make an Informal Outline

In your outline, jot down the types of evidence you will bring to prove your point (the thesis statement). The evidence should come from the book itself. In most cases, the reviewer summarizes the evidence from the book. Paraphrases or quotes should be used judiciously.

Write the Review

A book review is structured like an essay. It needs an introduction paragraph, body paragraphs, and a conclusion. Check the length requirements for your review. Generally, a book review runs about three to five pages (typed and double-spaced) or 500 to 1,000 words.

In writing your review, limit your summary of the book's contents to one paragraph. Identify the work's thesis statement or hypothesis, and discuss the evidence the author assembles in support of the thesis. State the author's conclusions.

The paragraphs that follow should bring evidence in support of your thesis statement and discuss the book's strengths and weaknesses. In a book review, it is likely that your thesis statement may incorporate your critique of the work, and so your defense of your thesis will incorporate an evaluation of the work. In any case, focus on analysis, not description, emphasizing your impression of the work. Make sure to critique the author's thesis statement or hypothesis (is it appropriate to the purpose and scope, grounded in the literature, and reflective of the most current thinking on the subject?), the supporting evidence brought in defense of the thesis (does it actually reinforce the argument being made, and is it current and relevant?), and the author's conclusions (do they emerge logically from the evidence presented and address the same unit of analysis as the evidence presented?).

In discussing a book's strengths and weaknesses, don't point out that the book is logical or well organized. That is much like praising a book because most of the words are spelled correctly. All books that get published are expected to be clearly and carefully written. Of course, a book with many misspellings, poor organization, or no index is fair game for your criticism.

Focus on substantive issues when evaluating a book's strengths and weaknesses. How important is the topic to sociology or society in general? Did the author cover the topic thoroughly? What is missing, if anything? What methodology did the author use, and what were its limitations? How about the quality and style of writing? Does it hinder or advance the purpose of the book? What contribution did the work make to the body of knowledge about this subject? What is the book's contribution to society-at-large?

Evidence is unnecessary in the paragraph covering content, but it is required when you analyze the work. Use your own words for examples and try to place them in context. Use quotes only when absolutely necessary to make your point, and then choose short ones, providing appropriate citations to the book.

There is no single format for a book review. The example presented in Table 10.1 incorporates the main features of book review, and is built around a thesis statement with three points. Adapt this model as necessary by subtracting paragraphs (perhaps

TABLE 10.1 Outline of a Book Review

Paragraph 1	Introduction Introduce the topic in a general statement. Identify the book and author. State the work's scope and purpose. State whether the purpose was accomplished. Present the thesis statement.
Paragraph 2	Give an overview of the book's contents. State how it compares to other books on the same topic.
Paragraph 3	First point of the thesis A. Give supporting evidence 1. B. Give supporting evidence 2.
Paragraph 4	Second point of the thesis A. Give supporting evidence 1. B. Give supporting evidence 2.
Paragraph 5	Third point of the thesis A. Give supporting evidence 1. B. Give supporting evidence 2.
Paragraph 6	Book's strengths (or weaknesses, whichever is more important) A. Give supporting evidence 1. B. Give supporting evidence 2.
Paragraph 7	Book's weaknesses (or strengths, whichever is less important) A. Give supporting evidence 1. B. Give supporting evidence 2.
Paragraph 8	Conclusion Summarize your main points. Describe how this book contributes to the sociological literature or body of knowledge on this subject. Describe how this book contributes to society-at-large. State who will benefit by reading this work. End with a flourish.

your thesis has only two points) or adding paragraphs (maybe you need more space to discuss the book's strengths).

The review written using the outline shown in Table 10.1 would be fairly long. Of course, it could be shortened by paring down the thesis to only two points, and made even shorter by making the book's chief strength or weakness part of the thesis. It could also be lengthened by adding more evidence to each of the paragraphs, or adding additional paragraphs to treat thesis points. You should not add paragraphs to describe the book's contents, however.

Revise the Review

The final step in writing any paper is to edit it through the 10 Revision Cycles discussed in Chapter 2. In finalizing your book review, pay attention to your tone and use of extreme language. When writing a critique, it is easy to get swept up in the moment and revert into informal tone and extreme terms. Watch out for this pitfall.

Lastly, if your book review will be read by people other than your instructor, take care to express your criticism in moderate language. The academic world can seem very small sometimes. A scathing review you publish as a student may come back to haunt you years later as you sit for a job interview and find a still-vengeful author on the search committee casting the deciding vote against you.

10c Provide a Complete Reference for the Reviewed Work

Every book review includes publication information about the reviewed book. This information is generally placed before the review begins. A double-space separates the publication information and the first line of the introductory paragraph. As illustrated in the following example, the "blurb" includes the number of pages, price, and ISBN of the book, in addition to the usual reference information.

> *The Homeless*, by Christopher Jencks. Cambridge, MA: Harvard University Press, 1994. 161 pp. $17.95 cloth. ISBN: 0-674-40595-1.

10d Text Citations and References in a Book Review

If no other works are cited in your review, you may skip giving full text citations for quotes and paraphrases. Instead, simply state the page number in parentheses following the borrowed material. You also may exclude a reference page, since the full reference is given in the publication information at the start of your review.

If you cite additional works in your review, give text citations and add a reference page with the other sources listed. Keep in mind that citing other sources, if permitted, is an often viewed as a sign of diligence and scholarly temperament.

 Avoid Internet sources unless you are citing data from a reputable database.

10e Final Check

Make sure you have . . .

1. an appropriate title.
2. a correct title page.
3. headers with your name in the upper right-hand corner of each page.
4. correctly numbered pages.
5. text citations following ASA documentation style.
6. a reference list, if necessary, following ASA documentation style.
7. spell-checked and personally proofread your document.
8. printed on good-quality, white paper with black ink.
9. stapled your paper in the upper right-hand corner, or placed it in a binder as instructed.

11 Writing a Critique or Text Analysis Paper

A **critique** is a paper that analyzes and evaluates a text. The analyzed texts may include journal articles, book chapters, published or unpublished papers, reports, other documents, or books. Critiques are similar to book reviews in that they describe and assess a work. Critiques, however, examine the text in greater detail and in a more intellectually rigorous fashion than would be appropriate (or publishable) in a book review, and therefore they also may be referred to as text or textual analysis papers. In a critique, the text is essentially put under a microscope, scrutinized from all sides, and then dissected. In a book review, by contrast, the text is either admired or criticized from afar, and its general contours and stylistic effects are observed and noted.

When you are assigned a critique or text analysis paper, you may be given instructions to focus on particular aspects of the text. If not, use the following guidelines to help craft your argument. (Note: A critique is an argument in which you attempt to persuade the reader that your point of view is the correct one.)

11a What Should You Talk About in a Critique or Text Analysis Paper?

Appropriate Depth

Before starting to write, check how in-depth your analysis of the text should be. Are you supposed to focus on the structure of the argument? The use of rhythm and paragraph structure and its purpose in the work? Word choice and its purpose? In Marx and Engels' ([1848] 1983) *The Communist Manifesto*, for example, all of these techniques were expertly used to create a powerful piece of writing. On the other hand, a critique could also focus on the authors' reasons for writing the piece, how they wrote it and for what immediate end, how it was received, and how it came to be recognized as an important work.

Background Information

As the example of *Manifesto* demonstrates, the more in-depth your analysis of the text itself, the less emphasis is put on the background information. The opposite is true as well. The more general your critique, the greater the importance of background information and source materials.

The Role of Personal Opinion

Check whether you are expected to express your personal opinion explicitly in your paper. Some instructors expect you will not, or do so in a very limited fashion, while others don't care. It is wise to find out before starting to write your paper.

Describing and Summarizing the Text

In your overview of the text's subject matter, generally the following questions are addressed: What is the author's main point? Who is the author? Is there a larger issue being discussed that may not be readily apparent? When was this text written and in what context (i.e., was it written as part of a larger debate on an issue and, if so, which one)? Does the author state his or her motives in writing it? Do you have reason to believe other motives were important? If so, you will need to cite an authoritative source for this point.

Analyzing the Text

What type of evidence does the author bring to support the main point? How are concepts operationalized in the text, and what is the relationship between the concepts? Are the same concepts operationalized differently in other works? If so, what does that tell you about this text?

Evaluating the Text

On balance, does the author accomplish his or her goal in the critiqued work? What implications does the work have for sociology or society in general? What has been its actual impact? Has it been used in ways the author did not intend?

To find answers to the preceding questions, you may need to review the literature, check your course readings, or look up the author in a sociological encyclopedia. Famous works or authors are likely to have been discussed a great deal in the literature, while new or fairly unknown authors may not. Check with your instructor to make sure you are on the right track.

11b Writing a Critique or Text Analysis Paper

To start a critique, review the steps for writing papers discussed in Chapter 1 and determine your entry point into the process.

Select a Topic

You may not need to choose a text if you have been assigned one. If you are given a choice, criteria for selecting a text is discussed in Chapter 10.

Review the Literature

You will need to read the text very carefully several times. Pay attention to the content, tone, the author's assumptions and conclusions, and your reactions to the text. If you have a strong reaction, think about why. You may want to address the reason for your reaction in your paper.

Also, check whether your assignment expects you to consult other articles or books for background or commentary on your text. If you paraphrase or quote them in your paper, remember to cite your sources.

Construct a Thesis Statement

A critique, like all papers, must have a thesis statement. Your thesis states your position on the text or what you plan to argue in your critique. In constructing a thesis statement, you do not need to explicitly state thesis points, although you certainly need to know these points yourself, since they will structure the body paragraphs of your critique.

Remember that your critique's thesis statement is not the same as the thesis statement of the text. Your thesis statement indicates the major point *you* intend to make in your critique of the text.

How do you find a thesis statement?

1. Think about what is distinctive about the text you have chosen, and focus on this uniqueness in your critique. The subject matter does not make a text distinctive. Rather, the author's innovative ideas or unusual point of view sets the work apart from others.

2. How is the subject matter treated by the author? Who the author is will influence the background, approach, knowledge, and style he or she brings to the topic.

3. Does the author accomplish his or her stated purpose in the book? Why or why not?

Make an Informal Outline

Construct an informal outline, noting down the evidence you will bring to support your thesis statement. Use quotes from the text to back up each point you make, where necessary.

Write the Paper

A critique is structured as an essay, with an introduction paragraph, body paragraphs, and a conclusion paragraph. If your assignment requires you to compare or contrast two works, see Chapter 9. Like all papers, your critique should begin with a title page, unless you are instructed otherwise. As you undoubtedly will paraphrase or quote passages from the text, you will need text citations and a reference page even for a single source, unless otherwise instructed.

Whereas a critique is always structured as an essay, there is considerable flexibility in the number of thesis points and amount of evidence brought in support of those points. Depending on the length requirements of the paper, you may decide to have two or more paragraphs for each thesis point (in the outline in Table 11.1, see paragraphs 3 to 5). The example shown in Table 11.1 is based on a thesis statement with three points.

TABLE 11.1 Outline for a Critique or Text Analysis Paper

Paragraph 1	Introduction Introduce the topic in a general statement. Identify the text and author. State the text's importance. State the text's or author's purpose, if known. State whether the purpose was accomplished. Present the thesis statement with three points.
Paragraph 2	Give an overview of the text's contents (what does it discuss?). State how it compares to other texts on the same topic.
Paragraph 3	First point of your thesis A. Give supporting evidence 1. B. Give supporting evidence 2.
Paragraph 4	Second point of your thesis A. Give supporting evidence 1. B. Give supporting evidence 2.
Paragraph 5	Third point of your thesis A. Give supporting evidence 1. B. Give supporting evidence 2.
Paragraph 6	Evaluation of the text, main point (i.e., positive attributes) A. Give supporting evidence 1. B. Give supporting evidence 2.
Paragraph 7	Evaluation of the text, secondary point (i.e., negative attributes) A. Give supporting evidence 1. B. Give supporting evidence 2.
Paragraph 8	Conclusion Summarize your main points. State how the text appears on balance. Describe how the text contributes to sociology or society-at-large. State who will benefit by reading this text. End with a flourish.

Prepare a Reference List

All works cited in your paper must be listed in the reference list at the end of your paper. If you compile citations as your write your paper, make sure to compare your list to the final version of your paper. Citations in footnotes or endnotes also are placed in the reference list. For help in creating reference list entries, see Chapter 4.

Revise Your Paper

Revise your paper using the 10 Revision Cycles discussed in Chapter 2.

11c Final Check

Make sure you have . . .

1. an appropriate title.
2. a correct title page.
3. headers with your name in the upper right-hand corner of each page.
4. correctly numbered pages.
5. text citations following ASA documentation style.
6. a reference list following ASA documentation style.
7. spell-checked and personally proofread your paper.
8. printed on good-quality, white paper with black ink.
9. stapled your paper in the upper right-hand corner, or placed it in a binder as instructed.

12 Writing an Essay Exam

An **essay examination** tests your ability to reflect on and synthesize your course notes and readings by requiring you to craft a thoughtful, well-organized response. A good exam answer indicates that you understand the main ideas and themes presented in the course well enough to compose a cogent response. An excellent exam answer accomplishes the points just mentioned, but also shows that you can integrate differing perspectives, see the big picture, and assess implications.

You may be relieved to know that most instructors do not expect essay exam answers to be highly creative or innovative, especially for "in-class" essay exams. They understand that the time pressure for writing exams tends to dampen originality. They do, however, expect that your work be thorough, well written, and display a mastery of the course material.

12a Formulating an Essay Exam Answer

Your essay exam answer must demonstrate that you can do the following:

- **Content** Grapple with the notes and readings, and not just write everything you can remember about the subject.
- **Organization** Formulate a logical, well-developed response, with appropriate supporting evidence and citations to sources.
- **Format** Write a coherent essay, with correct text citations and references, grammar and punctuation.

TABLE 12.1 Examples of What *Not* to Say in an Essay Exam—Or How Many Mistakes Can You Find?

1. I can prove this because . . .
2. This is true because my grandfather told me so and he loves me very much.
3. This is a social trend because it happened to my mother.
4. The books I read for a course with Professor Johnson last semester help explain this concept.
5. It is true because I learned it in Sunday school.
6. As *Wikipedia* explains . . .
7. *Encyclopedia Britannica* discusses this point, stating . . .

Content, organization, and *format* are the three keys to an excellent essay exam answer. Then there are the things you never should do in an essay exam. Take a look at the examples in Table 12.1 and see if you can identify the problems.

It's interesting to note that all of the examples listed in Table 12.1 are taken from actual student papers. Let's review them.

1. Don't use the word *prove.* It is questionable whether *anyone* can prove *anything.* Also, where is this sentence going to end?

   I can prove this because . . .   I am a wizard.

                                               it already has been proved last week.

                                               I know a secret no one else knows.

   As you can see, the sentence is headed for a bad ending. Here is what many students do to this sentence, which is wrong scientifically, logically, and grammatically.

   I can prove this because of three facts: *X, Y,* and *Z.*

2. Who is your grandfather? A known, recognized expert on the subject under discussion? Einstein, perhaps? If your grandfather was Einstein and told you the information, you may use the evidence but must cite your source, namely your personal conversation with Einstein. Follow the citation format shown in Chapter 4. And by the way, you don't need to tell us he loves you. We all know.

3. Social trends occur when something happens to lots of people, not just one person—even if it is *your* mother. You need to present statistics on how many other people have experienced the same thing.

4. Whether you did the readings for Professor Johnson is irrelevant. Cite only to the readings for this class. Your instructor will not interpret your references to a different course as a sign of your expansive intellect—only your lack of reading in *this* course.

5. Sunday school or grandfathers, when writing a paper in the social sciences you need to cite evidence that has been acquired using the Scientific Method (for more information, see Table 6.2). Knowledge—passed down by religious, familial or other authorities—may be true, but scientists don't accept it as evidence in scientific debate. However, you could cite to an article or book, pointing out that, for example, X% *of Catholics are reported to believe* Y, or *a fundamental belief of Buddhism is Z.*

6. Do not cite *Wikipedia* as a source. Mentioning this Web site suggests to your instructor that you did not read the assigned course texts and probably didn't have complete lecture notes, either. In your essay exam, only cite to your class readings and notes unless you are told otherwise.

7. *Encyclopedia Britannica* may have long words and give citations at the end of its articles, but read point 6—ditto.

12b Exams: Take-Home versus In-Class

An essay exam may be distributed for students to complete "at home" within a certain time period, or administered in class with time limits. In both cases, your essay exam answer should leave no doubt in the reader's mind that you have read, understood, and thought about the course readings and notes, organized your ideas logically, and presented your response in a clear, well-written manner. Needless to say, higher expectations prevail for take-home exams, as they are generally designated "open-book" (meaning texts and notes can be used), other resources can be consulted, and more time is theoretically available for revising and polishing the final version before submitting it.

The next sections show you how to write the best possible essay answer. Take-home exams are discussed first, followed by pointers for taking essay exams in class. The guidelines for take-home exam answers comprise the ideal against which in-class exam answers are evaluated, even though you will likely have less time for developing, revising, and polishing your answer in class.

12c Prepping for the Exam

Keep in mind that the remainder of this chapter focuses on *writing* essay exam answers. You need to have done your preparation for the exam by reviewing course readings and lecture notes before sitting down to write a single word. The reflection and synthesis mentioned at the start of this chapter is vital to your success. So do your prep work early. If you missed notes, get copies of classmates' notes well before the exam so you have time to review them several times. Even if you have a full set of notes, it is helpful to review a second set of notes. Consider exchanging a copy of your notes for a classmate's. Lastly, finish all the assigned readings. As you read, take notes or highlight your text so you can locate key points easily.

 Never give your original set of notes to anyone. If you wish to lend them, make a copy. Feel free to charge photocopying costs to the person requesting the copy.

12d Writing a Take-Home Essay Exam

When you receive a take-home exam, handle it like you would a term paper. Remember the steps for writing a paper discussed in Chapter 1? Follow those six steps here. Select a topic, review the literature, construct a thesis statement, outline, write a draft, and revise the draft. Of course, in the case of an essay exam, selecting a topic is easy. Either the question is assigned, or you will have a limited choice. If you can choose the exam questions to answer, consider your choices briefly, assessing which question you are best prepared to answer. Review the literature (look over your readings and notes), and then construct a thesis statement (formulate your answer to the question and the reasons you think so). Sketch out an informal outline of your essay (introduction, body paragraphs, conclusion), and write a draft. Finally, apply the 10 Revision Cycles in Chapter 2 to your draft, and you have a finished product!

Content

Generally, an essay exam will either pose a question and ask for a response, or make a statement and ask you to react. It also might make an assertion, and ask you to choose and defend one of several explanations.

As you think about the question, go back and reread it several times to make sure you are responding to what is being asked. It is not unusual for instructors to receive fine exam papers that simply don't answer the question. Such exams usually get low grades, so be careful. For each question, check to see if there are several parts that must be answered or only one. Students who skip one part of a three-part question will lose one-third of their grade for simply not answering one-third of the question.

Do not approach an essay exam as a freewriting assignment. Squarely attack the question and administer a laser-precise response. Check to see that your approach to the subject matter is correct. Usually, you will be required to do one or more of the following in your response:

- Describe and discuss a concept or process
- Examine and analyze trends
- Compare and contrast differing perspectives
- Assess or evaluate ideas or policies

Organization

A question asking you to describe, discuss, examine, or analyze involves expository (explanatory) writing. Structure your answer to this type of question as an essay. An outline of a so-called five-paragraph essay is shown in Table 12.2. For each point in the thesis statement, two supporting forms of evidence are provided, but three, four, or five forms would be even better.

For a question asking you to compare, contrast, assess, or evaluate, structure your answer as a compare/contrast paper, choosing either Version 1 or 2 depending on the subject matter. (For more information, see Tables 9.1 and 9.2.)

Sometimes, a question requires you to choose a side and defend it against the other side. An argument has its own structure—a twist on the essay—as those who have joined a debate team or argued with their parents can tell you (Table 12.3).

What kind of supporting evidence should be used? Draw on your course readings and lecture notes. What does the question ask you to do? Evidence generally used to support an essay answer includes definitions, descriptions, opinions of important sociologists, statistics, research findings, and examples. Be sure to cite your sources in text citations, and list the sources correctly on your reference page.

TABLE 12.2 Outline for an Essay Exam Answer: A "Describe"
or "Discuss" Question

Paragraph 1	Introduction (including a thesis statement with three points)

Paragraph 2	I. First point of the thesis
	    A. Give supporting evidence 1 (first subordinate idea).
	    B. Give supporting evidence 2 (second subordinate idea).

Paragraph 3	II. Second point of the thesis
	    A. Give supporting evidence 1 (first subordinate idea).
	    B. Give supporting evidence 2 (second subordinate idea).

Paragraph 4	III. Third point of the thesis
	    A. Give supporting evidence 1 (first subordinate idea).
	    B. Give supporting evidence 2 (second subordinate idea).

Paragraph 5	Conclusion (summary)

TABLE 12.3 Outline for an Essay Exam Answer: A "Take a Side
and Argue It" Question

Paragraph 1	Introduction (ends with the thesis statement)
Paragraph 2	All evidence in support of your thesis*
Paragraph 3	The main arguments that can be brought in support of the other side**
Paragraph 4	Rebuttal (why your side wins)
Paragraph 5	Conclusion

*If you have more evidence than fits well within paragraph 2, add as many paragraphs as necessary. In general, the more appropriate evidence you bring the better.

**To win, you need to show that you have considered the strongest arguments of the other side and found them less persuasive than your own position. If you never even considered them, how do you know they are no good? Obviously, your goal is not to argue for the other side, but simply to show that you are aware of and have rejected the arguments. In writing this paragraph, introduce the other side's arguments with phrases such as *of course . . . , granted that . . . , it is obvious that . . .* , and *no one disagrees that. . . .*

Finally, keep in mind that in writing an essay exam, your answer should *not* simply answer the question. For example, if you are asked about a cause of delinquency and you responded with three words—*the human condition*—you probably would not receive the stellar grade you felt you so richly deserved. Yes, stories circulate about the student who wrote an ultra-short exam answer and supposedly received an A. My favorite case was the student who, in response to a complex question on Henry David Thoreau, supposedly wrote the answer "simplicity, simplicity, simplicity" and received an A. Please be cautioned: Most of these stories fall in the category of urban legend. Instructors give essay exams so students can demonstrate what they have learned in the course. Your game plan should be to use essay exams as opportunities to showcase what you have learned from course readings, class lectures, and class discussions. Do not quote heavily from other course readings or outside sources. Instructors usually interpret such actions to mean you did reading for other courses, but not for this one.

Format

Your essay exam answer is essentially a short term paper. If you are given more than one question to answer, treat each as a separate essay and do not combine questions. Before beginning your response, restate the question, then triple-space and begin your introduction paragraph. Submit your exam with a title page and reference page(s). If you are answering more than one essay question, only one title page and reference page is needed for the whole exam.

After you have drafted your essay answer, apply the 10 Revision Cycles. Your final submitted version should look like a term paper.

12e Writing an In-Class Essay Exam

For the in-class essay exam, follow the guidelines for the take-home. When you are presented with the exam, you will need to make a quick choice about the question(s) to answer, and develop a thesis statement with two or three points. Take a moment and sketch out a brief outline to follow as you write. Then, start writing. Don't take time to revise and rewrite. For an in-class exam, once you start writing, keep going. Just remember to watch the time so you can finish all the questions on the exam.

12f Tips for Taking an In-Class Exam

1. When you receive your exam, read each question carefully. Check to see if a question has more than one part that must be answered. Students who skip one part of a two-part question may lose 50 percent of their grade on the question for simply not answering.

2. Identify the questions you tentatively plan to answer if you have a choice. You can always decide to change your plan if, while answering one question, you suddenly remember information that will help with another.

3. Create a game plan. How many questions must you answer? Pay attention to the point values of the questions. If some questions count more heavily toward your grade, spend more time developing and writing those answers. Figure out the total number of minutes allowed for the exam and allocate time for each question. You will need to pace yourself to finish all the required questions.

4. Answer the easiest questions first, and then move on quickly to the more difficult ones. As you start writing, you will find ideas come to you. Be ready to jot

them down on the inside cover of your exam book so you don't forget. You may write your answers out of order in your exam booklet, but sure to number (or letter) your questions following the exam format so your instructor can match up your answer to the correct question.

5. Before starting each question, pause for a moment. Decide on a thesis statement and make a brief outline for your answer. Even though it may take a minute or two to write, an outline will help you remember the points you want to include and the order you want to follow. Also, what evidence will you bring in support of those points? List anything appropriate that comes to mind, and then start writing! If you have studied for the exam, you probably will find that new ideas start coming quickly once you begin.

6. You don't need a fancy introduction for your answer. If you are not sure how to begin your question, try using some of the words from the question. Reorder them to begin a new sentence.

> Question: Discuss three theories of delinquency and their application to the case of female runaways.
>
> Opening sentence for the introduction paragraph: Three theories of delinquency that shed light on the case of female runaways are *X*, *Y*, and *Z*.

7. If you run out of time before finishing the question, you may want to try this idea. Conclude your answer with the remainder of your outline, demonstrating how you intended to complete the question. While there is no guarantee that your instructor will give you credit, you can increase the odds by including in the outline your main points, subpoints, and supporting evidence with citations. At least, this will show your instructor that you could have written a fuller answer had you been given more time.

12g Final Check

Make sure you have . . .

1. a correct title page.
2. headers with your name in the upper right-hand corner of each page.
3. correctly numbered pages.
4. text citations, if needed, following ASA documentation style.
5. a reference list, if needed, following ASA documentation style.
6. spell-checked and personally proofread your paper.
7. printed on good-quality, white paper with black ink.
8. stapled your paper in the upper right-hand corner, or placed it in a binder as instructed.

13

A Sample Student Paper

Those qualitative student paper incorporates field observations that are documented in footnotes throughout the paper.[*] The paper as a whole is a good example of the style and tone to be adopted in undergraduate papers. It brings together many of the elements discussed throughout this book to produce an informative, interesting, and well-documented paper.

---

[*]Used with permission.

The word *stuff* is too informal and unclear.

TAPS:

The "Stuff" That Goes into the Privatization of Space

Allison Fischer
Sociology 335
Production, Consumption, and the Policy of Public Space
May 3, 2008

New York and other tourist cities are defined by their public spaces. Cultural centers, subway stations, and parks are all available to the public, allowing for a diversity of uses and users. Along with the anonymity of public spaces, however, comes a lack of community that exists in privately owned neighborhoods. To cultivate a sense of community in an anonymous city, the public turns to informal mediators. Performance artists in tourist cities like New York work to bridge the differences that exist between residents and tourists, various ethnicities and races, as audiences gather together for the common purpose of an entertainment experience. This form of intimacy is initiated with a bottom-up transformation of public space to private as a TAPS, or temporarily appropriated public space(s), is created.

Various urbanists and sociologists have attempted to identify public and private spaces and their significance. Smithsimon (2004) categorizes spaces by the degree of privatization or publicity. A "private space" is owned by a private corporation or a "public–private authority," and allows for only a limited number of users. "Filtered space" is a less extreme form of "private space," which "often create[s] unequal ease of access" (p. 26) and is regulated by either a limitation of access or activities (p. 28). "Community space" is even more inclusive, but still limits a space to the community residents, while a "popular space" is loosely regulated and encourages diverse uses by a diverse population. Through this system of categorization, questions of inclusion or exclusion arise as a result of the way a space is regulated.

Kohn (2004) moves beyond categorization and discusses the shift from public to private spaces. She uses the example of the evolution from public marketplaces and town squares to privatized mega-malls in order to analyze the way public space has become private in an exclusionary way. Kohn traces the privatization of public space to the "growing phenomenon of private government" (p. 2). While she proposes defining space as "a cluster concept" composed of "ownership, accessibility, and intersubjectivity" (p. 11), her work speaks to the notion that government and the owner(s) of a space define its identity.

Kayden (2000) also addresses the question of ownership of space when discussing the phenomenon of privately owned public space, challenging their publicity and efficacy. Kayden defines this form of space as, "private ownership [that] would reside with the developer and successor owners of the property, access and use with members of the public, hence the appellation of 'privately owned public space.'" The zoning resolution that facilitated this concept was adopted in New York in 1961 (p. 1). This initiative offers private companies enticing incentives to build public plazas. Private owners of such properties navigate through a series of zoning codes and guidelines to create a public space. While some of these locations are inviting to the public and provide recreational space, open

Fischer

air, good seating, and food options, other spaces are ineffective and even hostile.

These two authors discuss the transformation of public space to private, and the top-down control of public spaces. Both authors ultimately arrive at the conclusion that the transformation of space occurs through the intention of the developer and legal acquisition, and that the real identity of a space lies in the hands of its owners.

The idea of a TAPS contradicts these notions in proposing that a space is temporary and transient, shifting from public to private and back again due to a break in the social norms of a space, not its legal contract. Control of a TAPS is not determined by the owner of the space, but by its users. A temporarily appropriated public space may be defined as the spontaneous creation of a temporary private zone within a larger public sphere. Performance artists are creators of such spaces.

The thesis statement should be more clearly identified as the thesis.

Defining a TAPS

To identify the definition, function, and parameters of a TAPS, I used field observations, interviews, and quantitative analysis of accumulated data. I visited many popular public spaces in New York where performers usually form a TAPS, such as Times Square; the south border of Central Park (the intersection of 5th Avenue and 59th Street); the steps of the New York Public Library; and Grand Central, Atlantic Avenue, Union, Times Square and Penn subway/train stations. I observed 16 separate TAPS between the dates of

This paragraph describes the methodology used in studying TAPS. This section SHOULD have been labeled METHODS.

Fischer

February 18 and April 11, 2008. The documentation of events with evaluations and photos, and interviews of police officers, performers, and observers, provided me with exposure to these forms of private spaces.

A TAPS is typically formed through the employment of several factors. All the leading indicators of an impending TAPS relate directly to the idea of disrupting the social norms of a public space, and defying its anonymity. Noise is often one such catalyst. Oftentimes entertainers will clap, shout, sing, play music, or cheer in order to draw attention to themselves. While the average noise in a public space is limited to traffic and minimal discussion, the performers' noises are an aberration, and identify the group as unique.

> First and second person pronouns should be avoided. Allison could have referred to herself as "the researcher" or "the author."

Another identifying factor of a TAPS is the homogeneous appearance of its participants. The race or ethnicity of a group, as well as their attire, marks them as identifiable among the anonymous mix of public space users. Of the observed performers initiating a TAPS, 80 percent are African American and 90 percent are male. Each performance group dresses similarly. In almost all break-dancing groups observed, the accepted attire is an oversized tee-shirt and baggy pants. Jewelry is frequently worn, and sneakers are mandatory. While other performers vary in garb, all the group members dress alike. The performers' similar appearances help distinguish them from a crowd.

The distinction that similar attire provides became evident when observing a break-dancing group in Penn Station. As the audience was warming up to a

Fischer

break-dancing performance, another dancer emerged from behind the crowd. He was clapping in sync with the rest of the audience, but due to his appearance, it was evident to the onlookers that he was a dancer, and they parted, allowing him to get through.[1] Although the "baggy jeans look" may serve to provide cultural and perhaps socioeconomic commentary, and may not necessarily be unique to break-dancers, it marks a homogeneous group among a multicultural audience.

A break in traffic flow also distinguishes a TAPS. As traffic on public sidewalks usually flows vertically, divided as those on the right side walk in one direction, while those on the left in an opposite direction, initiators of TAPS crowd around in a circlelike formation, thereby disrupting the linear trajectory of the masses. Instead of passers-by clashing with these deviants, people tend to diverge from their path, and swerve around the performers, in order to avoid confrontation. As people continue moving around the group, the flow of traffic shifts, allowing for an untrespassed, and therefore, temporarily private pocket of space to develop.

The exception to this rule is when the sidewalk or pathway is too narrow for people to pass by. In such a situation, the "privacy" of the TAPS might be compromised. It is important to note, however, that this loss of spatial integrity is not due to a flaw in the nature of a TAPS, but rather, to a poor decision of location. Oftentimes

---

[1]Observation of Penn Station, March 24, 2008.

break-dancers initiate their TAPS in narrow subway tunnels. While they successfully appropriate the public space, they are unable to retain a large audience or audience members for more than a minute or two because the space does not seem entirely private. The ratio of audience members to the trespassers of the TAPS is approximately 10:1, and although this number does not seem objectively significant, it affects the "private feel" of the space.[2]

To enhance the privacy of a TAPS as participants crowd around during the initiation process, they "warm up" by either tuning their instruments or displaying dance moves. The freedom with which these noises and movements are demonstrated signifies the privatization that is taking place. Onlookers acknowledge the implication of these actions (that would normally occur in private spheres) and act accordingly by allowing the performers more space. People slow down the pace of their stride to watch the performers. At this point onlookers assume the identity of "audience" as they observe the initiators of the TAPS, as if they are expecting a spectacle. This deference allows the TAPS even greater autonomy.

As all these catalysts merge together, a TAPS begins to take shape. The process of initiating a TAPS usually takes about 5 minutes, and the TAPS tends to last for about 10 minutes. The short lifespan of a TAPS emphasizes the temporal nature of space, and the ease of its fluctuation.

---

[2]Observation of Atlantic Avenue subway station, February 21, 2008; observation of Penn Station, April 9, 2008; observation of Times Square subway station, April 9, 2008.

The Social Contracts

The autonomy of a performer within a TAPS is based on societal consent. A TAPS is a mutually beneficial opportunity, as the performer creates a space in which he or she may perform for money, while the audience agrees to accept enjoyment in return for the power over space. During these impromptu shows, the audience members also relinquish a portion of their autonomy as they agree to follow the directions of the performer. When they are asked to clap, they do so. When an audience member is pulled into the center of the "stage" to dance with the group, he or she acquiesces.

The breaching of social norms for the sake of entertainment goes even further, as a TAPS encourages audience members to forfeit their anonymity and interact with other onlookers. Whereas interaction between two strangers in a New York public space is usually limited to informational conversations (regarding traffic, time, details of an emergency, etc.), viewers of a TAPS, and break-dancing groups in particular, are drawn into recreational interactions with the performers and other audience members.

In almost all TAPS, the audience seems highly fragmented, at first. People speak in hushed voices, and only to people they know. This lasts for the first few minutes of the performance. Usually one-third of the way through the show, the break-dancers begin encouraging audience participation through noisemaking (i.e., cheering, clapping, etc.) or by selecting an onlooker to participate in the dance. By breaching the social expectation to avoid recreational conversation with strangers, the performers open up multiple possibilities of interaction.

During an observation of a break-dancing group on the small plaza in the middle of the 5th Avenue and 59th Street intersection on April 11, 2008, I witnessed a consensual violation of an onlooker's personal space. The group was dancing for about seven minutes, and although the audience was clapping along, they did not seem involved with the show. There was a high turnover rate of audience members, as people stayed only for a minute or two before continuing on their way, while those who remained seemed distracted. To engage the audience, a break-dancer approached a young woman in the front line of the audience and began dancing right in front of her. He took her hand and led her into the "stage" area. While this was a clear breach of a well-known social contract that physical contact between strangers is inappropriate, she displayed her consent by laughing and beginning to dance before returning to her place in the crowd. She received a loud applause from the audience, and was congratulated by surrounding audience members. By the dancer violating a social norm, he nonverbally validated the same behavior between audience members. Onlookers took his cue, and began joking and chatting briefly.

Interaction between strangers is also fostered through the shared experience of the TAPS performance. When observing another crowd at the same location on March 24, 2008, I noticed that for the first five minutes of the show there was minimal interaction between the audience members, despite the performers' efforts. During a routine move, a dancer slipped and fell. He picked himself up quickly and continued dancing. This small mistake invoked an immediate response from the audience, mostly in the form of gasps and giggles, but continued to have an effect after the dancer had continued with the routine. Conversation began as people said "did you see that?" or those who had looked away asked others what they had missed. The common experience of watching a performer miss a step put the audience at ease, and allowed for the initiation of conversation between strangers.

This form of interaction is fostered by the creators of the TAPS, and the nature of a TAPS itself. When consenting to the appropriation of their public space, people provide nonverbal consent that other social norms may be altered, as well.

Identity of a TAPS

Initiators of TAPS not only appropriate a space, but they also identify with it. As TAPS are formed, there is an average distance of 6 to 10 feet that separates the performers and the audience. While single musicians might command only 5 feet of distance, multiperson break-dancing groups might require over 10 to 12 feet. It seems that once a group has familiarized itself with a certain amount of space, it continues to nonverbally demand it. The same break-dancing group in the tunnels between Herald Square and Penn Station, on two separate occasions, maintained the identical distance between the audience and themselves (the front line of the audience began approximately 10 feet away from the performers).[3]

Performance groups distinguish themselves not only by a certain amount of physical space, but with a specific location. The creation of a TAPS attaches an identity to a previously anonymous public space. When interviewing police officer Rob Savage regarding public norms and behaviors, he made reference to a specific platform at the Times Square subway station. When I asked him how I might identify the specific platform, he said, "y'know, where the guy with the guitar plays."[4] Another time, when asking for directions in Grand Central terminal, a woman pointed me toward a walkway and told me to keep walking straight, "until you reach the place where the dancers are usually set up, and then you make a left."[5] These comments reaffirm the common identity shared by a performance group and a location. Not only do performers appropriate public space when forming a TAPS, but they also imbue it with an identity. Even after the group has left and the space has been reclaimed by the public, it retains a sense of "privacy," as it is identified with a certain group of people.

The sense of "owning public space" is mutually respected among performance groups and initiators of TAPS. Spaces that are known to "belong" to particular performers are not

---

[3]Observation of Penn Station, February 26, 2008; observation of Penn Station, March 8, 2008.

[4]Observation of Times Square subway station, February 18, 2008.

[5]Observation of 5th Avenue and 59th Street, March 10, 2008.

Fischer

used by others. This "turf" mentality was highlighted in an
interview with James, a break-dancer in the Atlantic Avenue
subway station. He has been with his current group for four
years and with another break-dancing group for the previous
four years. He explained that the break-dancing community is
"like family," and that groups frequently trade members. This
communal sentiment breeds respect; as James stated, they
don't dance in our area and we don't use theirs."[6] In the same
subway station I met Dan, a stress-test administrator and
Scientology book seller, who had set up a card table with
some other volunteers. When asked if he had ever
experienced a dispute over use of the space, he said that
performers he had interacted with were understanding and
respectful. Earlier in the day, he mentioned, a group of
performers set up their boom-box and tip can directly adjacent
to his table. When he had difficulty talking to customers
because of the loud music, he went over to the group, told
them he would be there for another hour, and asked if they
could relocate and come back when he left. They agreed and
moved to another location. These interactions further
emphasize the respect and validation of TAPS by outsiders.

These temporarily appropriated public spaces are not
just socially accepted but sometimes they are even
encouraged by higher authorities. In New York, there are at
least two organizations that promote the use of public space
for entertainment purposes. Underground NY is a program

Here the first person is avoided.

---

[6]Observation of Atlantic Avenue subway station, February 21, 2008.

Fischer

that provides performance space in subway and train
stations, like Penn Station, Grand Central terminal, Times
Square subway station, and others. Performers are required
to provide a demo tape or an equivalent to apply to the
program, and if they are selected they are given a time slot
and location to perform. They may sign up for several times
slots and, if they wish, can even sign onto a semipermanent
schedule. This service is free of charge, and performers
retain all the tips that they earn. Symphony Space provides
a similar program to foster "artistically and culturally
diverse performing arts . . . that bring artists and audiences
together in an atmosphere of exploration and intimacy"
(Symphony Space 2007). While TAPS are usually developed
from the bottom up, these organizations break the mold, and
work from the top down to assist amateur performers.

Citations to interviews and field notes are correctly placed in footnotes.

Additionally, police officers generally support the use of
public space by performance artists. Most police
officers interviewed stated that they "don't mind" the
performers,[7] even though Officer Savage bluntly
stated that "police and music don't mix."[8]
When asked about the way performance space is
monitored, Officer Savage explained that if a performer is
using a space allocated to another group through the
Underground NY program, they are simply asked to
move, and they almost always comply. If the music

[7]Observation of Penn Station, February 26, 2008; observation at Union Station, February 28, 2008; observation of the steps of the New York Public Library on 5th Avenue, April 9, 2008. Three of five police officers interviewed stated, using exactly the same words, that "they don't mind" the performers.
[8]Observation of Times Square subway station, February 18, 2008.

Fischer

is too loud, he continued, "we ask them to turn it down, and they do." "Generally," he concluded, "it is not a problem."[9] When John, a break-dancer in the intersection of 5th Avenue and 59th Street, was asked to describe his relationship with police officers monitoring the area, he simply responded, "They watch us."[10] The officers' reaction to TAPS attests to their legality and right to exist. This relationship also emphasizes the use of social contracts rather than legal policing to enforce "rules" in this type of space. The performers are the local authority, not the police officers.

DISCUSSION/CONCLUSION

Privatization of space may happen in many ways. Low (2003) in *Behind the Gates* explores an exclusive form of privatization through gated communities. This form of privatization isolates outsiders by excluding those who cannot afford to live in such developments. This middle- and upper-class utopian ideal allows for the feeling of safety and distance from the anonymous public. A TAPS, however, privatizes space in an inclusive way. As Flusty (1994) notes, "the more inclusive the urban commons, the greater the diversity of interactions" (p. 12). This is the concept on which a TAPS is built.

In a TAPS, the anonymous public is invited and encouraged to interact with others. While this form of private space is initiated by a specific group that controls the space,

The literature should not be accented in the discussion section. Allison needs to follow the guidelines for developing this section of her paper.

---

[9]Ibid.
[10]Observation of Grand Central Station, March 10, 2008.

anyone may participate. Most initiators of TAPS are unaware of the implications of their actions, and are motivated to earn money, while the audience is motivated by the desire to enjoy a show. Although neither the performer nor the audience consciously decides to create an equal-opportunity private space, that is the forum to which they both nonverbally agree. If either participant would desire a more exclusive form of private space, they would opt out of this arrangement. Their participation signifies consent.

In a tourist city, or a city of diverse ethnicities, socioeconomic classes, races, and political persuasions, the "public" tends to remain anonymous. Whereas niche communities exist in a city like New York, oftentimes the larger identity of the city feels more fragmented than united. To establish communities, many have opted out of the "city life" and have moved to the suburbs. Others have formed exclusive gated communities in the city through apartment buildings with door attendants. It is difficult to find a truly inclusive private space in New York City that fosters community and simultaneously allows everyone to participate.

A TAPS is one place where these needs are being met. It is an opportunity for people to temporarily come together to enjoy a shared experience. Individuals do not have to commit to this community and may leave whenever they wish, but

Fischer

they are welcome to watch, applaud, howl, and mingle for the time that they are TAPS members. These aforementioned forms of behavior, which would normally be socially unacceptable in a public space, are awarded in a TAPS by applause and recognition. The TAPS of New York serve as a refuge from the large anonymous public spaces—the long tunnels from Herald Square subway station to Penn Station, the busy intersection between 5th Avenue and 59th Street— and allow a brief shared moment with others in a safe space before continuing on one's way. These temporary private spaces provide warmth to busy and unidentifiable public spaces, and it is for this reason that performer-initiated TAPS are found more frequently in busy, tourist cities. It is the lack of everyday community that fuels TAPS' existence.

Furthermore, TAPS challenge the urgency with which urbanists attempt to define space in concrete terms. The impermanence of space is conveyed through the temporary nature of TAPS and the ease with which they oscillate. While it is critical to reassess the top-down methods of controlling and monitoring space, more emphasis should be placed on bottom-up initiatives and nontraditional developments. Performance artists are just one group of many who form TAPS. Empowerment of the city's public space users is vital if a city is to have an identity that transcends its private skyscrapers and exclusive neighborhoods.

> **Limitations of the current study and directions for future research should have been included in the last paragraph.**

Fischer

REFERENCES

Flusty, Steven. 1994. *Building Paranoia: The Proliferation of Interdictory Space and the Erosion of Spatial Justice.* West Hollywood, CA: Los Angeles Forum for Architecture and Urban Design.

Kayden, Jarold. 2000. *Privately Owned Public Space.* New York: Department of City Planning of the City of New York, Municipal Art Society of New York.

Kohn, Margaret. 2004. *Brave New Neighborhoods: The Privatization of Public Space.* New York: Routledge.

Low, Setha. 2003. *Behind the Gates: Life, Security, and the Pursuit of Happiness in Fortress America.* New York: Routledge.

Smithsimon, Greg. 2004. "Types of Public Space." (Handout)

Symphony Space, Mission Statement. Retrieved January 5, 2007 (http://www.symphonyspace.org/institutional/description.php).

Interview data and field notes are correctly not listed in the reference list.

Adamson, Walter L. 1993. *Avant-Garde Florence: From Modernism to Fascism.* Cambridge, MA: Harvard University Press. Retrieved June 15, 2007 (http://name.umdl.umich.edu/HEB00462).

Adler, Patricia A. and Peter Adler. 1984. "The Carpool: A Socializing Adjunct to the Educational Experience." *Sociology of Education* 57(4):200–210.

American Federation of Teachers. 1998. *Survey and Analysis of Teacher Salary Trends 1998.* Washington, DC: American Federation of Teachers.

American Heritage Dictionary of the English Language. 1992. 3rd ed. Boston, MA: Houghton Mifflin.

American Institute of Public Opinion. 1976. *Gallup Public Opinion Poll # 965* [MRDF]. Princeton, NJ: American Institute of Public Opinion [producer]. New Haven, CT: Roper Public Opinion Research Center, Yale University [distributor].

American Psychological Association. 2007. "Guidelines for Avoiding Racial/Ethnic Bias in Language." Retrieved December 23, 2007 (http://apastyle.org/race.html).

American Sociological Association. 2007. *American Sociological Association Style Guide.* 3rd ed. Washington, DC: American Sociological Association.

"Americans Work More." Associated Press, September 1, 2001.

Anderson, Donald, ed. 1995. *Aftermath: An Anthology of Post-Vietnam Fiction.* New York: Owl Books.

Archer, Melanie and Judith R. Blau. 1993. "Class Formation in Nineteenth-Century America: The Case of the Middle Class." Pp. 17–41 in *Annual Review of Sociology,* Vol. 19, edited by J. Blake and J. Hagan. Palo Alto, CA: Annual Reviews.

Aries, Elizabeth. 1996. *Men and Women in Interaction: Reconsidering the Differences.* New York: Oxford University Press.

Aron, Raymond. 1998. *Main Currents in Sociological Thought.* Vol. 2, *Durkheim, Pareto, Weber.* New Brunswick, NJ: Transaction.

Association of Public Data Users. 2005. "Daytime Population." *APDU Newsletter,* December. Retrieved June 15, 2007 (http://www.apdu.org/resources/samplenewsletter.pdf).

Association of Religion Data Archives. 2006. "Denominational Family Trees." University Park, PA: Association of Religion Data Archives. Retrieved June 16, 2007 (http://www.thearda.com/Denoms/Families/).

Bandura, Albert. 1971. *Social Learning Theory.* New York: McCaleb-Seiler.

Becker, Howard S., Blanche Geer, Everett C. Hughes, and Anselm L. Strauss. 1961. *Boys in White: Student Culture in Medical School.* Chicago, IL: University of Chicago Press.

Bellah, Robert N., Richard Madsen, William M. Sullivan, Ann Swidler, and Steven M. Tipton. 1986. *Habits of the Heart: Individualism and Commitment in American Life.* New York: Harper and Row.

Bereday, George Z. F., ed. 1969. *Essays on World Education: The Crisis of Supply and Demand.* New York: Oxford University Press.

Berger, Peter L. 1963. *Invitation to Sociology: A Humanistic Perspective.* New York: Free Press.

———. 1967. *The Sacred Canopy: Elements of a Sociological Theory of Religion.* New York: Doubleday.

Blau, Francine D. and Lawrence M. Kahn. 1992. "The Gender Earnings Gap: Some International Evidence." Working Paper No. 4224, National Bureau of Economic Research, Chicago, IL.

Blau, Peter M. 1977. *Inequality and Heterogeneity: A Primitive Theory of Social Structure.* New York: Free Press.

Blau, Zena Smith. 1972. "Role Exit and Identity." Paper presented at the annual meeting of the American Sociological Asssociation, August 28, New Orleans, LA.

Bly, Robert and Marion Woodman. 1998. *The Maiden King: The Reunion of Masculine and Feminine.* New York: Henry Holt.

Bourdieu, Pierre. 1977. *Outline of a Theory of Practice.* Translated by R. Nice. Cambridge, England: Cambridge University Press.

Braverman, Harry. 1974. *Labor and Monopoly Capital: The Degradation of Labor in the Twentieth Century.* New York: Monthly Review Press.

Brim, Orville G., Jr. 1960. "Personality Development as Role Learning." Pp. 127–59 in *Personality Development in Children,* edited by I. Iscoe and H. W. Stevenson. Austin, TX: University of Texas Press.

Brim, Orville G., Jr. and Stanton Wheeler, eds. 1966. *Socialization after Childhood.* New York: John Wiley.

Caplan, Priscilla. 1997. "Will the Real Internet Please Stand Up?" *The Public-Access Computer Systems Review* 8(2). Retrieved June 12, 2007 (http://epress.lib.uh.edu/pr/v8/n2/capl8n2.html).

Carli, Linda L. 1989. "Social Influences as a Function of Gender and Language." *Journal of Personality and Social Psychology* 56:565–66.

Cicourel, Aaron V. 1970. "The Etiquette of Youth." Pp. 554–65 in *Social Psychology through Symbolic Interaction,* edited by G. Stone and H. Farberman. Waltham, MA: Xerox.

Clawson, Laura. 2005. "Cowboys and Schoolteachers: Gender in Romance Novels, Secular and Christian." *Sociological Perspectives* 48(4):462–79.

Colomy, Paul and J. David Brown. 1996. "Goffman and Interactional Citizenship." *Sociological Perspectives* 39(3):371–81.

Columbia University Archives, Morningside Heights Area Alliance Archives, Box 32. April 29, 1966. File: 6. Report of the Community Programs Committee to the Annual Meeting of the Board of Directors, Morningside Heights, Inc.

Cooley, Charles H. 1922. *Human Nature and the Social Order.* New York: Scribners.

Cose, Ellis. 2000. "What's White Anyways?" *Newsweek,* September 18, pp. 64–65.

Cuba, Lee. 2002. *A Short Guide to Writing about Social Science.* 4th ed. New York: Longman.

Curtis, James R. 1996. "Miami's Little Havana: Yard Shrines, Cult Religion, and Landscape." Pp. 485–94 in *Mapping the Social Landscape: Readings in Sociology,* edited by S. J. Ferguson. Mountain View, CA: Mayfield.

Eagly, Alice H. and Steven J. Karau. 1991. "Gender and the Emergence of Leaders: A Meta-Analysis." *Journal of Personality and Social Psychology* 60:685–710.

Ebaugh, Helen Rose Fuchs. 1988. *Becoming an Ex: The Process of Role Exit.* Chicago, IL: University of Chicago Press.

Elder, Glen H. 1977. "Age Differentiation and the Life Course." Pp. 165–90 in *Annual Review of Sociology,* Vol. 1, edited by A. Inkeles. Palo Alto, CA: Annual Reviews.

Emerson, Robert M., Kerry O. Ferris, and Carol Brooks Gardner. 1998. "On Being Stalked." *Social Problems* 45(3):289–314.

Epstein, Cynthia Fuchs. 1968. "Women and Professional Careers: The Case of the Woman Lawyer." PhD dissertation, Department of Sociology, Columbia University, New York.

Erikson, Erik. 1950. *Childhood and Society.* New York: Norton.

Etzioni, Amitai. 2007. "Basic Security Comes First." Amitai Etzioni Notes, November 19, 2007. Retrieved December 20, 2007 (http://blog.amitaietzioni.org/2007/11/basic-security.html).

Felmlee, Diane H. 2001. "From Appealing to Appalling: Disenchantment with a Romantic Partner." *Sociological Perspectives* 44(3):263–80.

Felsenthal, Edward. 1998. "Justices' Ruling Further Defines Sex Harassment." *Wall Street Journal*, March 5, pp. B1–B2.

Fennell, Mary L., Patricia R. Barchas, Elizabeth G. Cohen, Anne M. McMahon, and Polly Hildebrand. 1978. "An Alternative Perspective on Sex Differences in Organizational Settings: The Process of Legitimization." *Sex Roles* 4:589–604.

Foucault, Michel. 1977. *Discipline and Punish: The Birth of Prison.* Translated by A. Sheridan. New York: Vintage Books.

Garfinkel, Harold. 1967. *Studies in Ethnomethodology.* Englewood Cliffs, NJ: Prentice Hall.

Garfinkel, Irv. 1994. Review of *The Homeless,* by Christopher Jencks. *Contemporary Sociology* 23(5):687–89.

George, Linda K. 1993. "Sociological Perspective on Life Transitions." Pp. 353–73 in *Annual Review of Sociology*, Vol. 19, edited by J. Blake. Palo Alto, CA: Annual Reviews.

Glaser, Barney G. and Amselm L. Strauss. 1967. *Discovery of Grounded Theory: Strategies for Qualitative Research.* New Brunswick, NJ: Transaction.

Goffman, Erving. 1959. *The Presentation of Self in Everyday Life.* New York: Anchor.

———. 1961a. *Asylums.* New York: Doubleday.

———. 1961b. *Encounters.* Indianapolis, IN: Bobbs-Merrill.

Gordon, Milton M. 1978. *Human Nature, Class, and Ethnicity.* New York: Oxford University Press.

Gray, John. 1993. *Men Are from Mars, Women Are from Venus: A Practical Guide for Improving Communication and Getting What You Want in Your Relationships.* New York: HarperCollins.

Henslin, James M. 2005. *Instructor's Resource CD-ROM for Sociology: A Down-to-Earth Approach.* 8th ed. Allyn & Bacon (November 28, 2007).

Hewitt, John, P. 1984. *Self and Society: A Symbolic Interactionist Social Psychology.* 3rd ed. Boston, MA: Allyn & Bacon.

Hurtado, Aida, David E. Hayes-Bautista, R. Burciaga Valdez, and Anthony C.R. Hernandez. 1992. *Redefining California: Latino Social Engagement in a Multicultural Society.* Los Angeles, CA: UCLA Chicano Studies Research Center.

Hysom, Stuart J. and Cathryn Johnson. 2006. "Leadership Structures in Same-Sex Task Groups." *Sociological Perspectives* 49(3):391–410.

Inkeles, Alex. 1966. "Social Structure and the Socialization of Competence." *Harvard Educational Review* 36:265–83.

Jencks, Christopher, Marshall Smith, Henry Acland, Mary Jo Bane, David Cohen, Herbert Gintis, Barbara Heyns, and Stephan Michelson. 1972. *Inequality: A Reassessment of the Effect of Family and Schooling in America.* New York: Basic Books.

Johnson, Cathryn, Stephanie J. Funk, and Jody Clay-Warner. 1998. "Organizational Contexts and Conversation Patterns." *Social Psychology Quarterly* 61:361–71.

Kanter, Rosabeth Moss. 1979. "Women and the Structure of Organizations: Explorations in Theory and Behavior." Pp. 166–90 in *Social Interaction: Introductory Readings in Sociology*, edited by H. Robboy, S. L. Greenblatt, and C. Clark. New York: St. Martin's Press.

[Klein, Joe]. 1996. *Primary Colors: A Novel of Politics.* New York: Grand Central.

Kuhn, Thomas. 1970. *The Structure of Scientific Revolutions.* 2nd ed. Chicago, IL: University of Chicago Press.

Laurendeau, Jason. 2006. " 'He Didn't Go In Doing a Skydive': Sustaining the Illusion of Control in an Edgework Activity." *Sociological Perspectives* 49(4):583–605.

Linton, Ralph. 1936. *The Study of Man.* New York: Appleton-Century.

Lunsford, Andrea A. 2008. *The St. Martin's Handbook.* Boston, MA: Bedford/St. Martin's Press.

Lynd, Robert S. and Helen Merrell Lynd. 1959. *Middletown: A Study in American Culture.* New York: Harcourt, Brace and World.

Mannheim, Karl. 1936. *Ideology and Utopia: An Introduction to the Sociology of Knowledge.* Translated by L. Wirth and E. Shils. New York: Harcourt, Brace and World.

Marcussen, Kristen, Christian Ritter, and Deborah J. Safron. 2004. "The Role of Identity Salience and Commitment in the Stress Process." *Sociological Perspectives* 47(3):289–312.

Marx, Gary T. 1991. "Unintended Consequences of Undercover Work." Pp. 278–86 in *Down to Earth Sociology: Introductory Readings,* 6th ed. Edited by J. M. Henslin. New York: Free Press.

Marx, Karl and Friedrich Engels. [1848] 1983. *The Communist Manifesto.* New York: Pocket Books.

McGraw-Hill. 1979. *Guidelines for Equal Treatment of the Sexes.* New York: McGraw-Hill.

Mead, George Herbert. 1934. *Mind, Self, and Society.* Chicago, IL: University of Chicago Press.

Merton, Robert. 1957a. "The Role Set." *British Journal of Sociology* 8:106–20.

———. 1957b. *Social Theory and Social Structure.* New York: Free Press.

———. 1968. *Social Theory and Social Structure.* Rev. ed. New York: Free Press.

———. 1976. *Sociological Ambivalence and Other Essays.* New York: Free Press.

Merton, Robert K., Marjorie Fiske, and Patricia L. Kendall. 1990. *The Focused Interview: A Manual of Problems and Procedures.* 2nd ed. New York: Free Press.

Microsoft Corporation. 2005. "School of the Future: Understand the Vision." Retrieved December 19, 2007 (http://www.microsoft.com/Education/SchoolofFutureVision.mspx).

Miller, Warren, Arthur Miller, and Gerald Klein. 1975. *The CPS 1974 American National Election Study* [MRDF]. Ann Arbor, MI: Center for Political Studies, University of Michigan [producer]. Ann Arbor: Inter-University Consortium [distributor].

Mills, C. Wright. 1951. *White Collar: The American Middle Classes.* London, England: Oxford University Press.

National Center for Education Statistics. 2006. "Fast Facts." Retrieved June 15, 2007 (http://nces.ed.gov/fastfacts/display.asp?id=16).

New York Public Library, Manuscripts and Archives Division, Robert Moses Papers, Box 116. August 16, 1957. File: Committee on Slum Clearance 1957. Letter to Moses on the Development of the Polo Grounds, Dunbar McLaurin.

Parrado, Emilio A. and Chenoa A. Flippen. 2005. "Migration and Gender among Mexican Women." *American Sociological Review* 70(4):606–32.

Parsons, Talcott and Robert Bales. 1955. *Family, Socialization, and Interaction Process.* Glencoe, IL: Free Press.

Passell, Peter. 1996. "Race, Mortgages and Statistics." *New York Times,* May 10, pp. D1, D4.

Peter, Katharin and Laura Horn. 2005. *Gender Differences in Participation and Completion of Undergraduate Education and How They Have Changed Over Time.* National Center for Education Statistics: Report. Washington, DC: U.S. Department of Education. Retrieved June 15, 2007 (http://nces.ed.gov/das/epubs/2005169/references.asp).

Piliavin, Jane A. and Rachel R. Martin. 1978. "The Effects of the Sex Composition of Groups on Styles of Social Interaction." *Sex Roles* 4:281–96.

Ridgeway, Cecilia L. 1988. "Gender Differences in Task Groups: A Status and Legitimacy Account." Pp. 188–206 in *Status Generalizations: New Theory and Research,* edited by M. Webster, Jr., and M. Foschi. Stanford, CA: Stanford University Press.

Ridgeway, Cecilia L. and Lynn Smith-Lovin. 1999. "The Gender System and Interaction." *Annual Review of Sociology* 25: 191–216.

Robboy, Howard, Sidney L. Greenblatt, and Candace Clark, eds. 1979. *Social Interaction: Introductory Readings in Sociology.* New York: St. Martin's Press.

Rose, Arnold M. 1962. "A Systematic Summary of Symbolic Interaction Theory." Pp. 3–19 in *Human Behavior and Social Processes,* edited by A. M. Rose. Boston, MA: Houghton Mifflin.

Rosenfield, Michael J. and Byung-Soo Kim. 2005. "The Independence of Young Adults and the Rise of Interracial and Same-Sex Unions." *American Sociological Review* 70(4):541–62.

Rossi, Alice S. 1968. "Transition to Parenthood." *Journal of Marriage and Family* 30(1):26–39.

Sager, Rebecca. 2007. "The Faith-Based Initiative." *Footnotes*, April. Retrieved June 15, 2007 (http://www2.asanet.org/footnotes/ap07/fn4.html).

Sengupta, Somini. 2007. "Indian Officials to Rule How 'Backward' Group Is." *New York Times,* June 5. Retrieved June 17, 2007 (http://www.nytimes.com).

Shelly, Robert K. and Paul T. Munroe. 1999. "Do Women Engage in Less Task Behavior Than Men?" *Sociological Perspectives* 42:746–62.

Sherif, Muzafer. 1936. *The Psychology of Social Norms.* New York: Harper.

Shibutani, Tamotsu. 1962. "Reference Groups and Social Control." Pp. 128–47 in *Human Behavior and Social Processes,* edited by A. M. Rose. Boston, MA: Houghton Mifflin.

———. 1970. "On the Personification of Adversaries." Pp. 223–33 in *Human Nature and Collective Behavior,* edited by T. Shibutani. Englewood Cliffs, NJ: Prentice Hall.

Silverstein, Ken. 2007. "Their Men in Washington." *Harper's Magazine,* July 2007, pp. 53–61.

Singleton, Royce A., Jr., Bruce C. Straits, and Margaret Miller Straits. 1993. *Approaches to Social Research.* New York: Oxford University Press.

Skocpol, Theda, ed. 1984. *Vision and Method in Historical Sociology.* Cambridge, England: Cambridge University Press.

Speier, Matthew. 1970. "The Everyday World of the Child." Pp. 188–217 in *Understanding Everyday Life,* edited by J. D. Douglas. Chicago, IL: Aldine.

Thoits, Peggy. 1992. "Identity Structures and Psychological Well-Being: Gender and Marital Status Comparisons." *Social Psychology Quarterly* 55:236–56.

Thomas, W. I. and Florian Znaniecki. 1927. *The Polish Peasant.* Boston, MA: R.G. Badger.

Thornton, Russell and Peter Nardi. 1975. "The Dynamics of Role Acquisition." *American Journal of Sociology* 80(4): 870–85.

Tilly, Charles. 2004. "Observations of Social Processes and Their Formal Representations." *Sociological Theory* 22(4):595–602. (Retrieved from JSTOR on June 15, 2007.)

Timmermans, Stefan. 2005. "Suicide Determination and the Professional Authority of Medical Examiners." *American Sociological Review* 70(2):311–33.

Trochim, William and Sarita Davis. 1996. *Computer Simulations for Research Design.* Retrieved June 17, 2007 (http://www.socialresearchmethods.net/simul/simul.htm).

Turabian, Kate, L. 1996. *A Manual for Writers of Term Papers, Theses, and Dissertations.* 6th ed. Revised by J. Grossman and A. Bennett. Chicago, IL: University of Chicago Press.

U.S. Bureau of the Census. *Statistical Abstract of the United States: The National Data Book.* Washington, DC: U.S. Government Printing Office. Published annually.

U.S. Department of Health and Human Services, Public Health Service. 1990. *Healthy People 2000.* Washington, DC: U.S. Government Printing Office.

U.S. Department of Justice, Federal Bureau of Investigation. 2005. *Hate Crime Statistics, 2005.* Retrieved June 15, 2007 (http://www.fbi.gov/ucr/hc2005/index.html).

University of Chicago Press. 2003. *The Chicago Manual of Style.* 15th ed. Chicago, IL: University of Chicago Press.

———. 2007a. "Chicago-Style Citation Quick Guide." Retrieved December 21, 2007 (http://www.chicagomanualofstyle.org/tools_citationguide.html).

———. 2007b. "Electronic Manuscript Preparation Guidelines for Authors." Retrieved December 21, 2007 (http://www.press.uchicago.edu/Misc/Chicago/emsguide.html).

University of Wollongong. 2003. "Policy & Guidelines on Non-discriminatory Language Practice & Presentation Practice Policy." Retrieved January 2, 2008 (http://staff.uow.edu.au/eed/nondiscrimlanguage.html).

Wagner, David G. and Joseph Berger. 1997. "Gender and Interpersonal Task Behaviors: Status Expectation Accounts." *Sociological Perspectives* 40:1–32.

Walker, Henry A., Barbara C. Ilardi, Anne M. McMahon, and Mary L. Fennell. 1996. "Gender, Interaction, and Leadership." *Social Psychology Quarterly* 59:255–72.

Wallerstein, Immanuel. 1980. *The Modern World-System I: Capitalist Agriculture and the Origins of the European World-Economy in the Sixteenth Century (Studies in Social Discontinuity)*. New York: Academic Press.

———. 1988. *The Modern World-System III: The Second Era of Great Expansion of the Capitalist World-Economy, 1730–1840 (Studies in Social Discontinuity)*. New York: Academic Press.

Watson, John B. [1925] 1970. *Behaviorism*. New York: Norton.

Weber, Max. [1946] 1971. *From Max Weber: Essays in Sociology*. Translated and edited by H. H. Gerth and C. W. Mills. New York: Oxford University Press.

Whyte, William H. 1991. "Street People." Pp. 165–78 in *Down to Earth Sociology: Introductory Readings*, 6th ed, edited by J. M. Henslin. New York: Free Press.

World Energy Council. 2004. *Survey of Energy Resources 2004*. Retrieved June 15, 2007 (http://www.worldenergy.org/wec-geis/publications/default/launches/ser04/ser04.asp).

Yang, Song. 2006. "Organizational Sectors and the Institutionalization of Job-Training Programs: Evidence from a Longitudinal National Organizations Survey." *Sociological Perspectives* 49(3): 325–42.

Yellin, Linda L. 1999. "Role Acquisition as a Social Process." *Sociological Inquiry* 69(2): 236–56.

Zurcher, Louis A. 1979. "The Airplane Passenger: Protection of Self in an Encapsulated Group." *Qualitative Sociology* 1:77–99.